HOW TO COMPARE NATIONS
Strategies in Comparative Politics

MATTEI DOGAN
and
DOMINIQUE PELASSY

CHATHAM HOUSE PUBLISHERS, INC.
Chatham, New Jersey

How to Compare Nations: Strategies in Comparative Politics

Chatham House Publishers, Inc.
Post Office Box One
Chatham, New Jersey 07928

PUBLISHER: Edward Artinian
COVER DESIGN: Lawrence Ratzkin
COMPOSITION: Chatham Composer
PRINTING AND BINDING: Hamilton Printing Company

LIBRARY OF CONGRESS CATALOGING IN PUBLICATION DATA

Dogan, Mattei.
    How to compare nations.

    Translation of: Sociologie politique comparative.
    Includes bibliographical references.
    1. Political sociology. 2. Comparative government.
I. Pelassy, Dominique. II. Title.
JA76.D6313 1984   306'.2   83-20997
ISBN 0-934540-20-9 (pbk.)

CONTENTS

PART 1. THE COMPASS OF THE COMPARATIVIST   3
1. Comparing to Escape from Ethnocentrism   5
2. Comparing to Find Sociological Rules   13
3. Operational Concepts   20
4. Theoretical Frameworks   26
5. Functional Equivalences   31

PART 2. THE INTERNATIONALIZATION OF ANALYTICAL CATEGORIES   39
6. Social Classes: Different in Each Continent   41
7. Cultural Pluralism: Vertical Societies   50
8. Political Culture: From Nation to Nation   58
9. Political Socialization: From Generation to Generation   67
10. Political Clientelism: A Ubiquitous Phenomenon   75
11. Consociational Democracy:
An Elitist Model for Fragmented Societies   82
12. Political Crises: Historical Events or Stages of Development   92

PART 3. THE CHOICE OF COUNTRIES   99
13. On the Need to Segment Before Comparing   101
14. The Case Study in Comparative Perspective   107
15. The Binary Analysis   112
16. Comparing Similar Countries   117
17. Comparing Contrasting Countries   127
18. The Conceptual Homogenization of a Heterogeneous Field   133

PART 4. HOW TO STRUCTURE THE RESULTS OF THE COMPARISON   141
19. The Dichotomy as Clarification   143
20. Cross-National Typologies of Social Actors   148
21. Typologies of Political Regimes   157
22. The Dynamics of Models   163
23. From Comparison to Synthesis   171
24. From Comparison to Prediction   174

Name Index   179
Subject Index   183

FOREWORD

This book discusses strategies of comparison and explores some new perspectives in comparative research. The importance of the problems we are raising led us to voluntarily renounce dealing with methodological and technical issues, the exploration of which would require another book. We are focusing instead on the general strategy of comparative research. We do not intend to make an inventory of all the accumulated knowledge on political parties, pressure groups, parliaments, bureaucracies, elites, and so on. Rather our aim is to present a critical appraisal, a "state of the art."

Our American readers will find in this book many authors familiar to them. Indeed, the field of comparative politics is dominated by Americans. But the perceptions and perspectives of European scholars differ somewhat from those widely accepted on the other side of the Atlantic river.

This book is an adaptation of *Sociologie politique comparative* (Paris: Economica, 1982). Several transatlantic colleagues urged us to make the work available to Americans who do not read French. Since our English is like the Latin used in monasteries during the Middle Ages, we were helped immensely by Margaret Harrison, a Parisian American, and by two graduate students from UCLA, Rhys Payne and Dan Nataf. Many thanks to them.

As far as possible, throughout the book we cite the English edition of the books and articles to which we refer, even if they were orginally published in another language.

HOW TO COMPARE NATIONS

PART I

THE COMPASS OF
THE COMPARATIVIST

To COMPARE is a natural way of thinking. Nothing is more natural than to study people, ideas, or institutions in relation to other people, ideas, or institutions. We gain knowledge through reference. Scientific comparison is not of a different nature, although the intellectual level is higher. We compare to evaluate more objectively our situation as individuals, a community, or a nation. A sociologist who compares discovers the pitfall of ethnocentrism, and by the same token may find a way to overcome it.

But the comparativist does not seek a better understanding only of his or her own environment. By enlarging the field of observation, the comparativist searches for rules and tries to bring to light the general causes of social phenomena. Today there are about one hundred fifty independent nations in the world, each one presenting characteristics that can be viewed from different perspectives and combined in multiple configurations. In this kaleidoscope appear hundreds of questions that invite all kinds of analyses—descriptive or theoretical, limited or ambitious. This challenge to human intelligence provides the social sciences with the possibility of becoming real "sciences." *Cogito, ergo sum,* proclaimed René Descartes; paraphrasing him, we can say, "I think, consequently I am comparing."

International comparison requires an articulated conceptual framework. Social scientists who analyze only one country may proceed step by step, without structured hypotheses, building analytical categories as they go. Comparativists have no such freedom. They cannot advance without tools. Confronted with a variety of contexts, they are obliged to rely on abstractions, to master concepts general enough to cope with the diversity of the cases under consideration. When concentrating on a single country, a single culture, a single system, one may possibly grope. Comparativists, on the contrary, need a compass that will allow them to pass from one context to another, to select in each country the differences or similarities that can be integrated into their general scheme.

Every researcher decants reality. But such a decanting is a necessity for the comparativist, who must have a theoretical orientation from the start — with the understanding that it is precisely the purpose of the research to permit a refinement, a remodeling of the initial scheme. Even in the absence of a well-structured theoretical framework, the specialist on one country is not in danger of getting lost. But the comparativist may well go astray, and efforts to garner information may cruelly prove to have been in vain.

Perhaps there is no basic difference between the approach of the specialist and the approach of the comparativist. But there is an essential difference of degree. What is here latent is there bright; so much so that methodological and conceptual problems raised by international comparison appear to be specific.

CHAPTER 1

COMPARING TO ESCAPE
FROM ETHNOCENTRISM

An age-old idea of philosophers is that knowledge of the self is gained through knowledge of others. The ego affirms itself by the roundabout way of multiple comparisons. The child develops by imitating or opposing. The very stature of a person, original and unique, exists only in a relative sense. Hegel clearly states that consciousness recognizes itself in others, and knows the other in itself.

What is true for the individual is even more so for societies. There is no nation without other nations. This diversity, which actually contributes to the awakening of contrasting national identities, is the only element that permits the perception of what characterizes people and systems.

Let us imagine a country encircled for centuries by an unbreachable wall. Which of its inhabitants would be in a position to describe such a confined nation? What could be the reference point; how could one measure what is perceived; moreover, what *could* be perceived? Limited to a superficial and episodic chronicle, the observer would be incapable of understanding most of the fundamental and pertinent traits of the environment. With what rigidity are social groups constituted, what features characterize the mentality of the populace, to what degree is power centralized? The simple formulation of these questions presupposes comparison; denied the possibility of looking beyond his or her own world, the analyst is virtually blind.

Observers who cultivate a distance between themselves and the society in which they live will find new perspectives opening. It is not by accident that among the finest studies on so many countries, we inevitably find the work of a surprisingly perspicacious "stranger."

We can illustrate this proposition by many examples. A Frenchman, André Siegfried, half a century ago perceived how the mentality of the British ruling class could create a *Crise Britannique au XXᵉ Siècle*. An Englishman, James Bryce, at the beginning of the century showed in *The American Commonwealth* how the system of candidate selection for the Presidency of the United States could discard first-class talents. An American, Edward Banfield, during a relatively brief sojourn in the south of Italy, recorded the rules of behavior for a population distrusting the central power; later, Italian sociologists confirmed the main features of this analysis, at a moment when "amoral fami-lism" was already in rapid decline. The existence of 450,000 municipal coun-cilors in France is a fact not given great importance by French political scien-tists. But for a foreigner like Sidney Tarrow, it constitutes an extraordinary phenomenon that demands the revision of certain clichés nourished by many Frenchmen. To speak of a lack of participation in a country where one out of every sixty citizens is a member of a municipal council may seem a rapid and somewhat superficial judgment, especially if we look to rural areas. The decay of many American cities was perceived first by non-American observers. Even before World War II, books written by Europeans analyzed this decline, which scholars from the Western side of the Atlantic were so late in discover-ing. Australian geographers, for their part, marvel at the existence of villages in Europe. Thus sociologists and political scientists seem to have taken up the torch of a phalanx of illustrious writers, such as Kant or Goethe, Stendhal or Châteaubriand, Byron or Shelley, who in their time discovered at least one coun-try: Italy.

Expatriation has always been perceived as a key to more objective judg-ment. "Truth on this side of the Pyrenees, error on the other," commented first Montaigne, then Pascal. The most commonly accepted values, the most uncon-tested social structures or political institutions, are not necessarily universal. Throughout the eighteenth century, the pioneering comparativists appear to have been in search of models. Beyond the Channel, Montesquieu, Voltaire, and Diderot discover a political regime that they contrast to monarchical abso-lutism. With Tocqueville, the analysis turns purer; no longer does the observer look outside to polish weapons for his political combat. Rather, it is to sharpen his insight, to refine his perspectives by contrasting them. Some time later, the comparativist penetrates a new universe with the aid of anthropologists, recon-sidering some accepted generalizations and even asking new questions of the most familiar environment. Each foray out of his own country resounds like a revelation. He finally understands that there exists a plurality of values, struc-tures, and systems, which are not simply products of nature.

Such a revelation contains an explosive potential. There would not have been a French Revolution without the British example, or a Meiji era without the shock represented by the discovery of the Western world. Behind what they called the "big noses," the Japanese did see the vitality of another civilization, one built on other ideas, other behaviors, and other technologies, all worthy of imitation.

The historian has underlined how confrontations with other societies im-pose the burden of sometimes dramatically premature collective aspirations in well-established regimes. The Old World offers multiple illustrations of these disruptive pressures, and it is not surprising that so many countries in the Third World now try to protect themselves from what they feel to be dangerous contamination.

The contemporary totalitarian states, of course, have more ways to fight contagions that the monarchies had during the first part of the nineteenth century when they tried in vain to protect themselves against the virulent ideas of the French Revolution. The reasons, however, remain the same. The leaders of a well-known empire in the East have managed to restrict not only abstract communication but also the actual movement of people. They know that certain contacts can be dangerous. Any comparative knowledge risks becoming a factor of change simply because it contains the idea that what was originally perceived as proceeding from Reason or Providence is not a unique and absolute truth. Translated in terms of political demands, the perception of difference is one of the most important levers in history, as powerful perhaps as social conflicts within nations.

At a more prosaic level, it would be easy to provide instances of demands and solutions based on foreign examples that are diffused by contagion. We think, for example, of the institution of the ombudsman or the creation of a ministry of environment. Considered from a distance, the entire political and social history of Western Europe seems marked by congruence, as if the entire European continent periodically took the time from the same Big Ben. During the nineteenth century, many European countries wavered between the British and French models. But soon all countries tended to move to the same beat, voicing parallel demands for more freedom, more justice, more participation. Universal suffrage was extended at the moment the unions became powerful organizations. Women in eight countries simultaneously obtained the right to vote. A French student of labor legislation, Paul Louis, noted that "if we examine the historical evolution of labor law, we are struck by the fact that it proceeded in all countries along the same successive stages." In the aftermath of World War II, the nations of Western Europe built similar institutions for social security, welfare, retirement, family allocations; they gave the state increased means of intervention in economic life. For nearly half a century, Western democracies on both sides of the Atlantic have used fiscal means to increase progressively that part of the GNP controlled by the government. By the early 1980s, most "liberal" governments of the West collected and redistributed about 40 percent of the national product. At the present time, it is difficult to determine whether the budget-cutting endeavors of conservative leaders in the United States and Europe will mark a reversal of this tendency or not.

As international communication develops, so does synchronization. Agitation in one country awakens public opinion in the next, and ideas make their way. One country drops the voting age to eighteen, and five or six others seize upon the change. Legislation to protect the natural environment, to ease restrictions on birth control, and to adopt laws on divorce by consent was formulated and implemented at about the same time in France and Germany. The social reforms enacted in Italy during the first postwar decade were modeled on those of France.

Political leaders are themselves vectors of this parallelism. This is obvious in Third World countries where an entire generation of rulers tries to impose upon the masses ideas and models forged in advanced countries, whether Eastern or Western. But it is even more true for European nations. Tied together by strikingly similar economic and social problems, they tend to adopt solutions that are apparently beneficial in neighboring countries. The process of comparison becomes heuristic. It suggests political platforms—being clear that such mimicry does not guarantee that worthy solutions in one place are necessarily appropriate in another. A similar cure of liberalism will not result in the same benefits in Great Britain and in Japan; the capacity of the French social structures and organizations to regularize the functioning of the free market is probably not equal to that of the German system. A marvelous prescription here does not necessarily provide good results elsewhere. But an essential contribution of scientific comparison is precisely to shed light on the importance of original contexts, which actively assimilate the variable introduced.

Comparison is the engine of knowledge. Because the comprehension of a single case is linked to the understanding of many cases, because we perceive the particular better in the light of generalities, international comparison increases tenfold the possibility of explaining political phenomena. The observer who studies just one country could interpret as normal what in fact appears to the comparativist as abnormal. Even that which is most familiar can escape perception. *Was ist bekannt, ist nicht erkannt,* underlined Hegel. The problem is not merely to evaluate the banality or the singularity of these kinds of phenomena.

The discovery of the extraordinary invites the observer to try to explain why the rule that exists here is absent there, and vice versa. The historian would seek the reason for this or that uncommon delay in mobilization; the demographer would ask why fertility, here or there, is not affected by urbanization. The political scientist seeks the reason for instability in a particular context by progressively eliminating variables that do not produce instability elsewhere. The juxtaposition of cases is useful not only to situate each one in relation to others but also because it calls for generalizations, those wide melting pots that turn each particular experience into an exemplar, a deviant or a clinical "case," allowing in return a better understanding even of what is specific.

Although comparison may initially appear to be a quest for information, it also represents a quest for enlightenment, and thus it is one of the most fruitful ways of thinking. It helps to rid us of inherited fossilized notions, obliges us to reconsider the validity of undiscussed interpretations, and enlarges our visual field. Every researcher, even a comparativist researcher, belongs to a culture, and that can limit his or her capacity to perceive. These blinkers have not been easily recognized. Sociologists from the West have been slow to realize that they were taking their own measures for universal ones. For a long time, classic comparisons have implicitly incorporated the idea of progress, tending to consider each political system according to the place it occupied on an imaginary scale leading inexorably to "development," "democracy," or even "Westernization."

It is a natural risk, when one compares, to fall into ethnocentrism; and comparison may be the best antidote to this danger. Irresistibly, the perception of contrasts makes researchers sensitive to the relativity of knowledge and consequently helps liberate them from cultural shells. Indeed, the very concept of ethnocentrism simply cannot exist without the comparative exercise. Only with exposure to other cultures does one become conscious of possible intellectual occlusion. As Elie Halévy noted long ago, the differences between France and England, enormous for the European, are minimal indeed to the inhabitant of Peking or Calcutta. The perception of differences is a function of the proximity of the observer — a fact that can raise problems.

When researchers succeed in establishing a close relationship with a subject culture, the only dimension they really value is often that of specificity. For example, the works of Jacques Berque, who studied the Arab world from within, offer the reader an exceptional panorama of an original reality — but it is so original that a comparison becomes unattainable. As Edward Said asserts, difficulty with most writings about Islamic countries is that they overemphasize their pecularities, with the result that these writings deal more with the specificity of the culture than with comparisons. The intimate perception of a social universe, even if by a "foreigner," thus results in one precious quality — a lifelike knowledge — obtained through subjective complicity. But it is not always useful for generating comparisons and does not facilitate the induction from specific to general, which alone allows knowledge to progress.

Studying the Arab world, and considering the same transition to modernity, Daniel Lerner, in his book *The Passing of Traditional Society*,[1] perhaps commits the sin of excessive generalization; but such a sin could be considered minor in comparison to the overspecificity of so many experts. The objective of comparative sociology and political science, in their efforts to become more explanatory than descriptive, is precisely to insert each study — partial, regional, sectoral—into a larger context. The historian Paul Veyne went so far as to say, paradoxically, that even specific and individual knowledge passes through conceptual generalizations. It is necessary to conceive of imperialism in general in order to perceive what is particular about Roman imperialism, British colonial imperialism, Soviet imperialism by satellites, or American economic imperialism. "Only what remains constant individualizes, no matter how abstract and general it be."[2] Put differently, one needs the concept of a Gothic cathedral to appreciate what is original about the cathedrals of Burgos, Milan, Marburg, Strasbourg, or Cologne.

In their search for pertinent categories, social scientists have tried to rid themselves of the normative visions peculiar to their societies. How are we to measure "participation," "democracy," or "freedom" if we retain criteria that are particular to a certain political system? Some researchers from Eastern Europe, for example Jerzy Wiatr, have cited the difficulties of communication between Western scholars and their colleagues from the East. This normative bias is manifested even among Western comparativists. Charles Moskos and Wendell Bell have denounced some pernicious ideas—that democracy is inappropriate for poor people, for instance, or that military governments are more efficient than others at a given stage of development.[3] But how to conceive of a totally objective researcher? To be conscious of the values one holds may be more fruitful than to pretend to be totally free from preconceptions.

The contribution of anthropology to the "release" of political science from narrow cultural limits should be mentioned here. The study of primitive societies has permitted social scientists to comprehend their own universe in a different light. The integration of primitive groups into the recognized corpus of social systems has obliged them to draw back and elaborate more universal categories. It is not by accident that functionalism descends directly from anthropology.

Some authors, such as Jean Ziegler, have even proposed starting from the "non-Western" in order to return to the "Western" equipped with new concepts. This strategy has been criticized as excessive by Giovanni Sartori. It is as ridiculous to speak of political participation in Uganda or Yemen as it is to explain the functioning of advanced pluralistic democracies in terms of mobilization. One should not attempt to overcome one ethnocentrism by falling into another. In the best of hypotheses, the concepts will be swollen out of all proportion; they will be softened to such a degree that they will lose their accuracy even for the particular countries in which they were born. "All in all, it can hardly be held that our 'losses of specificity' are compensated by gains in inclusiveness. I would rather say that our gains in travelling capacity, or in universal inclusiveness, are verbal (and deceptive) while our 'gains in obfuscation' are very substantial."[4]

Sartori's critique is addressed to those who make indiscriminate use of what we have learned from non-Western societies. Nevertheless, one should not neglect how much some pages from anthropology have animated comparative political science. Parallels developed by Claude Lévi-Strauss between myths and ideologies in *Anthropologie structurale* have fertilized the analysis of both myths and ideologies. The research of Wilhelm Mühlmann and his colleagues on "nativism"[5] has nourished the comprehension of nationalism; in the same way, an analysis of "messianism" cannot be ignored by those interested in charismatic or revolutionary phenomena. Georges Balandier has rightly stressed how much the debate over power and politics in general has been stimulated by the anthropological approach.[6]

Sociology has also played an important role in pointing out the dangers of ethnocentrism. Societies across the world are infinitely varied. To account for the contrasts they observed between the behavior of Poles and Italians, Irish, and black people, sociologists from the Chicago School, at the beginning of the century, gave birth to the concept of culture.[7] They were among the first to emphasize how diverse societies are, how resistant and significant are the psychological frontiers imposed on them by history. A few decades later, Western social scientists, American and European, began invading the four corners of the world armed with erudite questionnaires; they rapidly discovered with bitterness the inefficiency of their "universal" concepts. Questions that were full of meaning in England or Scandinavia would shock the Japanese and could not be translated into Arabic. But these obstacles have stimulated serious reflection and have undeniably favored progress and maturation. To warn that a question or a research tool "does not fit," as Erwin Scheuch does, signifies "that the researcher from a foreign culture is usually unaware of the existential basis of his own thinking. Thus the 'pains' involved in doing cross-cultural research are reflections of the very corrective that cross-cultural research is supposed to provide for a social science developing within a particular social system."[8] Comparative studies point out and denounce ethnocentrism, and in this way they certainly contribute to its lessening. One must test one's own limits in order to transcend them. Like any scientific discipline, international comparison will progress by correcting a series of errors progressively revealed.

NOTES

1. Third ed. New York: Free Press, 1963.
2. Paul Veyne, *L'inventaire des Différences* (Paris: Seuil, 1976), p. 18.
3. In "Emerging Nations and Ideologies of American Social Scientists," *American Sociologist* 2, no. 2 (May 1967).
4. Giovanni Sartori, "Concept Misformation in Comparative Politics," *American Political Science Review* 64, no. 4 (December 1970): 1052.
5. *Messianismes révolutionnaires du Tiers monde* (Paris: Gallimard, 1968).
6. In *Anthropologie politique*, 2nd ed. (Paris: PUF, 1967), Foreword.
7. See infra, chapter 8.
8. Erwin Scheuch, "Society as a Context in Cross-National Comparisons," *Social Science Information* 6, no. 5 (October 1967): 15.

CHAPTER 2

COMPARING
TO FIND
SOCIOLOGICAL RULES

Political phenomena are not the object of an experimental science; that is all too clear. Social theories can sometimes be tested successfully. But the passage from micro- to macroanalysis is always risky, and the most important actors in political life are not those who can be manipulated for experimentation. Anyway, one cannot test the manner in which a social system regularizes itself under contradictory influences, the manner in which groups are formed or conflicts mature. The first sociologists rapidly understood how they could overcome these difficulties by using comparisons. The comparative method was perceived by John Stuart Mill, Auguste Comte, and Émile Durkheim as the best substitute for the experimental method in the social sciences.

In reality, it is not entirely satisfactory to speak of opposition between comparison and experimentation because the comparative approach is present in experimentation. It is the systematic comparison of the results of repeated experiments that constitutes the implicit key to the experimental method. The difference lies in the fact that the chemist or the bacteriologist has the means to provoke, in a closed setting, the phenomenon he wants to study. He can assure that no environmental variation interferes; by keeping constant those variables he does not want to study, he can eliminate them from his field. This kind of manipulation is clearly impossible in a human environment. The sociologist and the political scientist can study only phenomena that they themselves have not provoked.

In other words, in domains where experimentation cannot be applied, comparison is synonymous with an intellectual approach searching to make an inventory of similarities and differences between two or more situations; it is also the only way of collecting information and data in sufficient number to approximate a scientific approach. Comparison here means both description and thought. One cannot really know whether various electoral techniques have an impact on party systems without considering a sufficiently large series of concrete examples; in the same way, a study of different social contexts is needed for an analysis of the various agents of socialization, modernization, or party alignment.

"We have only one means of demonstrating that one phenomenon is the cause of another: it is to compare the cases where they are simultaneously present or absent." So wrote Émile Durkheim in *The Rules of Sociological Method,* emphasizing the difference between experimentation and comparison. "When the phenomena can be artificially produced by the observer, the method is experimentation in its proper sense. When, on the contrary, the production of facts is out of reach, when we can thus only bring them together as they are spontaneously produced, the method we use is that of indirect experimentation, or comparative method."

Comparison is a universal method in the social sciences; it is worthwhile not only to those who study an international field. Even if we intend to study electoral participation in a single country, we proceed by comparisons: between men and women, young and old, city dwellers and rural villagers, and so on. Even for this kind of study, international comparisons might provide supplementary support. One would better understand the behavior of French workers if one were to establish points of reference in some neighboring countries. It is easier to identify trends in the British economic development by analyzing what happened at the same time in Germany or France. It is not surprising that the historical method is so often combined with the comparative method.

All theories are syntheses. But the best ones find inspiration in multiple and contradictory analyses. The nature of totalitarian leadership or the process of military intervention in politics will become clearer if the study encompasses a series of cases in a variety of contexts. For the social scientist, comparing remains the main way of approaching the causes of observed phenomena, that is, of elaborating sociological rules.

Naturally, international comparison, like ecological analysis, does not guarantee the validity of the induced conclusions. The application of the methods of "difference" or "concomitant variation," as proposed by Mill, has its limits. Never will the context of the compared situations be sufficiently similar to permit considering as null the influence of the environment; never will the researcher be in a position to validly exclude from his conclusions those contextual variables that he cannot keep constant. Against the extreme consequences of such possible "overconscious" thinking, Giovanni Sartori has rightly reacted: What the researcher in social science should seek is not paralyzing perfection, but the most satisfying approximation to it.

In search of causal relationships, the comparativist encounters an additional obstacle: the relatively limited number of cases that can be treated. There are 150 independent nations in the world, but it is evident that we do not possess a large enough sample to study phenomena such as charismatic power, the decline of parliament, or the political role of top civil servants. In order to maximize the statistical significance of the analysis, several approaches are possible. Arend Lijphart has made some proposals.[1] A first possibility could be to multiply the number of situations by taking historical examples into consideration. Thus, one could study bureaucratization by integrating empires from ancient times into the comparative analysis, or study the process of urbanization by retrospectively looking at the experiences of historical Europe. Such a solution nevertheless has two limits: (1) the fragmentary character of the information at hand, even for the most recent past; (2) the distortions imposed by history, and the fundamental differences that often exist between identically labeled phenomena. It would certainly be useful to study the contemporary development of literacy in Africa or Asia, its modes and political consequences, in the light of what happened in Europe during previous centuries. But it would be a mistake not to consider the essential differences between the spread of literacy by print media at the time of Bismarck and the spread of literacy in an era of audiovisual media.

Another way of multiplying the cases available for comparison is to identify relatively homogeneous regions within each country. Juan Linz delineated eight Spains, Erik Allardt four Finlands, and Stein Rokkan as many Norways. Everyone knows that there are three Belgiums, four Italys, and five or six Frances. Those who are considering all of Western Europe might succeed in counting forty units. But, obviously, such a multiplication is valid only for problems that are sufficiently independent of the national polity. A supplementary advantage is that the internal homogeneity of each of the eight Spains or the four Italys will undoubtedly be greater than that of Spain or Italy in their entirety.

Another strategy consists in grouping together situations that are in fact not very different. One could thus contrast a number of one-party systems with multiparty systems, free market economies with planned economies, federal states with unitary ones, and so on. In this way, the number of cases grouped in each category necessarily increases. But what we gain statistically, we risk losing by reducing the incisiveness of the utilized concepts.

Another much advocated and practiced strategy consists in reserving comparisons for countries that present analogies sealed by history or geography. This strategy, known as "area study,"[2] seems to ensure in a natural manner the control of those environmental variables the observer would like to keep constant in order better to analyze the fluctuation of others. Thus, clearly one can better understand the influence of electoral techniques on political behavior or the structure of parties if the comparison is carried out in a culturally or structurally homogeneous universe. Douglas W. Rae proceeded in this manner in studying the political impact of electoral techniques. Taking up the prob-

lem formulated by Maurice Duverger, Rae extended the analysis to twenty pluralist democracies that could be considered relatively similar; his conclusions,
which essentially confirm those of Duverger, clearly reveal the effects of the
majority ballot and proportional representation.[3] In this example, the analysis
rests on a fairly large number of cases—or at any rate a sufficient number to
test Rae's theoretical proposals. When general laws are based on the comparison of only two or three countries, however, the conclusion induced may be
subject to question. In fact, in such cases, the best authors claim only to formulate hypotheses that need to be tested further in other countries. One cannot establish the conditions required for a stable democracy just by analyzing
Norway in the light of British and German experiences. Harry Eckstein knew
that.[4] Only when the original propositions are confirmed or refined by other
studies do hypotheses crystallize into rules.

Another means of maximizing the accuracy of the results of a comparison
is to carefully isolate the sectors on which the analysis will focus.[5] This "segmentation" of the political system usually precedes the selection of countries
to be compared. It permits the researcher to "forget," to a certain degree, those
contextual variables that make comparison so difficult. In concentrating attention on bureaucracies, unions, or women's votes, the analyst lessens the significance of environmental differences between countries, societies, or political
systems.

Researchers seek the most stable and invariant factors amid a profusion
of forms and events. That is why they look more for similarities than for differences. Wasn't it in the most trivial, persistent, and universal phenomena that
Newton and others discovered the greatest scientific principles? "The same thing
could be said about political phenomena," says LaPalombara. "Not only are
the persistent and enduring political patterns evidence of significant regularities
in human behavior or organization, they constitute as well an enormously important backdrop against which we can better interpret momentary deviations,
as well as unusual or seemingly esoteric patterns that may imply long-range,
more permanent changes."[6] Comparison helps separate the accidental from the
inevitable, the occasional from the regular. An accumulation of knowledge is
achieved through this movement, which shifts from particular to general, then
back from general to particular, with new hypotheses and progressively refined
concepts.

Only by examining multiple cases can we locate, rank, and build a hierarchy. Only by comparing can we order reality according to conceptual axes that
will perhaps become as many explanations. But comparison also permits the
induction of laws and the elaboration, sometimes slow, of generalizations. The
history of sociology is marked by laws discovered through more or less explicit

comparisons. The political scientist has often tried to elucidate the relation between the social and the political spheres, as well as to establish correspondences between strictly political variables. Xenophon early inquired as to the intrinsic logic of tyranny. The Anglo-Saxon theorists of nascent parliamentarianism later found the key to balanced power in the system of checks and balances. In a more empirical manner, Roberto Michels investigated the internal organization of parties in order to formulate his "iron law of oligarchy."

The analysis of behaviors has fostered a series of hypotheses, from the most general to the most specific. Max Weber has investigated the link between the Protestant ethic and the dynamic of a social system. Other sociologists have tried to understand the determinants of social mobility. While some authors have looked to the modes of socialization for an explanation of the adult's political attitudes, others have proposed sociological models that, for example, shed light on the moderating potential of crosscutting or overlapping cleavages.

As these few examples show, conceptualization can be performed at several levels. Considered at the highest degree of abstraction, political instability seems to involve variables as general as the distribution of ownership (an old hypothesis originally formulated by Tocqueville); or else the legitimacy of regimes, the relationship between socioeconomic and political development, the extent of cultural consensus, or the burden of political demands. The same question asked of parliamentary democracies alone would allow the identification of other decisive factors, such as the constitutional framework, the nature of governmental coalitions, or the number and cohesion of political parties.

Depending on the objective of the scholar who formulates the rule, its scope may vary greatly. Perhaps at midpoint between the two extremes—on one side the paradigm and on the other the description without interpretation—is located the most constructive propositions, those that Robert Merton calls "theories of the middle range": "theories intermediate to the minor working hypotheses evolved in abundance during the day-by-day routines of research and the all-inclusive speculations comprising a master conceptual scheme from which it is hoped to derive a very large number of empirically observed uniformities of social behavior."[7]

Each method available to the social sciences for establishing rules has its particular limits. For a long time, political scientists, particularly in Europe, remained enclosed in legalistic frameworks that undoubtedly did permit them to evaluate the impact of institutions. But the reverse should also be noted: By neglecting the social forces that influence the exercise of power, those scholars "proved to be relatively insensitive to the non-political determinants of political behavior and hence to the non-political bases of governmental institutions."[8]

On the other hand, the behavioral approach to political phenomena has tended to neglect the decisive role that institutions play.

Those who have given priority to the social forces at work in history have sometimes drifted into pure theory. The sclerosis of a certain Marxist school is, from this point of view, a sad example. But there certainly are criticisms to formulate against functionalists as well; they too are subject to the temptation to drown the multiplicity of events in unverifiable abstractions. The historical method has proved capable of demonstrating how political institutions have crystallized over time—in how many stages and under the pressure of what factors. But historical analysis must be transformed into asynchronic comparisons in order to be able to comprehend the essential originality, for instance, of the development of Europe in the nineteenth century. By quantification, it is possible to analyze rigorously the relations between political phenomena that were, for a long time, only presupposed. But quantitative methods have their own faults. The need for hard data may bias the questions asked and confine the researcher's capabilities to perceive. Bertrand de Jouvenel has rightly denounced this "new fatalism," which deduces everything from GNP per capita.

To give maximum consistency to results, the social scientist is obviously preoccupied with transcending the trivial comparison. In practice, this implies a constant effort to give more precision to the information and data used, to quantify all that appears to be quantifiable. But the social scientist must keep in mind that technical sophistication cannot be an end in itself. The development of technological means of investigation and the extension of the field of comparison should be accompanied by improvements in comparative methodology, by epistemological thinking, and by a careful formulation of concepts capable of absorbing, regularizing, and giving meaning to the stream of information. Without this, all technical progress achieved at the level of collection or treatment by computer of data will be in vain.

NOTES

1. In "Comparative Politics and the Comparative Method," *American Political Science Review* 65, no. 3 (September 1971).
2. See infra, chapter 16.
3. Cf. *The Political Consequences of Electoral Laws* (New Haven: Yale University Press, 1971), pp. 87-103.
4. *Division and Cohesion in Democracy* (Princeton: Princeton University Press, 1966).
5. See infra, chapter 13.
6. *Politics Within Nations* (Englewood Cliffs, N.J.: Prentice-Hall, 1974), p. 9.
7. *Social Theory and Social Structure* (New York: Free Press, 1957), pp. 5-6.
8. Roy Macridis, *The Study of Comparative Government* (Garden City, N.Y.: Doubleday, 1955), p. 15.

CHAPTER 3

OPERATIONAL CONCEPTS

Concepts have always been recognized as essential to knowledge. For a long time now, philosphers have argued about the origin of concepts and have debated whether they come down from a transcendent ideal world or up from real experiences. Today, such a debate would be futile, since it is generally admitted that there is an unending dialectic between the *a priori* and the *a posteriori*. All knowledge, as Kant has shown, results from the indissoluble coupling of sensitive intuition and concept: "intuitions without concepts are blind, concepts without intuitions are empty."

Applied to comparative analysis, the point could be briefly stated as follows: Without abstraction and intellectual construction, there are no common denominators between the several objects submitted to comparison. Because the concept is this very abstraction, there can be no comparisons without concepts. "Whereas the image is the representation of a particular object," posits the *Grande Encyclopédie,* "the concept represents all the objects of a given generis. The concept is an *abstract* idea, in that it considers only certain characteristics of the objects; and it is a *general* idea, in that it extends the considered characteristics to all objects of the same class." Abstraction first, then generalization—this is the natural behavior of the comparativist.

Comparative political science progresses with the help of conceptual instruments. Its path is marked by "buoys": participation, legitimacy, authority, anomia, integration, exclusion, alienation, populism, and so on. Social scientists have elaborated a lengthy list of concepts in order to dissect and master better the prolific diversity of reality. These logical categories are useful devices; they help researchers to represent intelligibly the phenomena they study. But they are as unobservable as the first microscopic particles imagined by Democritus or Anaxagoras. You cannot *see* social classes; you cannot *see* charisma. You cannot decide just by opening your eyes whether you should analyze "power" in terms of domination, as Weber did, or in terms of exchange, as Parsons did. In fact, as R.T. Holt and J.M. Richardson state, "concepts are judged not by their truth or falsity, but by their theoretical utility."[1] They add that there would be little sense in arguing, for example, "whether or not there are such things as demands, supports and functional requisites." The only important thing is to know how useful the concepts are in understanding reality.

The number of concepts that could be analyzed in a work dealing with international comparisons necessarily exceeds the size of any book. Nevertheless, numerous neighboring concepts are differentiated only by their label. In their search for originality and precision, sculptors of neologisms do not always make inventive contributions. It would be easy to denounce the amalgamation under one rubric of characteristics or processes that do not necessarily belong to a single analytical category. The concept of secularization, for instance, as utilized by Gino Germani to study the transition from the old to the modern, in fact covers a great variety of traits. Indeed, they concern the political system as well as the family, social reforms as well as demographic trends. Secularization is explicitly conceived by Germani as a complex process, implying three fundamental modifications of the social structure. They encompass, first, a transformation in behavior and models of action; second, the passage from the institutionalization of tradition to the institutionalization of change; and third, the shifting from undifferentiated structures to differentiation, specialization, and a growing autonomy of structures.[2] Those who speak about development or modernization are referring to the same processes as does Germani. These nuances in conceptual definition do not necessarily denote a substantial originality in approach.

Trying to analyze change, the concept passes from the static to the dynamic. But how to integrate movement? The point is worthy of reflection, since the concept naturally tends to rigidify the reality it orders. The great sociologist Max Weber was highly conscious of this problem. Elaborating his analytical categories, he took care to indicate how much they were "ideal types," references serving to situate relatively the concrete cases under investigation. There is no rational authority that is not also founded on tradition—be this tradition "democratic" or "republican"—and any traditional authority admits some innovation. Isn't *bon vouloir* included in the definition of monarchical absolutism?

Related to the idea of change are the problems of maturation and decay. Political systems, like societies, are living entities; they are constantly evolving. Charismatic power survives by weakening, since its routinization profoundly transforms its essence. Weber also imagined a certain number of dynamic concepts in introducing secularization between the sacred and the profane, *Vergesellschaftung* between *Gemeinschaft* and *Gesellschaft*. Today, it is possible to mention scores of concepts that are embedded in the idea of change, such as development, modernization, nation building, integration, legitimation.

The concept of structural differentiation, embryonic in the writings of Weber and developed by Parsons, has known a notable success among functionalists, who use it as a classificatory axis to distinguish various kinds of political regimes.[3] The sociologist Robert Marsh has applied this concept with a view to ranking the totality of known societies, from the Ibo tribe to the mastodon-like Soviet Union. Marsh's goal was to show that significant political and social phenomena change according to this fundamental variable of "structural differentiation."[4] But he did not really indicate how to measure it. To this difficult question, no one has yet brought a satisfactory reply. Here is an important lesson for the comparativist: The most general analytical categories, the most ambitious ones, are not necessarily the easiest to operationalize. In reality, under the façade of words like integration, socialization, politicization, and modernization, we find an extremely large number of complex phenomena, whose analysis would require refined models and subtle interpretations.[5]

The development of dynamic concepts has acted as an incentive to epistemological thinking. Reinhard Bendix, for example, proposes to see in each analytical category a complex of "contrast-conceptions," taking a different meaning according to the context and the prospect of the analysis. The nascent bureaucracy, he says, was remarkable for features that are no longer remarkable today. What originally distinguished it from feudalism — its impersonal and rational characteristics — could not be considered as a satisfactory definition for those who study the American "imperial Presidency" or the French Fifth Republic.[6] The argument could be extended widely. Is it possible to analyze, with concepts formulated in Europe in a completely different context, what is happening now in Burma or Zaire? What really is a "nation" or a "social class" in sub-Saharan Africa? Are not the words that we use surreptitiously leading us to misinterpretation?

Verbum dat esse rei announced the scholastic philosophers. But words do more than capture reality; they reveal or even enhance it. We see what we are looking for. That is why many comparativists have advocated and continue to defend the necessity for precise conceptual instruments. If everyone is to include a different content under words such as "dictatorship" or "freedom," no theoretical debate can progress. Giovanni Sartori became the passionate adversary of these dangerous approximations, engaging in a fierce battle against this Tower of Babel open to all historical connotations, to all bastards of interdisciplinarity, where the definition of concepts finally gets lost. "Our purpose," Sartori wrote with Fred W. Riggs and Henry Teune, "is to find a strategy that favors cumulative innovations precisely because it impedes the endless regression toward anarchic disruption and confusion."[7]

To coin a terminology both neutral and precise has been the goal of many researchers, a goal often pursued and sometimes achieved. But Stanislav Andreski has rightly pointed out how it may be in vain to "fabricate neologisms to eliminate normative nuances whereas the psychological and sociological vocabulary, as soon as it begins to be diffused, becomes the object of gross simplifications and deformations."[8] As he has stated in another place, "terminological confusion cannot be dispelled by convening committees to legislate on the matter, but only by adjusting and inventing terms whilst constructing theories which genuinely explain real events. Terminological confusion is just an aspect of the general lack of understanding."[9]

The search for neutral and incisive concepts is frequently the result of exchange and collaboration. The concept of political pluralism, for instance, marks a progress in relation to that of liberal democracy. That of polyarchy, imagined by Robert Dahl,[10] opens still different perspectives. Undoubtedly these categories fill a function that could not be ensured by the concept of democracy, which is now too vague and subject to dispute. But how much energy has been lost in this quest for neutrality and precision! And why not admit that a certain amount of ambiguity is not necessarily conducive to intellectual sclerosis? "Equivocity," noted Roger Caillois, "an imperfection for a code of signals, is for the language, on the contrary, a symptom of richness, the source of a greater variety of possible combinations among signs."[11]

The analytic capacity of social scientists is often proportionate to their capacity to imagine a series of hypotheses that they constantly refine to carve out "operational" concepts oriented toward practical efficiency rather than abstract beauty or philosophical coherence. William J. Goode is certainly right when he says that the success of such an instrument does not depend only on its clarity or etymological precision "but on how much fruitful research a new concept generates. Most concepts new or old are not killed by attack but by neglect."[12]

There are imperfectly defined concepts around which an entire literature has grown—the concept of charismatic power is a case in point. Some concepts have provoked lengthy polemics, even though they may have been conceived as neutral instruments by their "inventors"—an example is the notion of working-class authoritarianism formulated by Seymour Martin Lipset.[13] There are concepts that continuously occupy the front of the stage, like the concept of power, and others that have cyclical fortunes, such as the notion of social movement.[14] Not all are instruments of equal value; but they all foster a continual process of conceptual adjustment in the social sciences. None of them is sufficiently perfected to escape the need for constant revision. One reformulates the concept of social class or "revisits" the civic culture;[15] one critically reconsiders the notions of revolution or counterrevolution. The comparative perspective steadily favors this process.

That comparison needs concepts has already been sufficiently argued. What is equally important to emphasize is the determinant role played by comparative analysis in the elaboration of concepts that rapidly appear indispensable even in noncomparative studies. The concepts of culture or political socialization stem from comparison.[16] The same could be said about the articulation or aggregation of interests. Comparative paternity is clear as well in the concept of underdevelopment. Raymond Aron put it perfectly: "The notion of under-development was born from a comparison. It qualifies what certain societies are not (i.e., developed), and does not characterize what they are. The concept of under-development, indeed, applies to old civilizations (India), as well as to tribal areas (some parts of Africa), or even to backward regions within developed countries. I will go further: it is not reasonable to expect a direct and positive definition of under-development, because this concept is comparative in its very nature."[17]

International comparisons sometimes engender very general and vague concepts. The distance that the comparativist must maintain between himself and the field of investigation multiplies these kinds of risks and demands critical vigilance on the part of even the best analysts. Good concepts are needed to open the door of comparison. But in this primary quest, the social scientist is confronted with many obstacles and temptations. He must avoid the trap of conceptual imperialism, which pushes some to explain everything in terms of culture, class, profit, personality, and so on. In the social sciences, there is never one single determining factor that can explain all historical trends; there are always several or many causes involved.[18]

Social scientists should guard against slipping from theory to doctrine, from clarifying caricatures to distortion, from concept to myth. The temptation of oversimplification does not spare the scientific spirit; nor does the temptation of irrationality. Aron once accused certain intellectuals of also having their opium.[19] Reality is to be discovered beyond ideologies, common ideas, and the too obvious "evidence." In his *Règles de la méthode sociologique,* Durkheim exhorted researchers to protect themselves against these recurrent elements of pseudo knowledge. Illusionary knowledge and false truths often appear, in the field of international comparisons, as prejudice, cliché, and national stereotype.

NOTES

1. "Competing Paradigms in Comparative Politics," in *The Methodology of Comparative Research,* ed. R.T. Holt and J.E. Turner (New York: Free Press, 1970), p. 24.

2. Gino Germani, *The Sociology of Modernization: Studies on Its Historical and Theoretical Aspects, with Special Regard to the Latin American Case* (New Brunswick, N.J.: Transaction Books, 1981).

3. See infra, chapter 23.

4. Cf. *Comparative Sociology: A Codification of Cross-Societal Analysis* (New York: Harcourt, Brace, 1967).

5. See infra, chapter 22.

6. Cf. "Concepts in Comparative Historical Analysis," in *Comparative Research across Cultures and Nations,* ed. Stein Rokkan (Paris: Mouton, 1968), pp. 70-72.

7. *Tower of Babel: On the Definition and Analysis of Concepts in the Social Sciences* (International Studies Association 1975), p. 1. See also G. Sartori, *Democratic Theory* (Westport, Conn.: Greenwood, 1973).

8. Stanislav Andreski, "Classifications et terminologies: des outils à manier avec circonspection," *Revue Internationale des Sciences Sociales* 3 (1974): 525.

9. Stanislav Andreski, *Elements of Comparative Sociology* (London: Cox and Wyman, 1964), pp. 85-86.

10. Robert Dahl, *Polyarchy, Participation and Opposition* (New Haven: Yale University Press, 1971).

11. In R. Caillois et al., *Le robot, la bête et l'homme* (Neuchâtel: La Baconnière, 1965), p. 20.

12. In Peter M. Blau, ed., *Approaches to the Study of Social Structure* (New York: Free Press, 1975), p. 67.

13. In a famous article, reprinted in *Political Man: The Social Basis of Politics,* expanded ed. (Baltimore: John Hopkins University Press, 1981), pp. 87ff.

14. Besides the classic book by Rudolf Heberle, *Social Movements: An Introduction to Political Sociology* (New York: Appleton-Century-Crofts, 1951), a large literature has been devoted to the concept of social movements. See, for an encompassing view of the subject, Louis Kriesberg, ed., *Research in Social Movements: Conflicts and Change* (Greenwich, Conn.: JAI Press, 1979).

15. See infra, chapters 6 and 8.

16. In fact, the pioneering work of Charles Merriam has taken a comparative look at socializing processes. Cf. *The Making of Citizens: A Comparative Study of Methods of Civic Training,* 2nd ed. (Chicago: University of Chicago Press, 1935).

17. Raymond Aron, "La théorie du développement et l'interprétation historique de l'époque contemporaine," in *Le développement social,* ed. Raymond Aron and Bert Hoselitz (Paris: Mouton, 1965), p. 89.

18. Against that *illusion du trait dominant,* see Léo Hamon, *Acteurs et données de l'histoire* (Paris: PUF, 1970), 1:41.

19. Cf. *L'opium des intellectuels* (Paris: Calmann-Lévy, 1955).

CHAPTER 4

THEORETICAL FRAMEWORKS

Concepts are indispensable but not sufficient for the comparativist, who must not only analyze and dissect reality but also coherently structure data. It is in the creation of logical frameworks that the comparativist can make knowledge cumulative. Thomas Kuhn, in his classic work *The Structure of Scientific Revolution,*[1] has shed light on the role of paradigms in scientific progress. This role is significant not just for the physical sciences.

A great variety of theoretical constructions interest comparativists. While some models can be tested, others are highly abstract paradigms that borrow their theoretical components from cybernetics, biology, or mechanics. There are theories imbedded in reality that do not claim to explain everything; and other, more generous ones sometimes have the tendency to lose themselves in the stratosphere.

Joseph LaPalombara called the comparativist's attention to the "widening chasm" he observed between theories too general to ever be tested and empirical research without direction. Comparative political science, he argued, lacks theories at a median level of abstraction, which would permit a translation of the accumulated findings into effective and testable knowledge. Taking up Robert K. Merton's ideas, LaPalombara called for a return to greater empiricism and segmentation. "It strikes me as enormously telling," he said, "that at precisely that moment in the profession's development when methodological tools will permit the rigorous comparative testing of hypotheses the distance between hypotheses and general theory should be widening, and that the linkage between hypotheses and macrotheory is either terribly obscure or of such problematical logical construction that theory itself cannot be falsified."[2] If the conceptual scheme escapes verification, how can it be refined or remodeled? If the distance between theory and social reality is too great to be bridged, is there not a risk of a comfortable intellectual sterility, or even of "mystification," to use a word suggested by Maurice Duverger?[3]

The critical remarks by LaPalombara should be heeded. There is much that could be said about the proliferation of ambitious schemes, while our knowledge of so many fields remains incredibly poor. "I find it instructive, for example, that political scientists are loath to make high-flown generalizations about the American political system (the one about which we have the greatest amount of information) while they will at the slightest stimulus generalize about large-scale societies in Africa, Asia and Latin America, concerning which our lack of historical and contemporary information is perhaps the most striking thing we can say."[4]

It would be dangerous to turn the theoretical construction into a means of filling lacunae in our empirical knowledge. In his *Governmental Process,*[5] David Truman long ago advocated the formulation of a conceptual framework that would help us master the flux of gathered information; since then, however, theoretical frameworks have themselves tended to proliferate.

This is not to deny a positive contribution to holistic theories. Whatever problems they pose, they have certainly helped comparative political science face the enormous problems raised by the emergence of so many new nations in the last third of the century. One could probably take issue with the utility of including in the same analysis countries such as Indonesia and Britain, or India and the USSR. But when the comparativist proposes such a heterogeneous field, when he claims to compare American and Chinese political systems, he is naturally led to adopt notions whose degree of abstraction is related to the immense gaps existing in the reality. The farther apart the compared countries are, and the more sharply contrasting, the greater the need to rise on the scale of abstraction.

To establish a common matrix is precisely to find the means of comparing, of locating in the same diagram, the multiplicity of national political systems. That is why all great paradigms, whatever they may be, have attracted comparativists' attention: Hegel's or Marx's dialectical schemes, Easton's mechanical model, Deutsch's cybernetic paradigm, Almond's pseudo-biological or Parson's psychological models. The theoretical construction is more than a mere temptation to the scientific spirit; it is a necessity, since only the bouquet of hypotheses proposed by a researcher gives meaning to facts, events, and figures. For this reason, such a collection accompanies any research, even if noncomparative.

Order is intellectual, and it imposes itself more stringently as the volume of unorganized data increases. The need to systematize grows in relation to the accumulation of information, the problem being to master its anarchical spreading. Do we not see today even the world of signs and symbols reduced to "systems," and a profusion of literatures to "theories"? Unfortunately, this propensity is full of danger. Theory orders, but it also guides. If perception influences theory, the opposite is equally true. "In order for an object to be accessible to analysis, it is not enough to perceive it," noted the Nobel prizewinner François Jacob. "It is also necessary that a theory be ready to accommodate it. In the exchange between theory and experience, it is always the former that initiates the dialogue."[6] That is to say, theory may also be a source of biased perceptions or erroneous interpretations.

Max Weber presented himself ostensibly as an "antimetaphysician." In this manner, stressed Julien Freund, "he intended to manifest his dislike for these broad romantic syntheses, which claim to systematically explain the world, life or society, on the basis of some unique element or concept. Weber was an adversary of the philosophers of history, who like Hegel, Marx or Comte, have attempted to give one complete and holistic explanation of reality."[7]

No sociologist and no political scientist involved in comparative research can avoid becoming, at a certain point, a theorist; but both should resist becoming prisoners of "grand explanations" that are all too encompassing not to arouse doubts. The temptation is often great to imagine theoretical frameworks that are capable of integrating, like a splendid puzzle, all the findings and data accumulated in pieces. Indeed, the development of statistical techniques, made excessively simple by the computer, has rendered more pressing the need for articulated logical schemes. The refinement of these theoretical and conceptual tools is the point at issue if we are to prevent the progress of data collection from resulting in a grandiose void. "One of the greatest difficulties in cumulative research," writes Alfred Grosser, "is precisely to find the level of generalization which permits the simultaneous avoiding of sterile theory on the one hand, of useless accumulation on the other hand."[8]

The inability to integrate the accumulated materials in a constructive manner can also result from too much inertia in the explanatory schemes. The most brilliant models often become pallid as soon as one tries to move beyond static description in order to comprehend movement. It is symptomatic that structuralism, for instance, found it difficult to pass from "synchronic" to "diachronic," although Claude Lévi-Strauss did recognize the importance of this historical dimension. It is also a fact that the "epistemological projections" described by Michel Foucault in Les mots et les choses communicate between themselves rather badly across time. The confrontation of theoretical schemes with changing reality frequently and cruelly marks their limits.

Critiques against the "overly static" characteristics of many theoretical frameworks, functionalist or systemic, are in a sense paradoxical, since most promoters of these paradigms are sensitive to problems of change and development. Karl Deutsch summarized these grievances: "Altogether, in the world of equilibrium theory, there is no growth, no evolution; there are no sudden changes; and there is no efficient prediction of the consequences of 'friction' (between parts of the system) over time."[9]

In reality, theorists of the "political system" generally include the idea of change in that concept.[10] But their perspective leads them to represent the political body as naturally tending to restore its equilibrium indefinitely. This remark is as valid for the extremely rigid scheme of David Easton as for the theories of Talcott Parsons, whose concern with change is indisputable and who passionately sought out the axes around the directions in which societies tend to evolve.

The cybernetic approach has permitted Karl Deutsch to propose a model specifically designed to integrate movement, making room for the idea of autonomous goals, of reaction to information from outside, of internal adjustments or transformations.[11] Curiously enough, this audacious scheme, perhaps too abstract, has hardly found an audience to date among comparativists. Its application has remained limited to the domain of international relations.

One could not make this kind of reservation in regard to functionalism, as elaborated by Gabriel Almond and others from ideas developed by Merton, Parsons, and Easton. To identify the universal functions that should be filled by any social or political system is to provide the analyst with the means of making significant global comparisons. In fact, this approach has permitted a notable development in the comparison between advanced and developing countries. For the comparativist, undoubtedly, functionalism is the most useful of all theoretical frameworks. By liberating comparative analysis from its formal shackles, it permits progress that remains above criticism.

NOTES

1. Chicago: University of Chicago Press, 1965.
2. J. LaPalombara, "Macrotheories and Microapplications in Comparative Politics, A Widening Chasm," *Comparative Politics* 1, no. 1 (October 1968): 56.
3. Cf. "De la science politique considérée comme mystification," *Revue Française de l'enseignement supérieur* 4 (1965).
4. LaPalombara, "Macrotheories," p. 63.
5. New York: Knopf, 1951.
6. François Jacob, *La logique du vivant* (Paris: Gallimard, 1970), p. 24.
7. Julien Freund, *Max Weber* (Paris: PUF, 1969), p. 14; see also, by the same author, *The Sociology of Max Weber* (New York: Random House, 1968).
8. Alfred Grosser, *L'explication politique. Une introduction à l'analyse comparative* (Paris: Colin, 1972), p. 55.
9. Karl Deutsch, *The Nerves of Government* (New York: Free Press, 1963), pp. 89-90.
10. See on that aspect John McKinney, "Social Change: Theoretical Problems," in *Constructive Typology and Social Theory* (New York: Irvington, 1966), pp. 140-55.
11. Deutsch, *Nerves of Government*.

CHAPTER 5

FUNCTIONAL EQUIVALENCES

The notion of functional equivalence descends directly from the concept of "function."[1] The idea that a political system necessarily fulfills certain fundamental tasks helped functionalists move to an important stage. They have indeed emphasized with particular clarity, first, that different structures may perform the same function, and second, that the same structure may perform several different functions.

The search for functional equivalences passes through this analytical disassociation of roles and functions. The same performance may be accomplished in various countries by different organs; and similar or comparable institutions may fulfill, in various countries, different tasks. In some places a tribe can assume the function of political recruitment that a well-organized political party performs elsewhere. But the presence of such a party does not impede other organs from contributing to the recruitment of political elites, as do, for example, unions in Great Britain or Catholic Action in Italy. The higher administration not only plays an executive function; it is well known that it also intervenes in the legislative process upstream, although to varying degrees. This intervention is particularly important in France, Austria, Sweden, Norway, Denmark; it is much less so in Belgium, Italy, or the Netherlands.[2]

By way of simplification, one could say that the president of the French Republic, in his role as supreme magistrate, fulfills three functions: a symbolic one, which makes him the representative of the nation; an executive one, which makes him the chief executive; and a partisan one, which makes him the leader of the majority coalition. If one asks who fulfills these three functions in Great Britain, one finds two officials: the monarch for the symbolic function and the prime minister for the two others. In Italy, these three functions are distributed among three persons: one for the symbolic function (the president of the Republic), one for the executive function (the president of the Council of Ministers), and one for the partisan function (the general secretary of the dominant Christian Democratic party). A similar division occurred in Germany in 1974 when Helmut Schmidt succeeded Willy Brandt to the Chancellory, leaving Brandt with the effective presidency of the Social Democratic party. Once the comparativist has identified the person who fulfills the various functions, he can tackle the field, however large, that he wishes to investigate, asking identical questions of systems that are as different as the Soviet, the Dutch, and the Albanian.

For the comparativist, functionalism starts with the search for equivalences. But it is necessary to emphasize here how much this concept is a tributary of functionalist theory and systems analysis. Only the universal matrix of the political "system," such as Easton in particular has imagined it for the study of political phenomena and processes, has rendered possible the development of comparisons in terms of functions. Knowledge of these functions did not exist prior to the discovery of this allegorical system. This fact alone testifies to the usefulness of theoretical elaboration; without it, it would have been impossible to construct the marvelous "instrument" of functional equivalence.

No one is obliged to accept the parable of the "black box" in which the energy of demands and supports is transformed into legislative texts, governmental orders, or symbols; still, everyone would agree that all political systems engender decisions. Who makes them? The parliament, as under the French Third Republic; party headquarters, as in Italy; a military nucleus, as in Argentina; the high bureaucracy, as in Austria at the time of the Habsburgs; powerful groups like Opus Dei in Spain under Franco; a tyrant like Idi Amin Dada in Uganda; a dictator resting on a solid party; or the crowds in the street, as in revolutionary Saint Petersburg or Teheran? To identify these organs across a diversity of situations is a primary duty for the comparativist. Indeed, by locating the site where political decisions are made, the comparativist will not only differentiate between various political systems but will also bring to light the specificity of certain problems. LaPalombara stressed in his introduction to *Bureaucracy and Political Development*[3] that the seizure of power by bureaucracy brings about significant consequences. Its intrusion signifies that decisions will be taken according to processes marked as much by obscurity as by expertise; furthermore, its growth may also represent a serious obstacle to the development of an autonomous political authority. In this example, we see how the functional perspective can elucidate even the history of political institutions.

One could make the same observations about communication. The existence of a network of mass communication, as Daniel Lerner showed in *The Passing of Traditional Society*,[4] naturally brings about political processes that are very different from those engendered by the old mediated and fragmented system of oral communication. It is true that in both cases, functions of communication are fulfilled. But they are performed so differently that the political scientist has come to explain on that basis a part of the enormous contrast that exists between political systems in the age of audiovisual media and those that rely on mouth-to-ear relays. These observations bring us to the question of the nature of "equivalence," which should never be confused with similarity.

Most vital functions of a political system can be treated in the same way; socialization, for instance, may be fulfilled by the family, the church, the public school, or a political youth organization; and to these different patterns will correspond different political consequences. Comparing as a functionalist has the advantage of getting rid of misleading labels. Comparing "White House and Whitehall,"[5] Richard E. Neustadt suggests that the American and British machines are not at opposite poles, but rather "near the center of a spectrum stretching between ideal types, from collective leadership to one man rule." But the similarities between the two systems are not to be detected by conventional comparison: "We [Americans] have counterparts for their top civil servants — but not in our own civil service. . . . We have counterparts for their Cabinet ministers — but not exclusively or even mainly in our Cabinet. . . . We make ourselves much trouble, analytically, by letting nomenclature dictate our analogies."

Functional equivalence is not a trivial equivalence; it implies conceptualization, that is to say, it appears only after an in-depth analysis of the political processes. Who articulates demands in Poland and Italy? By what channels is information transmitted? How much independence is enjoyed by the courts or the socializing agencies? Functional equivalence allows for a comparison that automatically sheds light on the manner in which the political system "functions" in general and in its various sectors. This conceptual matrix calls for generalization. Because each function is conceived of as a part of a living complex, even the most empirically oriented research eventually nourishes the theoretical framework.

Among the universal and fundamental functions, two in particular attract the attention of the comparativist interested in a great variety of political systems because they permit a significant differentiation between them. They are (1) the articulation of interests, which consists of the translation of diffuse interests into explicit demands (claims, petitions, proposals, amendments, etc.); (2) the aggregation of interests, which consists of converting these demands into global and coherent alternatives (party programs, congressional platforms, parliamentary majorities, etc.)

For example, the interests of winegrowers from southern France, or those of metalworkers, can be expressed by organized associations such as unions or by more spontaneous groups that will block highways, damage official buildings, or demonstrate in order to arouse public opinion. These interests can also reach the ears of those in power by more diffuse means, by mass media, or even by direct contact.

Once articulated, the interests need to be aggregated, that is, integrated or included in wider programs capable of winning a majority with various ideally compatible goals. The institutions or organizations that fulfill this aggregating function could be unions at national or regional levels, political parties or a coalition of parties, or some conciliatory committee.

Let us imagine, in various countries, interests already articulated by feminist, ecologist, or consumer movements. These interests will not be integrated in the same manner in a multiparty system, in a two-party system, or in a one-dominant-party system. In the first case, several majorities are possible simultaneously, according to whether the issues of the day concern foreign policy or legislation on birth control, taxation, unemployment, and so on. Usually, a party will have to take the initiative in defending this or that particular interest, but its minority position will oblige it to find allies through a series of negotiations and compromises. The process of interest aggregation will find its final stage in the parliament, or during negotiations among leaders of parties representing a virtual majority.

In a two-party system, on the contrary, the site of aggregation will normally be the leadership of the party in power, after debates and even fights among factions. In a one-dominant-party system, the aggregation is still fulfilled within the party; but, sometimes, external interventions such as those by the higher administration, the church, or the army make themselves strongly felt. This happened, for example, in Franco's Spain. In a political regime with strong personalized power, it may be the leader himself who reconciles divergent interests. That is to say that according to the context, the same function could be fulfilled by structures as specialized as parties, unions, parliaments, and so forth; whereas elsewhere it could fall to the hands of a single man or to his immediate entourage, according to ethnic, tribal, clientele, or familial ramifications.

Functional equivalence is most useful when we consider highly contrasting countries. Functionalists have, in fact, purposefully designed it to make possible comparison between two countries when one is structured in an embryonic way and the other has reached a high level of structural differentiation. For example, it would be easier to compare Germany and Austria without the concept of functional equivalence than it would be to compare Indonesia and Canada.

Necessarily, the more a system develops, the more it becomes differentiated; the specialization of structures tends to grow until each particular function is performed by a specific institution. It is incumbent upon the comparativist to bring to light the way in which various specialized political agencies have historically crystallized—executive power, legislatures, bureaucrats, courts—and to indicate which different functions could be fulfilled by similar structures in various historic, cultural, or systemic contexts.

The function of mobilization, for instance, frequently escapes the central political structures. It is well known that this role may be played by institutions outside the political sphere, such as religious ones (we think of the Hussites in the past or, more recently, of the Ayatollahs); newspapers (the name of *Al Ahram* should suffice); universities (from Al Azhar in Cairo to Teheran); unions; the army; or even sports associations.

In the same way, it could be admitted that no one institution is limited to a single function. A union, for instance, may depart from its normal role (i.e., to articulate specific interests) in order to become the representative and symbol of an entire population, as happened in Poland in 1980-82. These substitutions occur with particular frequency in certain specific situations. A fascinating task for comparativists would consist in pinpointing the link that exists between various contexts and the probability of such substitutions. When the English dissolved the party of Kenyatta in 1955, the trade union of Tom Mboya took up the banner. Similarly, in Algeria or Cameroon the union became the flagship of nationalist claims at the moment when French authorities forbade their political expression.

Religious organizations may compete with political channels everywhere. Nevertheless, as Guy Hermet noted, the political presence and activity of the hierarchy, the clergy, and the organized Catholic militants are notable "especially in regimes characterized at the same time by an authoritarian exercise of power, and by the incapacity or refusal to implement a sufficient and generalized participation of the citizen in the political system. . . . In these countries, religious organizations are the only ones capable of offering host structures, leadership, and means of expression distinct from those controlled by the power or dominating oligarchy."[6] The political role of religious organizations seems thus to correspond to a particular systemic situation.

In the same way, in the particular setting of Eastern Europe discontent is manifested through various specific channels, which have been well analyzed by G. Ionescu.[7] It is expressed through magazines and intellectual circles (as in Czechoslovakia during the Prague Spring); in the universities (in Budapest in the 1950s); around religious leaders (and not only in Poland and Hungary); through the army, which is often less subservient to Moscow than the party; around factions, particularly when the classic opposition crystallizes between "dogmatics" and "Moscovites" or "revisionists" and "nationalists"; or around strong personalities.

The significance of functional equivalences may vary not only according to the distance existing between the countries compared but also in relation to the place and importance of the observed function within the political system. To pose the equivalence of the modernizing bourgeoisie in nineteenth-

century Europe with the bureaucracy studied by Eisenstadt, or with the army
in certain Third World nations, is certainly more difficult than to note the equivalence between the secretary of state in France and the senior minister outside
the Cabinet in Great Britain.

On the other hand, the search for equivalence should not be limited to
the most important functions. It could be enlightening, for instance, to consider primary elections in the United States as accomplishing a function similar
to the first round in French elections. In the same way, it would be possible
to see in the practice of surveys, as introduced in Great Britain, an equivalent
to this first electoral round. If one fails to consider these equivalences, one com-
prehends neither how electoral behaviors are formed nor how the selection of
political leaders is accomplished.

The utility of the concept of functional equivalence is obvious but its empirical application is sometimes difficult. The idea, theoretically precious, that
certain vital functions are fulfilled everywhere has certainly helped the comparativist in perceiving the importance of certain structures, in discovering their
hidden tasks, their secondary roles. At the same time, certain shortcomings
should also be mentioned. It is not certain, in fact, that all the functions considered crucial to the existence of a political system are really performed everywhere. Obviously, it will always be possible to maintain that interests all over
the world are necessarily filtered, articulated, or aggregated; but how far can
we go in this direction? What "interests" really exist in the Yemenite or Afghan
political arena? It would certainly be fruitful to trace a parallel between the
electoral participation of, say, the English or Dutch citizen and that, more symbolic, of the Argentine *decamisado* or Algerian *fellah*. These kinds of comparisons would lead the researcher to reconsider the significance of the electoral
act in the context of true polyarchies and to point out, for example, its universal symbolic dimension. But one will not discover grand truths by advancing
very far along this road. As noted, Giovanni Sartori has contested the utility
of applying such concepts as "participation" to systems in which it is practiced
in such formal ways. An evident risk of the use of functionalism would be the
dilution of concepts, which might lose their analytical power as efforts are made
to have them cover the greatest variety of political regimes.

NOTES

1. See Gabriel Almond and G. Bingham Powell, Jr., *Comparative Politics* (Boston, Little, Brown, 1966). A revised edition of this now classic book was issued in 1978, but it remains to be seen whether an increase in volume has brought about a new vision or a more accurate definition of the concepts utilized.
2. See Mattei Dogan, ed., *The Mandarins of Western Europe* (New York: Halsted, 1975).
3. Princeton: Princeton University Press, 1963.
4. Daniel Lerner, *The Passing of Traditional Society* (New York: Free Press, 1958).
5. In *The Public Interest* 2 (1966).
6. Cf. "Les fonctions politiques des organisations religieuses dans les régimes à pluralisme limité," *Revue Française de Science Politique* 23, no. 3 (June 1973): 440.
7. *The Politics of the European Communist States* (New York: Praeger, 1967), pp. 190ff.

PART 2

THE INTERNATIONALIZATION
OF ANALYTICAL CATEGORIES

ANALYTICAL CATEGORIES are not born "operational." Those that attract the attention of scholars and demonstrate an ability to cross national boundaries and decades owe their power and longevity to the continuous adjustments they manage to absorb. That is to say, too rigid a definition may well be found sterile.

International comparison has had a great influence on some analytical categories that originated in the West, even if they were originally forged with a comparative perspective. In this section we consider these perpetual adjustments, first, apropos of social class.

The inclusion of developing countries in the research field has led many scholars to reformulate many concepts. At the four corners of the world, researchers have found that vertical stratifications are often more important than horizontal cleavages. Thus they have emphasized, for instance, the ubiquity of cultural pluralism or political clientelism. We follow this maturing process by considering political culture and socialization.

The concept of consociational democracy certainly deserves special attention. Indeed, it illuminates in a particularly interesting way the functioning of several European polities and even brings to light common features among countries that, from many points of view, appear very different. Finally, we have selected the concept of political crisis, which helps us analyze a great variety of critical situations and illuminates how analytical categories may contribute in capturing the most dynamic processes.

Many significant concepts could be considered from the point of view of internationalization. It was necessary to make a choice, guided partly by the existing literature. Several books deal with the problem of the internationalization of analytical categories. Some focus on it directly, for example the book by Sidney Verba and Lucian Pye on participation,[1] or that by Dankwart A.

Rustow on nation building.[2] Some deal more implicitly with this international-ization process; this occurs when an author reviews the "state of the art" in one field, for instance the book edited by Arnold J. Heidenheimer on corrup-tion,[3] or that by Glenn D. Paige on leadership,[4] by Marvin E. Olsen on power,[5] by Richard Rose on electoral participation,[6] Bertrand Badie on development,[7] or Karl W. Deutsch on nationalism,[8] to mention only a few examples.

The concepts selected here are intended to exemplify with particular clarity the way in which comparison helps refine the intellectual tools that, in their turn, permit comparison to progress further. Knowledge as it is acquired must be appraised critically, permitting rectification and reformulation of original analytical categories. The concept becomes more accurate throughout this proc-ess of continuous exchange between reality and abstraction, between words and substance. Applied on a worldwide scale, international comparison plays the role of a powerful tool in these readjustments precisely because it is difficult to fit into a single and often rigid mold so many nations, systems, and societies.

NOTES

1. *The Citizen and the State: A Comparative Perspective* (Stanford, Calif.: Grey-lock, 1977).
2. *A World of Nations: Problems of Political Modernization* (Washington, D.C.: Brookings Institution, 1967).
3. *Political Corruption: Readings in Comparative Analysis* (New York: Holt, Rinehart and Winston, 1970).
4. *Political Leadership: Readings for an Emerging Field* (New York: Free Press, 1972).
5. *Power in Societies* (New York: Macmillan, 1970).
6. *Electoral Participation: A Comparative Analysis* (Beverly Hills, Calif.: Sage, 1980).
7. *Le développement politique,* 2nd ed. (Paris: Economica, 1981).
8. *Nationalism and Social Communication* (Cambridge, Mass.: MIT Press, 1953).

CHAPTER 6

SOCIAL CLASSES:
DIFFERENT IN EACH CONTINENT

All societies are stratified. Nowhere in the world can one find a flattened society. This fact, evident to the lay observer, engenders the crux of sociological inquiry: On what basis is a society structured? Is there a criterion that will permit rigorous comprehension of social hierarchies?

Even when we consider social classes within only advanced Western societies, we are struck by the evident heterogeneity of social constellations. Categories important in some countries may be negligible or nonexistent elsewhere. Sharecroppers here, fishermen there, aristocrats here, ethnic *lumpenproletariat* here—one would find it difficult to compare the patterns of social stratification in Italy and Norway, in England and Finland.

For those who attempt a comparative analysis of social structures on the two sides of the Atlantic, problems become even more thorny. The analyst is impressed by the fact, simple but significant, that the word "class" is absent from the current vocabulary of both workers and sociologists in North America. This finding suggests, even to the uninitiated, that self-identification is an essential element in class stratification. A second distinction impresses itself on the comparativist who finds that the gap between the lower and upper classes is much smaller on the American side of the Atlantic than the gap between the working class and the bourgeoisie in old Europe. It is not only a matter of income; even the ways of life indicate a less significant psychological distance between groups, as many sociological studies show. To the subjective dimension of social consciousness is thus added a more objective dimension concerning the differences between standards of living and life styles. Nowhere in the world does the industrial manual worker have such a high salary in comparison with other social strata as in the country considered the most capitalistic.

If one extends the comparison to include Japan, one notices the contrast between the rigidity of Japanese social structures and the very high mobility— horizontal as well as vertical—in the United States. This observation brings a third dimension to light, one in which Europe occupies a median position. A Japanese is likely to spend his entire life in the same place and in the same company, and to perceive and conceive of social climbing as possible only within these stable parameters.

These examples, and they could easily be multiplied, suffice to lead the observer to question the capacity of the concept of social class to make a comparison between the fifteen or twenty most advanced Western countries. The reply to this question is included, it seems to us, in the observations we have just made: Only the analytical category of social class permits us to say that social hierarchies are more or less rigid, that social distances are more or less significant, and that social consciousness is more or less developed. The concept of class is sufficiently abstract to allow for comparisons between very different situations.

In handling the concept, however, one encounters very serious difficulties as soon as one leaves the relatively homogeneous Western world. The hurdle of internationalization is arduous to cross.

If we were to follow Marxist theses, social classes should be easy to identify. Certainly the importance of phenomena like social consciousness engenders some uncertainty regarding the preponderance of objective factors over subjective ones in the social realities. Alerted by some historical circumstances, Georg Lukacs points out the distinction between class *in* itself, which can be identified by the relations of production, and class *for* itself, which is revealed to consciousness by social and political conflicts. This is a nuance, however, on which most Marxist theoreticians do not insist. Nicos Poulantzas indeed traces a distinction between the "structural determination" of classes and their "conjunctural position," which could lead them to act in a way that was not in accord with their own interests; but he rejects the contrast that could be inferred between economic and politico-ideological situations. If we are to believe him, the process of production remains the "main determinant" of class alignment.[1]

The rigidity of such a definition runs into many difficulties, particularly for the comparativist whose work encompasses the five continents. Private ownership of the means of production does not exist everywhere, and domination is not linked everywhere to the monopoly of such property. Far from it.

The Polish sociologist Stanislaw Ossowski clearly indicates the limits of the traditional Marxist view. According to him, it helps in the clarification of only one social context: "The closer the social system to the typical model of capitalist free enterprise, the more the social classes will define themselves according to their relations to the means of production, and the more will human relations be conditioned by the ownership of the means of production."[2]

Already the spectacular development of the "technostructure," and the dispossession (as analyzed by various authors from James Burnham to John Kenneth Galbraith) of the owners of capital by a new class of managers, poses in advanced societies a series of difficulties of interpretation, which Marxist theory has also had trouble overcoming.[3] These problems loom even larger when the comparativist considers the socialist countries of Eastern Europe, which claim to ban individual ownership of the means of production. Other difficulties arise for the analyst who includes in the comparison countries of the Third World, where the mechanisms of the national economic system are often dominated by external forces. Specialists in developing countries have shown how social classes have been established here according to processes largely unrelated to economics. The place of what Richard Sklar calls the "managerial bourgeoisie,"[4] and what Irving Markovitz calls the "organizational bourgeoisie,"[5] in the constitution of a new ruling class in Africa illustrates the originality of a process of social stratification, which takes root as much in the political superstructure as in the economic infrastructure. Curiously enough, the consolidation of the state engenders the development of this stratum of bureaucrats, who with businessmen and some traditional elites share status, power, and wealth. Structurally heterogeneous, this dominant group finds coherence essentially in its strategic privileged situation. It is united not so much in regard to the means of production, which may escape its control, as it is in terms of political power, which controls the distribution (or confiscation) of goods produced.

Certain Marxists have tried to evade these facts—troubling for those who believe that social class should be defined exclusively in relation to the means of production—as they move their analyses from the national to the international level. The "center-periphery" model proposed by Edward Shils has been transposed to the planetary level by Immanuel Wallerstein, Johan Galtung, and Samir Amin, among others. Class struggle remains for them the driving force of history; but the context of the struggle has become international. In these models the national bourgeoisie has been reduced to local representatives of imperialist interests. Though with more subtlety and greater respect for the autonomy of social and political local institutions, theorists of "dependence," such as F.H. Cardoso, also state that the structures of developing countries are conditioned by the interests of foreign capitalist classes. For certain Marxist authors, the ultimate consequence of such interpretations, analyzing the situation on the periphery from the vantage point of the domination of the center, is the elimination, sometimes contrary to the evidence, of the role of the national bourgeoisie and of the concept of ruling class for the developing countries. We thus arrive at the paradoxical but frequent result of an analysis that claims to be radical but offers little insight and relatively superficial explanations of social changes. "Not unfrequently," stresses Richard Sklar, "an elite theory is the unknown and unrecognized premise of a professed 'Marxist' analysis. 'Marxists' who refuse to acknowledge the existence of a ruling class on the so-called 'periphery' of international capitalism are left with little more than a doctrine of elites and cannot effectively analyze the inner structural drives of non-industrial societies."[6]

Confronted with the reality of the existence of social classes in extremely different national contexts, the comparativist is naturally led to ask how relevant the concept of social class, as formulated by Marx in the nineteenth century, really is. In the search for a common conceptual category, Stanislaw Ossowski has admitted the importance of factors that cannot be reduced to the economic sphere. The division into classes reflects, according to him, social stratification related to all "non-natural" systems of privileges and discriminations. His definition thus reintroduces, in a striking fashion, the notions of power, status, and wealth.

How could one combine these various elements in order to apply them, at an intercontinental level, to the concept of social class? The question at this stage is whether the definition of class should be unidimensional or multidimensional. Gerhard Lenski[7] advocates a very broad concept of social stratification, defining class as "an aggregation of persons in a society who stand in a similar position with respect to some form of power, privilege or prestige." He insists, in addition, that hierarchies, since they are derived from resources like power, privilege, and prestige, never totally coincide. Canadian or Brazilian citizens would be stratified differently according to what we consider first: wealth, political influence, economic activity, or even skin color. There is some congruence among these various hierarchies. But Lenski also develops the interesting idea that, according to the system, the main key to social stratification is to be found either in ethnicity, status, ownership, or in power. "In totalitarian nations, repeated efforts have been made to increase the importance of the political class system at the expense of other kinds of class systems, especially the property class system."[8]

Many survey studies have been carried out in order to measure the prestige of various professional categories. W. Lloyd Warner showed a long time ago,[9] and many others have confirmed since, that there exists in the United States a strong relationship between hierarchies of status and income. Studies done by Alex Inkeles on the Soviet Union,[10] and those by Robert W. Hodge, Donald J. Treiman, and Peter Rossi,[11] among others, have shown that professional hierarchies tend to be more or less the same everywhere; that is, the doctor or the professor is effectively ranked higher than the shopkeeper or the artisan, who in turn ranks above the manual worker or the peasant. All this is interesting in itself, but it does not advance us very far along the road toward a universal definition of "social class." Things get seriously complicated when original groups appear in various national contexts—specific social categories that draw their prestige from irreducible sources such as tradition, religion, or even more simply, power or ownership. We thus find that party bureaucrats in some countries, corporation managers in others, and religious leaders elsewhere occupy a privileged place that cannot be analyzed in identical terms.

These considerations indicate the difficulty of comparing, in space and time, the structure of classes. It is easier to conduct a comparative analysis of class systems in relatively similar countries. This has been done for advanced industrial countries, for Latin America, for Africa, and for communist countries. As soon as one tries to analyze these continents together, however, all difficulties multiply, in large part because the determinant criteria in one place are not those that are significant elsewhere. That is why we rarely see intercontinental studies. Those who have attempted them have been obliged to divide their analyses according to various kinds of societies: industrial, agrarian, ex-colonial, and so on. [12]

As Albert A. Simkus states, comparative research on stratification has been neglected: "Much of what we know is based on analyses of crude data of questionable comparability, secondary analyses of data whose methodological bases are poorly documented, and impressionistic contrasts between studies of individual societies." [13] It is significant that Larry Isaac, discussing the literature in *Comparative Economic Inequalities,* [14] found, on the contrary, that interest in the matter was great and that "there has been a wide variety of strategies for organizing this vast literature."

Only the study of the distribution of wealth has permitted the expansion of the analysis to cover the entire planet. In effect, this is a rare criterion that one could hope to measure empirically. And as the multiple aspects of social stratification often overlap, with all modern social systems tending to express inequalities in monetary terms, one might hope that an analysis of income distribution, for instance, could constitute one of the very few practical means of approaching the phenomenon of social class around the world.

One method consists in drawing so-called Lorenz curves, translated in Gini's "indexes of inequality." To do that, specialists perform analysis by deciles of personal income, dividing the population into these deciles and determining the proportion of the population pertaining to each group. Because the technique of analysis is identical for all countries, comparison is possible. Naturally, the precision of available data varies greatly from country to country. For many countries, it is more a matter of evaluation done by experts than of solid statistics. This technique has been utilized by economists for many years. But only recently did the World Bank publish a report covering eighty-one countries [15] and present it in such a way that it is possible at a glance to compare such different situations as those of Gabon and Canada, or of India and France. One example among others: In West Germany the poorest decile in 1970 received 2.2 percent of the national income, whereas in East Germany, its share was 4 percent. At the peak of the pyramid, the most privileged decile reserved for itself in West Germany 29.1 percent of GNP, as against 16.9 percent in East Germany. If we push the analysis further, we may note that the highest 5 percent of the scale in West Germany gets 18.2 percent and in East Germany 9.2 percent of GNP.

The most interesting finding at the global level is that the poorer the country, the greater the inequality. There are notable exceptions, interesting deviant cases, which underline the importance of political orientations. But the ratio between the first and the last decile is in general smaller in the richer countries than in the poorer. The higher the standard of living, as measured in GNP per capita, the smaller the inequalities.

This phenomenon is all the more remarkable because it cannot be explained by the portion of the GNP controlled by the state. There is no significant relation between the degree of redistribution of wealth and the size of the national budget measured as a portion of GNP. In effect, some Third World governments control as high a proportion of the GNP as do the governments of Bonn, Paris, Washington, or London. Thus it is necessary to look elsewhere for an explanation. But where? In the amount of social demands authorized in a democratic system or in the very richness of the countries?

It was Gerhard Lenski's hypothesis that inequality in the distribution of wealth is inversely proportionate to the size of the "social surplus": The more wealth increases in a given society, the more wealth there is to be redistributed. Several examples in contemporary history seem to confirm such an interpretation. Many great social reforms have been adopted in periods of prosperity by conservative governments, the decisive factor appearing to be favorable historical circumstances rather than the political color of the government that is in office.

Nevertheless, pressure by the masses on the political system remains an essential factor. When the political system is open and competitive, the redistribution of the national revenue operates more effectively—by means of direct and indirect taxation, social security, familial allocations, state education systems, and so forth.

Should we infer that the class system is more rigid in developing nations than in postindustrial societies? No, and herein lies a paradox. Western society, which is slowly but significantly moving toward more homogeneity—whose citizens live at the same rhythm, consume the same goods, flock to the same beaches—remains eminently more conscious of its divisions than any other society. The perception of social inequalities has not declined along with the reality of these inequalities. To the contrary.

Naturally, the criterion of national income redistribution does not clarify completely the phenomenon of social classes. Neither does exploitation or domination appear in the distribution by deciles. In this sense, the perpetuation of a class consciousness in the European countries, for instance, also points to the inherent weakness of the indicator chosen.

But how could one explain the fact that such a social consciousness does not really characterize the profoundly inegalitarian societies? The first hypothesis is that the emergence of social consciousness implies the existence of a certain level of development. The miserable masses in India or Latin America hardly constitute a "vanguard" of the proletariat. They often lack all that is needed for a political awakening. Centuries of servitude and failure nourish resignation rather than revolt; persistent illiteracy keeps them away from ideological currents; their precarious situation turns them into a gigantic rural or urban *lumpenproletariat*. Finally, geographical isolation can influence socioeconomic conditions. In countries where 80 percent of the population lives in a relatively homogeneous context, as in sub-Saharan Africa or on the Peruvian plateau, the emergence of social consciousness is much more difficult a process than in a heterogeneous context, where the oppressed are directly confronted with an inequality that is thrown in their faces.

But the essential reason for the difficulty of making operational at the world level a concept like social class is the fact that the context profoundly shapes perceptions. Most developing societies are characterized by vertical stratifications that are more visible, solid, and easily recognized than the partly hidden horizontal cleavages. Stratification into social classes is obviously less likely to be perceived in a society vertically divided into racial, ethnic, tribal, religious, linguistic, or clientelistic pillars.

Advanced nations have largely eliminated vertical cleavages as a result of unified educational systems, mass media, and political party networks at the national level. In these countries, the significant cleavages are at the level of socioeconomic interests; even ideologies are rooted in these conflicting interests. Religious or regional allegiances, except in consociational democracies, have lost much of their weight; social stratification is primarily horizontal.

This is not true for most of the developing countries, which retain very important and deeply rooted vertical structures. One would certainly find, from this point of view, very great differences between Latin America and Black Africa, for instance. In the one area, there exists a tremendous amount of religious and linguistic homogeneity. Almost all Latin Americans are Roman Catholics, and most of them speak either Spanish or Portuguese. As long as the people of the Andean islets, who are generally excluded from political participation, do not fuse into self-conscious political subcultures, Latin America will continue to remain an original continent compared to the rest of the developing world. On the other side of the southern Atlantic, a mosaic of tribes, dialects, and indigenous or imported religions turns Black Africa into what specialists call a world of "cultural pluralism." Unlike the situation in Mexico or the United States, it is not a matter of mixed and assimilated heritages melting into a relatively homogeneous culture. It is a question of spatially distributed subcultures. The majority of African nations are vertically split into cultural segments that are more significant than the diversity of horizontal structures to be found in each one. It is obviously rare for the various ethnic groups to be equal from a social point of view. The economic and political domination of some over others is a well-known fact, one that has led some comparativists to suggest the principle of an equivalence between ethnicity and class. This interpretation is in many cases excessive, as becomes clear when spectacular reversals occur in the hierarchy of ethnic groups by coups d'etat, civil wars, or more progressive processes.

M. Crawford Young rightly points out that it is precisely when class cleavages coincide with ethnic cleavages that their explosive potential is greatest.[16] That means that the two concepts do not overlap. For most African or Asian countries, a concept such as cultural pluralism[17] or tribalism could be as useful and operational as that of social class. Nathan Glazer and Daniel Patrick Moynihan note also that ethnicity may be a source of stratification that is more fundamental than class.[18]

Other vertical stratifications should be considered from this perspective. Clientele chains, which link clients and patrons of different statuses in various social contexts, sometimes play a counterbalancing role in the recognition of horizontal solidarities. The concept of clientelism,[19] formulated in order to elucidate the way in which essentially different groups and strata coagulate around a network of persons, does not prohibit a parallel recourse to the concept of class domination. All specialists know that the patron-client link can obscure a case of real class domination. "The important issue then," says René Lemarchand, "is not whether class or ethnicity are more relevant than clientelism but how they interact with each other. . . . The problem can be approached in one of two ways. In one case the focus is on the transition from a vertical ordering to one in which horizontal solidarities predominate; in the other, attention is drawn to the opposite phenomenon, that is, the resurgence of clientelistic ties in the pursuit of a dominant class or ethnic objective."[20]

Why has the class struggle not yet "changed the face of the world"? Analytical categories such as cultural pluralism, political culture, socialization, and clientelism, among others, can greatly help us in the search for an objective reply to this question, which has provoked so many impassioned polemics.

NOTES

1. Nicos Poulantzas, *Les classes sociales dans le capitalisme d'aujourd'hui* (Paris: Seuil, 1974), p. 18; the book was later published in English as *Classes in Contemporary Capitalism* (New York: Schocken, 1978).
2. Stanislaw Ossowski, *Class Structure in the Social Consciousness,* rev. ed. (London: Routledge and Kegan Paul, 1979).
3. See, for example, Ralph Miliband's theses on the homogeneity of the ruling groups in *The State in Capitalist Society: An Analysis of the Western System of Power* (New York: Basic Books, 1969).
4. *Corporate Power in an African State* (Berkeley: University of California Press, 1975).
5. *Power and Class in Africa* (Englewood Cliffs, N.J.: Prentice-Hall, 1977), esp. pp. 204-7.
6. Richard Sklar, "Socialism at Bay: Class Domination in Africa" (paper delivered at a joint meeting of the African Studies Association and the Latin American Studies Association, Houston, Texas, November 1977), p. 21.
7. Gerhard Lenski, *Power and Privilege: A Theory of Social Stratification* (New York: McGraw-Hill, 1966), pp. 74-75.
8. Ibid., p. 81.
9. W.L. Warner, *Social Class in America* (Chicago: Science Research, 1949).
10. "Social Stratification and Mobility in the Soviet Union," *American Sociological Review* 15, no. 4 (1950): 465-79.
11. "A Comparative Study of Occupational Prestige," in *Class, Status and Power,* ed. R. Bendix and S.M. Lipset, 2nd ed. (New York: Free Press, 1966), pp. 309-21.
12. See, for example, André Beteille, ed., *Social Inequality,* 4th ed. (Baltimore: Penguin, 1974).
13. "Comparative Stratification and Mobility," *International Journal of Comparative Sociology* 22, nos. 3-4 (1981): 213.
14. *International Journal of Comparative Sociology* 22, nos. 1-2 (1981): 62.
15. Shail Jain, *Size Distribution of Income: A Compilation of Data* (Washington, D.C.: World Bank, 1975).
16. "Cultural Pluralism in the Third World" (communication to the IPSA World Congress, Moscow, August 1979).
17. See infra, chapter 7.
18. *Ethnicity* (Cambridge: Cambridge University Press, 1975), p. 17.
19. See infra, chapter 10.
20. In S.N. Eisenstadt and René Lemarchand, *Political Clientelism: Patronage and Development* (Beverly Hills, Calif.: Sage, 1981), p. 12.

CHAPTER 7

CULTURAL PLURALISM: VERTICAL SOCIETIES

The word "pluralism" has had a rich history. Today it is used in many different ways, two of which are important for the comparativist: political pluralism and cultural pluralism. Political pluralism was born under the influence of English theoreticians like John Neville Figgis and later Harold Laski. It was subsequently taken up in the United States under the influence of David Truman and Edward Shils. These authors have stressed the important role played by groups in political life. The organizations of which they speak mobilize citizens in defense of specific interests. One essential consequence of this pluralism is that it should normally lead to moderation and compromise. Caught in a network of multiple affiliations, the individual should progressively realize that some of his interests may be conflicting, and thus learn to moderate his demands. The multiplicity of organizations is not sufficient to establish political pluralism; it implies that each individual be involved in several associations.[1]

When J.S. Furnivall[2] formulated the concept of "plural society," the social segments to which he referred were of a different nature altogether. The concept had to do with closed groups, separated by cleavages that, far from cutting across the population in a variety of ways, isolate retrenched camps. The communities "possess" their members in an exclusive fashion, imparting a particular sensitivity to them that competes with the national allegiance required of them by the central state. Like Furnivall, many authors have related this particular structure to a situation of domination by one group. M.G. Smith thus defines plural society as "a politically autonomous unit ruled by a culturally distinct and politically privileged minority."[3] If we are to believe Smith, unequal access to central institutions is the defining criterion of cultural pluralism. But this perspective is reductionist. Indeed, not all plural societies are subject to the preponderant influence, to the domination of one group. A more neutral and appropriate criterion therefore could be the coexistence, within a national state, of impervious social segments, cultural collectivities aware of their particularism (ethnicities, castes, or religious or linguistic communities). This much broader definition makes it possible to enrich the analysis with all situations in which cultural pluralism has not engendered the clear domination of one group over the others.

Today a great number of states are vertically divided into antagonistic segments. With some exaggeration in the formula, David and Audrey Smock saw in the 1960s not so much the decade of "development" as that of "politicization of pluralism." "Country after country, both industrialized and developing, some before and many after 1960, have experienced strains wrought by the competing demands of communal groups within their borders. Attachment to parochial communities within the state . . . have become more salient reference points in the political process."[4] From this point of view, the fragility of many African or Asian nations is an obvious fact, and it is also true that even old and well-consolidated states (e.g., Great Britain or Spain) have again been confronted with the agitation of ethnic, linguistic, or religious communities at their peripheries. As M. Crawford Young states, "significant elements of cultural pluralism characterize the overwhelming majority of nation-states; the truly homogeneous polity, such as the two Koreas, is the deviant rather than the normal case."[5]

The number of countries to be considered in a study on pluralism depends on the criteria chosen. In less than one out of five countries in the world does the entire population speak the same language. However, four countries out of five are certainly not characterized by several vertically divided communities, each conscious of its identity. Between Libya on the one side and Lebanon on the other, between Costa Rica and Ireland, between Japan and Nigeria, there is a wide spectrum with multiple gradations.

Cultural pluralism should be clearly distinguished from social pluralism. The United States is a "melting pot"—to borrow the title of a famous book. But its constituting communities have accepted a common set of fundamental values and basic beliefs that certainly make "conviviality" easier. The great difficulty for the comparativist is precisely to evaluate what makes the difference and the similarity between, say, Great Britain and Chad, or Belgium and Cyprus. Since the concept of cultural pluralism is highly abstract, fruitful confrontations become possible.

Even though it seems of interest primarily to the sociologist, the notion of a plural society is in fact a crucial concept for the political scientist as well. David Nicholls has pointed out that, even if apparently sociological, "it is essentially a category of political science."[6] It could even be argued that cultural pluralism exists only in relation to the nation-state, since the social groupings are "plural" only in comparison to a unified national entity. The assemblage of these segments is a "society" only insofar as the primary collectivities are grouped under a common state structure.

R. Jackson, who analyzed societies of this type, noted that "paradoxically, the plural society is not a society at all. . . . It is rather a medley of stateless societies: an assemblage of contiguous, closed communities in which membership is ascriptive and mandatory."[7] The distinctive features of cultural pluralism appear here clearly. To describe this particular kind of allegiance, some authors have utilized the word "communalism." In the search for his identity, the individual naturally tends to confer an essential significance on the ties that Clifford Geertz calls "primordial."[8]

But M. Crawford Young emphasizes that the cultural groupings that weigh on the cohesion of many states are modern realities. "Contemporary cultural pluralism is not usefully viewed as a resurgence of 'primordial' sentiments."[9] Indeed, the Kabyle community in Algeria or the Indian segment in Malaysia are entities that are much broader, much more structured, self-conscious, ideologically enclosed, and at the same time geographically open than the tribes of another time. Modernization has simultaneously brought about a territorial opening and a redefinition in more abstract terms of cultural identities. In this sense, one can effectively say that cultural pluralism is "a quintessentially modern phenomenon."[10]

For a conscious feeling of belonging to a subculture to crystallize, it is necessary that the nation-state be established, that an impersonal bureaucracy develop, that a dominant language spread, and that a body of national legislation be implemented. The development of media, transportation, school enrollment, or urbanization paradoxically does not necessarily favor a homogenization of society. Indeed, these very elements that objectively unify styles of living at the same time provide minorities with the means of subjectively recognizing themselves as conscious entities.

All the analysts who have considered cultural pluralism seriously have denounced the naiveté of those who expected that industrialization and the extension of communication would directly counteract segmentation. In reality, economic, social, and political development often engenders a reawakening of competition between rival groups, competing for the new services offered by the state. Modernization brings with it an overgrowth of main cities, a consolidation of political centers that control mass media, as well as a redistribution of incomes. Such developments arouse rebellion at the periphery—what Jean Gottmann calls the "challenge to centrality."[11] Urbanization, education, and communication, far from radically opening the cultural collectivities, offer them the means of creating an elite, of developing a consciousness, of transforming their dialect into a true "language" and their legends into cultural patrimony. Even living in the town may have contradictory effects. As a matter of fact, the urban milieu generally exacerbates feelings of solitude and insecurity that may paradoxically reinforce the solidarity of original cultural collectivities.

The pretensions of the central power do the rest. Lured on by the myth of homogeneity, new states follow the same path as multinational states of yesteryear. Most of the time, their efforts to cultivate unity rebound against them by stimulating the crystallizaton of cultural identities. Like the Ottoman Empire or that of the Habsburgs, some new nations inadequately respond to the demands of their peripheries. The policy of arabization pursued in Sudan has ripped the country apart; in the past, russification aroused the Polish national consciousness. In the most dramatic hypothesis, cultural pluralism can lead to the breaking apart of the nation-state. The secession of Bangladesh from Pakistan is an extreme case; but Nigeria at the time of the Biafran war, and Chad a bit later, only narrowly avoided this kind of definitive dislocation. Naturally, all situations are not so dramatic. But, in all cases, the reinforcement of cultural solidarities weighs directly on the solidity of the political system.

At the level of political structures and processes, and in spite of the great variety of situations, pluralism favors some specific formulas, such as patronage, clientelism, factionalisms, and a personalized administration. These phenomena result from the preeminence of "communal" allegiances over a more homogeneous citizenship.

The concept of cultural pluralism is in fact extremely broad; it includes in the same basket solidarities that take root in very different kinds of communities and are based on race, ethnicity, religion, language, region, and caste. These solidarities may be more or less politically structured, felt with more or less intensity, and variously colored by ideology. There are situations in which segmentation is extremely rigid; this rigidity occurs when several cleavages are "superimposed." Other situations are more fluid. For example, J.A. Nagata[12] insists on the multiplicity of possible combinations and on the flexibility of allegiances in Malaysia, where racial and religious affiliations cut across one another.

Would it be possible to apply the perspective of "cultural pluralism" to situations of rigid ideological segmentation? Probably in Northern Ireland, where ideological affiliations have developed on the basis of religion. Imperial Germany was certainly a case of partial segmentation, since the socialist subculture was protected from contradictory influences and represented an efficient counterculture to the "official Germany."[13] The division in several self-conscious *Länder* and the opposition between Catholics and Protestants added elements of pluralism.

The profound identification that ties the individual to the segment community may have two general consequences. First, the citizen tends to reserve "patriotism" more for the community than for the enlarged collectivity, and this tendency often results in tensions that endanger the solidity of the national unity. Empirical surveys have confirmed the link conceived by theoreticians between vertical segmentation and instability, intensity of conflicts, and violence.[14] Cultural pluralism also contributes to the relative anesthetization of horizontal conflicts between classes, thus favoring a certain social conservatism. Conflicts of interests are often hidden and sometimes totally inhibited by the clientelistic ties instituted within the cultural segments.

Cultural pluralism naturally results in the crystallization of vertical solidarities. The individual who feels that he belongs to the Ibo or Hausa community will tend to align his political behavior on that of his ethnic brothers, even if they do not represent his own class interests. More or less, he reacts like the Parisian employee who approves of his government's position on the necessity for reevaluation of agricultural prices in the Common Market, in spite of his losses as a consumer.

This example shows how speaking about a "false consciousness" in describing relationships between members of the same subculture may be misleading. Such arguments do not help us understand why, in fact, inferior strata of dominant ethnic groups find it so difficult to ally themselves with dominated groups. "The persistent failure of Blacks and poor Whites to form durable alliances is eloquent testimony to the analytic necessity of conceptualizing the problem both in terms of cultural pluralism and social stratification. One needs only to imagine General Yahya Khan telling Sheik Mujibur Rahman in 1971 that Bengalis were deluded by 'false consciousness' to appreciate the inadequacy of this formulation."[15]

The disruptive ultimate consequences of cultural pluralism explain why most leaders of new states view homogenization as a crucial goal. Strategies of "unification" generally use the classical device of the diffusion of a common language. James Coleman has shown the fundamental role played by education in this process.[16] Others, like Dankwart A. Rustow,[17] have emphasized the place of symbolic elements in the gestation of a national "feeling." After independence, a revolutionary language, preserved to direct the group's aggressiveness against a common enemy such as "imperialism," has sometimes acted as a substitute for the former anticolonial struggle. The figure of the charismatic leader has fulfilled the same kind of unifying function.

But even totalitarian methods of unifying a population may prove ineffective. Such efforts at homogenization may foster a deep cleavage between public and private lives, the individual obeying the laws and norms of the imposed culture only in a superficial manner. This trend, which has been recognized clearly by observers in many developing countries, is also evident in countries where an intense policy of "massification" has been pursued for a long time. Hélène Carrère-d'Encausse's book on the Soviet Union, L'Empire éclaté,[18] has

shown how subcultures can perpetuate themselves behind the façade of ortho-
dox behavior.

In all cases where leaders perceive cultural pluralism as a serious handicap,
they work toward a mixing of the ethnic groups or other segments. The military may help bring about such integration. Parties and unions are also moti-
vated to serve this purpose. From this perspective, David and Audrey Smock
have noted the efforts made by Ghana's leaders, Nkrumah in particular, to turn
the Convention People's party into a pluri-cultural party, that is, a fully national party. That it rapidly loosened into branches organized along ethnic lines
attests to how difficult it is to stem such profound currents institutionally.

The problem takes on a different aspect in states where cultural segments
cohabit, that is, where various ethnic, racial, or religious communities are not
segregated geographically. In this regard, Malaysia and Lebanon are obviously
in a situation that is quite different from that of Nigeria. The geographical
dispersion of such various communities may create very different political problems. The mixing may revive antagonism by multiplying occasions for conflict
or, on the contrary, may accustom groups to the idea that they are compelled
to live together, and so convince them of the virtue of compromise and moderation.

Some authors have found unsatisfactory the dichotomy between political
and cultural pluralism and have tried to trace some possible bridges between
them. In considering the distance that separates the harmonious model of political pluralism on the one hand and the conflictual pattern of cultural pluralism on the other, Leo Kuper has insisted that it could prove most valuable to
orient research toward understanding what the two kinds of pluralism may have
in common. Such a study might reveal to social scientists how it is possible
to pass, without revolution, from deep segmentation to some degree of homogeneity, from domination to negotiation, from exclusion to participation.[19] Ralf
Dahrendorf has in the same way stressed the idea that there is no real discon-
tinuity; rather, there is a progression between the situation of cultural pluralism, which he characterizes by the concept of "superimposition," and situations of political pluralism.[20]

It is often by challenging the overly categorized approaches proposed by
theoreticians that comparativists arrive at the idea of a continuum. The isolation of cultural segments in fragmented societies is rarely total. As for pluralist
democracies, it is not necessary to search very far to find that none is perfectly
homogeneous, that the common code which cements the nation is never equally
accepted by all social strata. "The idea that a state can exist only when the
people share a common set of values is mistaken," writes David Nicholls.[21]
"Even in a relatively homogeneous state like the United Kingdom, values differ

quite radically from one section of the population to another." For this reason, Leo Despres proposed to call "heterogeneous" those societies that escape significant vertical fragmentation; and to call "homogeneous" the "primitive," nonstratified societies. In his classification, "plural" societies constituted a third group, characterized by particularly significant cultural sections.[22]

By following a dynamic policy of national integration, a state may well bring on itself the very disintegration "which it was the purpose of the policy to avoid."[23] It depends on the circumstances and conditions of this policy of unification. Cultural pluralism has sometimes proven to be perfectly compatible with political pluralism, as we shall see by analyzing consociational democracy.

NOTES

1. See, for example, William Kornhauser, *The Politics of Mass Society* (London: Routledge and Kegan Paul, 1960), pp. 79ff.
2. John S. Furnivall, *Colonial Policy and Practice* (New York: New York University Press, 19456.
3. M.G. Smith, "Institutional and Political Conditions of Pluralism," in Leo Kuper and M.G. Smith, *Pluralism in Africa* (Berkeley: University of California Press, 1971), p. 36.
4. D. Smock and A. Smock, *The Politics of Pluralism: A Comparative Study of Lebanon and Ghana* (Amsterdam: Elsevier, 1975), p. 1.
5. "Cultural Pluralism in the Third World" (paper presented at the IPSA World Congress, August 1979).
6. *Three Varieties of Pluralism* (New York: Macmillan, 1974).
7. *Plural Societies and New States: A Conceptual Analysis* (Berkeley: University of California Press, 1974), p. 8.
8. *Old Societies and New States* (New York: Free Press, 1963), p. 104.
9. M. Crawford Young, *The Politics of Cultural Pluralism* (Madison: University of Wisconsin Press, 1976), p. 34.
10. Ibid., p. 23.
11. *Center and Periphery: Spatial Variations in Politics* (Beverly Hills, Calif.: Sage, 1980), pp. 11ff.
12. In *Pluralism in Malaysia: Myth and Reality* (Leiden: Brill, 1975).
13. See, for example, Guenther Roth, *The Social Democrats in Imperial Germany* (Totowa, N.J.: Bedminister Press, 1963).
14. See, for example, D.G. Morrison and H.M. Stevenson, "Cultural Pluralism, Modernization and Conflict" *Canadian Journal of Political Science* 5, no. 1 (1972).

15. Young, *Politics of Cultural Pluralism,* p. 40.
16. *Education and Political Development* (Princeton: Princeton University Press, 1965).
17. In *A World of Nations: Problems of Political Modernization* (Washington, D.C.: Brookings Institution, 1967).
18. Paris: Flammarion, 1978.
19. "Plural Societies: Perspectives and Problems," in Kuper and Smith, *Pluralism in Africa,* pp. 19-22.
20. Ralf Dahrendorf, *Class and Class Conflict in Industrial Society* (Stanford: Stanford University Press, 1959).
21. D. Nicholls, *The Pluralist State* (New York: Macmillan, 1975), p. 122.
22. Leo Despres, *Cultural Pluralism and Nationalist Politics in British Guiana* (Chicago: Rand McNally, 1967), pp. 122-23.
23. Nicholls, *Pluralist State,* p. 121.

CHAPTER 8

POLITICAL CULTURE:
FROM NATION TO NATION

The concept of political culture has animated a wide debate among political scientists over the course of the last two decades. Rarely has a concept been so frequently used and so often contended. The choice of the word "culture" denotes the concept's derivation and emphasizes how comparativists have followed a road opened by anthropology, sociology, and psychology. At the same time, this borrowing has involved difficulties, which Almond and Verba, the fathers of the concept, have recognized: "We appreciate the fact that anthropologists use the term culture in a variety of ways, and that by bringing it into the conceptual vocabulary of political science we are in danger of importing its ambiguities as well as its advantages."[1]

What is political culture? It refers to the set of political beliefs, feelings, and values that prevail in a nation at a given time. Because it filters perceptions, determines attitudes, and influences modalities of participation, culture is a major component of the political game. "Looked at this way," writes Sidney Verba, "it can be seen that political culture represents a system of control vis-à-vis the system of political interactions . . . A new constitution, for instance, will be perceived and evaluated in terms of the political culture of a people. When put into practice in one society it may look quite different from the same constitution instituted in another nation with another political culture. Similarly, political ideologies are affected by the cultural environment into which they are introduced. History is full of examples of constitutions that did not 'take' as the constitution writers had hoped because their application was mediated through a particular political culture, and history is full of examples of the ways in which political ideologies have been adapted to fit the pre-existing culture of the nation into which they were introduced."[2] To those who contest the existence of anything that could be referred to as "political culture," one could reply that many political phenomena would remain inexplicable in the absence of such a concept.

In the literature, the concept is often globally applied to nations. The topics are then French, Italian, English, or Algerian political cultures. But the perspective may also be adjusted in order to encompass subcultures of various categories, or to locate general types designed to transcend the social entities under investigation. International comparison makes use of all these strategies. Across national boundaries, the comparativist may oppose the political culture of youth to that of adults or modernized social strata to those that remain attached to tradition; or he may shed light on what makes unique this or that subculture in different nations. The comparativist may choose to aggregate the political cultures of several countries he considers to be rather similar, as does Jacques Lambert, when he speaks of a Latin American culture. Or the comparativist may try to characterize what is specific about a particular national culture in regard to others.

It is when the researcher globally invokes national political cultures that the difficulties raised by the use of the concept appear clearly. The instinctive mistrust of the "native" about the way in which he is classified and labeled reflects real problems. In the search for a national common denominator, the observer naturally tends to neglect what differentiates various components within a nation. This may lead to distortions. It is already difficult to speak of a French or American political culture; it becomes even harder when the process of homogenization is not so advanced as in these two countries. A Scot is not an Englishman, as he himself claims. Nowhere does the small peasant react as does the white-collar worker, nor the practicing Catholic as the Freemason. It should also be admitted that problems concerning this heterogeneity do not disappear at a lower level; after all, the Basque culture is not uniform. Many young people, many workers, and many women would not recognize themselves in studies where the subcultures to which they belong are treated as entities.

The irritation of the native is aggravated by the impression that a sophisticated analysis more or less carries all kinds of stereotypes about him. The German sociologist Erwin Scheuch has confirmed this feeling by noting that "it is rare that the characteristic attributed to a foreign culture which a social scientist 'discovers' in his research differs from the folklore or prejudices about the foreign country which already exist in his own society."[3] The sophistication of modern survey analysis has not really diminished this risk. The apparent objectivity of quantified data far from guarantees that the researcher is immune to ethnocentric views that condition his perceptions and even his approach: "At present, the possibility exists that certain myths of everyday thinking, especially ethnic stereotypes, may be re-introduced into the social sciences as knowledge supported by evidence from cross-cultural comparisons."[4]

It could be damaging, nevertheless, to push that criticism too far. A survey is normally more reliable than the remarks of the observer of yesterday, who was obliged to trust subjective impressions: travel discoveries, contacts, and impressionistic reading of the literature or newspapers. But it remains true that questions asked in a modern intercultural survey normally focus on what seems essential to the comparativist, not to the person analyzed; and interpreting the answers is necessarily an active and possibly distorting process. Only Italian people could evaluate the role of humor or cynicism in their replies, which specialists of political culture often too directly contrast with German or American replies.

But these difficulties alone attest — as a demonstration in absurdity — to the existence of a "national culture." For if Italians generally do not express themselves as Germans do, it is precisely because they speak another "language," in every sense of the word. This does not solve all problems. Unresolved questions remain, which concern not only the methods by which cultural phenomena could be analyzed more scientifically but also the theoretical elaboration of fundamental proposals concerning the manner in which political culture influences the political game and is reciprocally influenced by it.

An explanation in terms of "values," "culture," or "personality" always risks falling into the trap of circular thinking. "The real difficulty with value explanations," states Robert Marsh, "is their circularity. The analyst typically knows something to begin with about the behavior of the members of the societies being compared; he tends to infer 'values' from this behavior and to use the 'values' to 'explain' the behavior."[5]

The difficulties encountered by the researcher who is comparing cultures are enormous. Our purpose here is not to present them. We simply point out the problems raised by the extraction of variables from their contexts. The comprehension of cultural realities logically implies that culture is perceived as a coherent whole. But the treatment usually imposed by researchers on their sample tends to neglect this requirement. So when Almond and Verba, to come again to *The Civic Culture,* lump the Revolutionary Institutional party, which is almost unique in the Mexican political system, with the German Social Democratic party or the Italian Communist party in order to evaluate traits such as tolerance or partisan involvement, they paradoxically disregard the notion of functional equivalence. "To compare structures with different functions has no meaning," write Jean-Pierre Cot and Jean-Pierre Mounier;[6] "and it is clear that the structure 'party' does not perform the same political functions in Mexico as in the other countries considered. The attitude of Mexicans toward the PRI thus could not be integrated into the comparison." These considerations could be extended to other countries. Many elements of the Italian system do not fill the same functions as do the nominally corresponding organs in the British or American system. To know the name of the chief of state, whether Eisenhower or Segni, does not test the same degree of political participation.

The task of the comparativist, at this level, is to pinpoint real functional equivalences in order to control and master distortions raised by inevitable contextual differences. The point for the researcher is to make sure that no systemic interference spoils the validity of his inductions. "System interference occurs when the inferences from the same direct measurement statements to inferred measurement statements are not equally valid in all systems under investigation," say Adam Przeworski and Henry Teune.[7] That a person admits his reluctance to see his child marry someone with adverse political ideas does not everywhere constitute an equally valid indicator in measuring the psychological distance between parties. "In the United States, such an inference may be valid, while in Italy the underlying attitude may be the authoritarianism of family rather than perceived distance between parties." A system is a complex made up of interdependent elements. When we utilize, as indicators of some general phenomenon, one or another of its elements, we extract them from their context, and so run a constant risk of misinterpretation. "For example," state again Przeworski and Teune, "it is obvious that the systemic context determines whether voting is a valid indicator of participation." The elaboration of really comparable measures could make necessary a diversification of propositions serving to guide induction.

The true problem is thus to construct general models that permit comparison without dangerously reducing the complex texture of the nations being considered. To do so, the first rule should be to avoid taking the conceptions of one of the parties—American in this instance—as universal referents. The study by Almond and Verba does not demonstrate the central idea of the authors, which is that the functioning of a stable and efficient democracy is a function of an "open and moderate partisanship"; that "it implies taking sides, having convictions and feelings, (but also assumes) a limited partisanship."[8] Participation and respect for the opinions of others without doubt belong to the philosophy of any good democrat. But it is not certain that the German Federal Republic, born by obligation, so to speak, and in a climate of skepticism, has proved less "efficient" than the Italian Republic, which was joined with enthusiasm. Everyone tempted to see a hypothetical precondition of political development in these "feeling correlates" should consider that the most durable of French political regimes, the Third Republic, began in doubt and distrust, with a majority of a single vote!

Largely useful for description and analysis, the concept of political culture may not have all the qualities required to sustain causal models. Durkheim used to say that every sociologist should search for the key to the phenomena he studied in structures and observable processes. But is there not a risk, with concepts like "political culture," of reintroducing explanations irreducible to social reality, that is to say of regressing scientifically? It could be excessive to follow this criticism to its logical end. After all, subjective data, no matter how difficult to observe, belong to reality; and a sociologist who neglected their influence would have little chance of proposing a comprehensive analysis.

This is so true that even Marxist authors have been led to grant greater consideration to the study of cultural phenomena. In the derivation of the concept of dominant ideology, developed in the writings of Antonio Gramsci or Louis Althusser, a debate over the nature and role of these "superstructural" elements has been opened. This theoretical approach clearly poses the question of the relationship between the socioeconomic infrastructures and culture. The society "secretes" the dominant ideology, which in turn fulfills a precise integrating function, along with the coercive instruments at the disposal of the state. For the sociologist, obviously, such a theory is not entirely satisfactory. Indeed, the idea of a purpose, as expressed in a statement like "the ideology works for the profit of . . . ," cannot serve as a substitute for a causal explanation. But the reverse is certainly equally true. It is undoubtedly necessary to renounce making "political culture" a reservoir of easy explanations, which would make up for any lack of understanding and even discourage further efforts to discover other possible causes. In too many models, culture remains an independent variable that unilaterally influences political phenomena. That is why we must applaud when research is done in order to understand what political culture itself depends on—how it is fashioned, along what processes, under the pressure of what conflicts, events, conscious policies.

The mechanisms of socialization today are studied with increasing care, giving a dynamic dimension to the concept of "culture." An effort has been made to comprehend how culture can change as a result of conflicts between various social categories, generations, or ethnic groups. "Not all political cultures are well integrated and consistent," writes Sidney Verba. "There may be many sources of strain within such cultures: sets of beliefs that are incompatible with other beliefs, sets of beliefs held by one segment of society and not another, or unmanageable incongruities between belief and reality. Under such circumstances the culture may accelerate change as part of a search for a new and more integrative set of beliefs."[9]

The concept of culture has aged like good wine. Cultural elements are considered less and less as the rigid framework within which political action develops; on the contrary, researchers increasingly stress how important it is to refer the analysis of change to that of fundamental creeds or "primitive beliefs," to borrow a term from Milton Rokeach.

Those who have studied the problems of development have stressed that no political system can survive unless a certain harmony exists between the political practices, the rules of the game, on the one hand, and what people expect, what they recognize as legitimate, on the other. It is certainly important and valuable to search in economic underdevelopment for the key to political unrest and instability. But it is certainly useful too to consider the maturation of what Daniel Lerner called individual "empathy," to grant attention to the "modernizing" mood that Alex Inkeles and D.H. Smith tried to measure. For if a linkage between structural and cultural development does exist, it is clear also that this relation is not a mechanical one. We cannot explain why the democracy of Bonn rests on more solid pillars than the Weimar Republic without noting the impact of factors irreducible to steel production, circulation of newspapers, or rates of unionization. An analysis in terms of institutions would be equally insufficient.

The political system itself is obviously a major agent influencing culture. As Sidney Verba states, "basic political attitudes have of course always been in part the objects of conscious manipulation. . . . But the new cultural policies involve attempts to create new patterns of beliefs, not merely to transmit established patterns to new generations. And these attempts are being made at a time when technological changes in the realm of communications and symbol manipulation may make such policies particularly effective."[10] Culture is exogenous to the system, but there exists between the two an indissoluble interaction. Culture influences the system. Michel Crozier has shown that it conditions the manner in which decisions are taken;[11] Jean Meynaud has indicated how much it fashions the physiognomy of parties and groups.[12] But the system affects culture in its turn, and it is deplorable that too many scholars interested in political culture still neglect this impact.

Reconsidering the "civic culture" nearly two decades after the pioneering "visit" by Almond and Verba, one can see that cultures have evolved; the West German system has taken root in the minds of the German people, whereas confidence in central governmental institutions has significantly declined in the United States and Great Britain. It would not be difficult to show that these evolutions are related to the performances of the systems.[13]

It is indeed the *sotto governo*, perceived by Italian people as corrupted, inaccessible, and inefficient, that engenders people's distrust in their government. In some pluralist democracies it is dissatisfaction with political parties that makes citizens willing to breach the dikes of formal institutions and long-recognized practices, such as voting or partisan membership, in order to give preference to other kinds of actions, such as blocking highways, occupying churches, or squatting in unoccupied lodgings.[14] That Austrian citizens appear relatively inactive in politics in the Barnes and Kaase study devoted to these new attitudes, while Austria keeps breaking all records concerning party membership (40 percent of Austrians are members in one of the two big parties), probably points to some deficiencies in the survey. It is surprising to see some political scientists neglecting how much the characteristics of a regime may profoundly influence a culture. But it is also a weakness because this perspective biases their perception of the problem and thus preconditions their results. No culture develops in the abstract. The feeling manifested by the Italians that the government is "incompetent" is intimately related to the features of the system. Those who are familiar with Italian politics have difficulty accepting some of the conclusions from the Almond and Verba book. The idea that Italians would participate less than the British, or even the Mexicans, may surprise one who considers that the number of party members or parapolitical organizations in Italy is one of the highest among pluralistic democracies; moreover, politics are omnipresent throughout Italy. Politics affect the allocation of jobs, the distribution of public housing, the attribution of agricultural subsidies, and even leisure or sport. "The little world of Don Camillo," even if a caricature, certainly reflects a profound reality.

When asked what they would do if confronted with an unfair political decision, Italians who reply that they would do something, that they would take an individual or collective initiative, are less numerous than the British or the Mexicans. Should we conclude that Italians "participate" less? Their affiliation to parties and parapolitical organizations explains part of the apparent abstention. They expect these parties and organizations to take the initiative, to seize it, so to speak. The network is there, ready to function and to launch the appropriate reaction. It is the system itself, organized around groups, factions, and clienteles, that dissuades the Italian citizen from adopting the same pattern of behavior as the American citizen, who is propelled toward more active and individualistic participation by the very inconsistency of the skeletal parties in the United States. To be sure, the hypertrophy of partisan politics in Italy can only nourish attitudes of defiance or even rejection toward the state, the "system," and "those in Rome." But are we to accept conclusions that credit or blame political culture alone for the good or bad health of the political system? There is a confusion here that international comparisons have not yet dissipated.

Some popular subcultures have demonstated a stubborn resistance in the face of a maturing national culture. Particularisms have been found in very different contexts. For instance, Edward Banfield observed a unique subculture in the south of Italy. He called it "amoral familism"[15] and described a situation in which allegiance to the primary familial group is so strong and deeply rooted that it determines a very particular kind of political participation, which the author analyzed along seventeen points. He stressed, for example, that only civil servants and politicians—who are paid to do so—are expected to get involved in public affairs. For the common citizen, such an involvement would look improper and abnormal. As a consequence, "no one will take the initiative in outlining a course of action and persuading others to embark upon it. . . . And if one did offer leadership, the group will refuse it out of distrust." The control over politicians is incumbent on other professional politicians. The law will be respected only if one fears punishment. The one who shares a bit of power will not hesitate to line his pockets; whether he does so or not is irrelevant anyway because the amoral family will actually believe that he does. The vote takes on a clientele form; one looks for immediate advantage. The distrust evoked here is the product of a secular experience. Recent history has proved that such a subculture is not to be dissolved easily by urbanization, industrialization, or the development of mass communication. Political culture transmits itself from generation to generation by socialization.

NOTES

1. Gabriel Almond and Sidney Verba, *The Civic Culture* (Princeton: Princeton University Press, 1963), p. 14.
2. Sidney Verba, "Comparative Political Culture," in *Political Culture and Political Development,* ed. Lucian Pye and Sidney Verba (Princeton: Princeton University Press, 1965), p. 517.
3. Erwin Scheuch, "Society as a Context in Cross-Cultural Comparisons," *Social Science Information* 6, no. 5 (October 1967): 8.
4. Ibid.
5. Cf. Robert Marsh, *Comparative Sociology* (New York: Harcourt Brace, 1967), pp. 28-29.
6. Jean-Pierre Cot and Jean-Pierre Mounier, *Pour une sociologie politique* (Paris: Seuil, 1974), 2:52.
7. Adam Przeworski and Henry Teune, *The Logic of Comparative Social Inquiry* (New York: Wiley, 1970), pp. 104ff.
8. Almond and Verba, *Civic Culture,* p. 123.
9. *Political Culture and Political Development,* p. 520.
10. Ibid., p. 121.
11. Michel Crozier, *The Bureaucratic Phenomenon* (Chicago: University of Chicago Press, 1964).
12. Jean Meynaud, *Les groupes de pression en France* (Paris: Colin, 1958), esp. chaps. 1 and 5.
13. See, for example, Alan Abramowitz on the United States and David P. Conradt on West Germany, in *The Civic Culture Revisited,* ed. Gabriel Almond and Sidney Verba (Boston: Little, Brown, 1980).
14. On this evolution, see Samuel H. Barnes and Max Kaase, eds., *Political*

Action: Mass Participation in Five Western Democracies (Beverly Hills, Calif.: Sage, 1979).

15. *The Moral Basis of a Backward Society* (New York: Free Press, 1958). See also the critical appraisal by A. Pizzorno, "Amoral Familism and Historical Marginality," *International Review of Community Development* (1966): 55-89.

Chapter 9

POLITICAL SOCIALIZATION:
FROM GENERATION TO GENERATION

Human societies perpetuate themselves through acculturation. Talcott Parsons says that the arrival of each generation looks like an invasion of barbarians; only socialization can permit the inculcation of rules of collective living on these "invaders." By defining culture as a "common code," Pierre Bourdieu emphasizes the need for a socialization process. Societies are not naturally destined to survive, as David Easton stresses;[1] rather, they survive only if this code is inculcated in each individual, if some minimal behavioral rules are imposed on her or him.

"The youngest are pushed in flocks to school," Max Stirner acidly accuses, "so that they may learn the old rituals by heart, and when they know the verbiage of the elders, they are declared adults."[2] Because societies can instill only those values, rules, and recipes that have already been tested, the socialization process necessarily takes on a conservative aspect. Many studies could be mentioned here, some along the lines of the Gramscian thesis on hegemony, which denounces the perpetuation of a situation of domination by control of the cultural message. In a perspective not far from this, Pierre Bourdieu and Jean-Claude Passeron show how the French university, under the banner of neutrality and independence, in reality functions as an agent of conservation, for the "reproduction" of a given class system.

Political culture is transmitted by acculturation. Thus, socialization assumes a function of stabilization in a vertical sense between generations, as well as in a horizontal sense between social groups.[3] But people are not entirely passive; their disposition is not absolute. The child reacts with a personal dynamism to the impulse of society. Relations between social groups are generally tense, if not conflicting. Finally, culture evolves; it changes with the times. In many cases, this alteration of traditional culture may even become an explicit goal of political leaders.

All societies do not assume the function of socialization with an equal amount of assiduous and conscious effort. Between the absolute control in the totalitarian state and the formation that the family or tribal elites spontaneously provide in the heart of Africa, there is whole array of intermediary situations. The bourgeois state of Jules Ferry was designed to awaken a certain kind of citizen; so was the ancient Republic of Sparta. But such is not always the case. Most contemporary states are aware of the importance of socializing processes and try to influence them. But what proportion of children, or students, or even adults will really be reached? The differences are so considerable from one country to another that we should ask to what measure *political* socialization, as opposed to socialization in general, is truly a universal phenomenon. Mali and Bolivia have neither the same ambitions nor the same possibilities as Hitler's Germany or Stalin's Soviet Union. The development of a political consciousness is part of the normal maturation of the French or American child. But it is not necessarily the same in the heart of the Congo or in the mountainous north of Burma.

As long as the political sphere has not reached a significant autonomy, as long as the means of enforcing power are minimal, and as long as the central institutions have not managed to secure a real penetration, political socialization will remain embryonic—unless it develops in a completely subversive way, as in revolutionary China or newly independent Angola.

Confronted with a variety of situations, the comparativist is led to focus attention on two points. He may first study the contents of the socialization; may question what it carries in terms of values, attitudes, political beliefs, and determine whether these beliefs and values are homogeneous or tolerate contradictory influences. He may then ask what the vectors of the acculturation are, and to what degree the various channels are allowed to diffuse potentially conflicting messages.

Generalizations are difficult to formulate. It seems nonetheless possible to say that the predominance of traditional channels, such as parents, religious leaders, or local elites, denotes a weak autonomy in the political sphere and consequently a feeble process of political socialization. Some ideal representations of the nation, the state, and the government do permeate these traditional channels, but they can rarely withstand sophisticated formation. The more education he receives, the more the young Kenyan or Tanzanian becomes skeptical of values propagated by the central system.[4] That is not the case with the young American[5] or Soviet Russian,[6] who adheres with more conviction to the national political credo as he climbs educational and social ladders. If we were to consider countries of Eastern Europe in this perspective, we would certainly differentiate between Poles or Czechs on the one side and Russians or Bulgarians on the other. Young *kolkhozians* appear to be more distrustful of "socialism" than educated *apparatchiki*. But it is not so evident that the student from Warsaw trusts the Polish system more than the peasant does. An interesting question would be to ask if a political system is not increasingly fragile if citizens become more skeptical of it as they climb higher in the social hierarchy.

Were he still alive, Vilfredo Pareto would undoubtedly find new data to confirm his theory of elite circulation by introducing into it the concept of stratified socialization processes.

The influence of the primary vectors of socialization tends to be decisive everywhere. But the family does not constitute, in all contexts, an equally important agent of socialization. It is in the nature of totalitarian states to strive to reduce as much as possible any competing influence on the "state's youth," which is viewed as its own possession. Robert d'Harcourt tells how regimented members of the Hitler-Jugend were forbidden to recognize or salute their relatives in the crowd when marching in their uniforms.[7] Margaret Wylie quotes this song, mumbled by small children in a Chinese kindergarten:

> "The kindergarten is my home
> The teacher is my mother;
> She teaches me so many things
> I am so happy learning here,
> I do not need another."[8]

Not to "need another" is the ideal of any totalitarian state. The unique party is granted all power. It dominates the schools and the whole process of youth formation, fighting against the development of contradictory pluralist influences. Determining the extent to which these regimes really succeed in counterbalancing all competing influences might constitute an interesting subject of comparison. It is evident that the Polish church here, the Tadjik family there, can represent efficient counterweights to the powerfull will of the state.

In developing countries, the channels of socialization represented by the media, unions, or factories are sometimes very important. The socialization of adults indeed is significant in every context. But in these new states it can represent the single or most effective means of forming modern political individuals.[9]

It may be very difficult to evaluate how much ideas inculcated during childhood continue to mark the behavior of adults. Researchers rarely ask this question, and when they do, they are obliged to rely on the vague memories of those interviewed and are therefore faced with the defects of any retrospective survey. Distortions, even involuntary, emerge naturally in narrative accounts and can bias the replies. At least these analyses propose a dynamic scheme, which informs us not only on the manner in which attitudes are formed but also on their longevity. Robert Lane has thus shown that an adolescent oppressed within the family, either in the United States or Germany, later tends to commit himself less than the youth allowed more freedom at home; on the other hand, the attitudes of the restricted adolescent are generally more in conformity with those of the family.[10] Clearly, the autonomy of the "citizen," as well as the content of his or her convictions, takes root in a social milieu.

S. Krauss and J.M. Fendrich also asked how the attitudes of the young later influenced their views as adults. Analyzing the manner in which the extremist youth establishes himself in adult roles, they noted that it is easier to maintain extremist opinions in the United States than in Japan, because the cost of marginality is somehow lower in America.[11]

Sure enough, pluralist societies tend to admit a plurality of contradictory influences. Families, friends, schools, churches, unions, or mass media are not expected to nourish and diffuse the same values and opinions. Specialists on fragmented societies, however, have depicted situations in which competing vertical groups succeed in protecting their members from intergroup communication and conflicting influences. The pattern is as follows: The family sensitizes the small boy to what the priest will later tell him, what the newspaper will repeat, and what the party will declare once again. The result is a very original cultural configuration.

Those who study the content of the education or information diffused by various agencies of socialization know very well that the explicit message is not always the most important one. Like the family, the American school is not built around the same models of authority as the French school. It would be difficult, without falling into caricature, to summarize in a few sentences what makes the difference between the two models. We may simply say that the description Jesse Pitts gives of the "delinquent community," forged on the benches of French schools,[12] is not applicable to America. To be convinced about this, one has just to read M. Kent Jennings and Richard G. Niemi[13] on the family and schools in the United States.

A very interesting comparison would be to analyze the effects of educational systems respectively in American high schools and their European counterparts. It has been said that the Trafalgar victory was prepared in aristocratic public schools. Even if this is an exaggerated statement, there is some truth in it. Those who have had the opportunity to teach on both sides of the Atlantic have seen to what degree youths aged eighteen to twenty are unequally prepared for life and citizenship. The European high school, whether it be *lycée* or *gymnasium,* is an institution primarily for instruction in the French-German-Italian-Swedish-Spanish sense of the word, which means the accumulation of knowledge and the learning of a method of thought — not a general education as in the United States. A test given to a sample of youths at the age of seventeen or eighteen in Europe and in the United States would undoubtedly demonstrate the better intellectual preparedness of the Europeans. But if the same persons were tested again four years later, at the end of their college training, the results would be reversed. By their early twenties, the American graduates would appear, each in his or her own field, much better prepared than their European counterparts. Simplifying things a little in order to make them clearer, one could say that in the United States the public high school is one of the weakest institutions, at least from a comparative point of view, while the university is among the very best (second only, perhaps, to the Supreme Court, would say observers from the other side of the Atlantic). These observations not only suggest that the socializing role of the high school and university is not the same on the two continents but also that the strength of one institution may compensate for the weakness of the other.

Many interesting surveys about the attitudes of parents and educators could be used in a comparative perspective.[14] A fundamental question to be considered would be how much harmony exists between the school and the family, and more generally, among the various socializing agencies. James Coleman has pointed out the importance of the question of the presence or absence of "congruence" between the educational system and other agents or channels of socialization.[15]

The problem of partisan socialization has real meaning only for states that admit a plurality of beliefs and attitudes. In order for these beliefs to develop without endangering the cohesion of the group, it is necessary to achieve some consensus on the most fundamental norms. Researchers who are interested in the dynamic of change have an immense field open to them in seeking to understand how a revolutionary counterculture can develop, able to alter or replace the previously accepted "common code." Why was the counterculture of the German "socialist ghetto" less explosive than the Nazi subculture? Why did the Black Power movement in the United States have less impact on the system than the Francophone movement in Canada? Phenomena related to the emergence of ideologies, perceived as substitutes for traditional culture, remain to be analyzed from this perspective.

Political socialization is an interdisciplinary domain, as Herbert Hyman points out in his poineering work.[16] One cannot understand the process of acculturation without appealing to psychology or sociology. But it remains to the political scientist to analyze the manner in which socialization supports or hinders, contributes to perpetuate or undermines the political system.

Totalitarian situations offer researchers interesting clinical cases. "Your help doesn't matter," shouted Hitler to the hesitant Germans, "we will grab hold of your children anyway!" The way that totalitarian regimes have taken, or have tried to take, possession of youth attests to the importance of controlling the means of socialization. Education is the natural support of propaganda in assuring the complete authority of the state over the individual. It is a fact that the modern tyrant is brought down only by external intervention. From the moment the dictator who intends to mobilize the mob is given the help of the modern technological means of penetration, his power is almost unsubvertible. This fact eloquently demonstrates the superiority of control over consciousness, in comparison to exclusive police control.

We shall not here give details about the tactics of totalitatarian educators. Let us just stress—because the phenomenon is of general relevance—that the earliest socialization seems to be the most efficient. It is on the soft clay of infancy one engraves most deeply the message of the day. The *Ballila,* the *Pimpf,* and the Soviet *pioneer* are not really in a position to resist the violence of the totalitarian credo. In order to be attractive, the new ideology generally utilizes the myth of youth, which is destined to comfort the rising generation in the face of parents or elders. It also appeals to the most natural trends and aspirations of the child, the sense of self-sacrifice and devotion to the Cause or idol.

Even revolutionary systems that eulogize Reason and Enlightenment have the tendency to take root in the unconscious, the irrational, and the emotional, as though they rested on the most solid rational ground. People are leashed by myths and images, such as the "locomotive of history," or better, the nation's "father" or "guide." The idolatry taught on school benches is, for the outside observer, an object of profound amazement.[17] One could nevertheless seriously ask if it is not necessary to have recourse to such sacred images and magic words in order to propel the masses and anchor the new legitimacy?

Examination of the socialization process in totalitarian countries brings to light three important elements. First, an awareness of the decisive importance of political socialization. Second, the absolute supremacy conferred upon the collective vectors—schools, party, army—to the detriment of all other possible competitors, against whom a ferocious struggle is waged. Churches are forbidden to say anything but prayers; local subcultures are domesticated, if necessary by violence; families soon become silent, as a result of the defiance instituted between parents and children. The third particularity of the totalitarian socialization pattern is the extraordinary simplification of political discourse. The phenomenon almost resembles intellectual regression. Whereas the modernization of societies implies the multiplication of sources of information and the development of cross-cutting messages, the totalitarian state returns to a single and indivisible Truth. The arts and sciences reflect the *Weltanschauung* of the day. Ideological slogans learned at school and repeated in youth organizations are again declared or preached in factories and delivered over the air waves. Public censorship and private cowardice contribute to make up a world where the youth, once he or she reaches adulthod, remains subject to the same socializing processes.

In reality, the control of socialization is never total. Communist party bureaucrats, according to Viktor Kravchenko's memoirs, opened wide eyes of astonishment when, sent by the authorities to travel on the Volga, they saw the backwardness of the area. With the new technology of mass media, even the most protected nation encounters difficulties in controlling messages from outside. The East German population has the possibility of seeing different modes of life through West Berlin telecasts. To a lesser degree, the Leningrad population has access to Helsinki programs. Protesters in Gdansk may be kept informed by Stockholm broadcasts; the Munich-based "Voice of America" certainly manages to reach a limited but influential audience in Eastern Europe. The fragmentation of the totalitarian society into multiple impermeable castes can, in a way, immunize against the consequences of such internal or external revelations. But the distance between ideology and reality may also become a source of fragility. What the regime gains in temporary legitimacy can rapidly be lost at the level of efficiency as soon as indoctrinated generations, deprived of any critical sense, arrive in controlling positions. It could be argued that the fall of the Nazi regime was in part due to the enclosure of the leaders and the masses in a sea of chimera in which they drowned—a sea of chimera that assured them that they were the strongest simply by virtue of "blood" or "will."

An interesting topic of comparative research would be to find out if each kind of socialization corresponds to specific weaknesses. Too much permissiveness could bring inconveniences of a different nature, but perhaps they would prove as important as too much rigor.

NOTES

1. In David Easton and Jack Dennis, *Children in the Political System* (New York: McGraw-Hill, 1969).
2. In *Der Einzige und sein Eigentum,* new ed. (Munich: Freie Gesellschaft, 1982).
3. According to the image developed by J.P. Cot and J.P. Mounier, in *Pour une sociologie politique* (Paris: Seuil, 1974), p. 68.
4. Cf. D. Koff, G. von der Muhll, and K. Prewitt, "Political Socialization in Three East African Countries," in *Socialization to Politics,* ed. Jack Dennis (New York: Wiley, 1973), pp. 231ff.
5. With the exception of the young black; see on that aspect, Dwaine Marvick, "Political Socialization of Black Children," in *Political Socialization,* ed. Edward S. Greenberg (New York: Atherton, 1970), pp. 178ff.
6. Alex Inkeles, *Public Opinion in Soviet Russia: A Study in Mass Persuasion* (Cambridge, Mass.: Harvard University Press, 1950).

7. *L'évangile de la force* (Paris: Plon, 1936), pp. 23-25.

8. *Children of China* (Hong Kong: Dragonfly Books, 1962), p. 17.

9. Cf. Roberta Sigel, ed., *Learning about Politics* (New York: Random House, 1970), chap. 7.

10. "Political Maturation in Germany and America," in *European Politics,* ed. M. Dogan and R. Rose (Boston: Little, Brown, 1971), pp. 101ff.

11. Cf. "Political Socialization of U.S. and Japanese Adults," *Comparative Political Studies* 13, no. 1 (April 1980): 3-32.

12. *In Search of France* (Cambridge, Mass.: Harvard University Press, 1963).

13. *The Political Character of Adolescence* (Princeton: Princeton University Press, 1974).

14. See, for example, the comparative data published by the EEC; particularly, *Les Européens et leurs enfants* (Bruxelles, October 1979).

15. *Education and Political Development* (Princeton: Princeton University Press, 1965), pp. 19ff.

16. *Political Socialization* (New York: Free Press, 1959).

17. See, for example, George Urban, ed., *The Miracles of Chairman Mao* (London: Pindar, 1971).

Chapter 10

POLITICAL CLIENTELISM:
A UBIQUITOUS PHENOMENON

"The clientelistic relationship is one of personal dependence, unrelated to kinship, which links two persons who control unequal resources, the patron and the client, for a reciprocal exchange of favors," writes Jean François Médard.[1] This definition stresses three fundamental features of clientelism, which indeed implies dependence, reciprocity, and personalization.

Clientelism forges a relation between two persons of unequal status, prestige, and influence, thus constituting an original factor of vertical stratification. The clientele relationship is engendered by an asymmetry in the situations of patron and client. John Duncan Powell[2] has analyzed various aspects of the client position in rural societies. On the economic level, the peasant's dependence appears in the fact that he possesses only his labor, not the land; he lacks also the capital that would allow him to use better technical tools. In addition, he is intellectually ill equipped to understand or even know the law. He is often unaware of his rights and obligations, and is accustomed to endure arbitrary injustice as if it were a natural calamity. In such a context, recourse to a patron is a way to surmount handicaps, to pass from what Vincent Lemieux calls "infra-power" to the immediately superior level of "under-power."[3]

The patron who grants protection will lend agricultural equipment and advance needed funds. He will give the advice expected from him, he will use his influence to moderate the severity of policemen or tax collectors — always adjusting his help in such a way that the patron-client hierarchy remains unchanged. Examining in detail relationships in a small town of Mezzogiorno with the fictitious name of Colleverde, S.E. Silverman[4] has shown how the economic dependence of the tenant-farmer vis-à-vis the owner, generally a landlord living in a distant city, has given rise to stable relationships that confer on the patron the role of a true mediator. The key to the patron's power is the linking position he occupies in a chain of relationships that extends beyond the small world of the client. This is clearly true for rural elites in Italy, as well as in Spain, Greece, or Latin America; but it applies also to prominent representatives of cultural subgroups in many areas characterized by ethnic, linguistic, or religious pluralism. In Colleverde, "the most valuable patron was neither the wealthiest nor the most generous, but the one with the best connections."[5] In exchange for his influence, he receives services in kind and ostensible deference from the tenant-farmer, which further nourishes his privileged situation and promotes him, to use again Lemieux's expression, from an "over-power" situation to "supra-power."

The reciprocity of exchanges between patron and client is observed everywhere, each one expecting to gain an advantage from the other. This means that the established relationship is of a contractual nature, even if the "contract" remains totally tacit. There is between the *compadre* and the *padre,* the patron and the father, the very distance that separates elective relationships from those between relatives. LaPalombara[6] has expressed this for Italy by contrasting *clientela* and *parentela.* Those who have analyzed patronage situations have pointed out that the protection accorded to this or that individual is generally extended to his family and that the wife of the patron normally becomes the "patroness." But this is not necessarily true. One does not enter into a clientelistic chain if one is not willing to play one's part; furthermore, one can more or less easily leave the chain.

Clientelism is a concept that generally interests political scientists because the patron everywhere occupies a preeminent place and plays the role of the principal intermediary between the center and the periphery. He is an important actor in most political processes, playing a part in the articulation of interests, communication, allocation of resources, rule adjudication, and so on. Certainly one may suspect some political scientists of practicing a kind of conceptual imperialism, of seeing clientelism everywhere. It is nevertheless significant that in the last decade or so, clientelistic phenomena have been studied in a wide variety of countries including India, Tunisia, Colombia, Senegal, Greece, Canada, Japan, Spain, Venezuela, Italy, Ireland, the Philippines, Turkey, China, Mexico, Lebanon, Malaysia.

J.F. Médard has stressed the apparently universal character of clientelism and has insisted that it is indispensable in understanding polities inside and outside the Third World: "It is necessary to admit that the modern political societies are penetrated by phenomena of this order to various degrees and in different forms."[7] We know of great mass parties that have reactivated in an ideological and impersonal manner the system of contractual exchanges practiced in former times around local notables.[8] This transformation of political machines into producers of services occurs even in parties that are not in a dominant position at the center of the political system. An opposition party, in cities where it has a majority, may reserve the allocation of municipal jobs or housing for political sympathizers. This practice is not unusual in many advanced countries. The political history of Boston, Chicago, Philadelphia, or other North American cities could certainly be analyzed from this particular point of view.

Clientelism is embedded in the political processes of many countries. But what do the patronage systems that so profoundly characterize Rwanda or Saudi Arabia have in common with the intermittent clientelistic practices one discovers in Marseille, Leningrad, or Bari? Here again, we are confronted with the crucial task of operationalizing concepts at the world level. One could make progress in this direction by distinguishing societies where clientelism is essential from those where it functions in connection with well-developed institutional relationships.[9] It would then be necessary, as suggested by René Lemarchand,[10] to ask which kind of clientelistic chain penetrates the formal institutions, when, and to what degree.

There are several ways to get a general view of the phenomena grouped under the concept of clientelism. One way consists in bringing the structural variables of clientelism to light in order to define their salient traits comparatively. One could thus juxtapose situations where client dependence on the patron is great with those where the hierarchy vanishes; one could see, for instance, how the adoption of agrarian reforms or universal suffrage, or the development of a modern bureaucracy, or the growth of literacy might change the client's situation. Other distinctions could be traced according to whether the clientele relationship is personalized or disappears into an anonymous political machine. For the face-to-face relationship may dissolve into a more complex network, and "affectivity" may be counterbalanced by rising "instrumentality."

Another way to comprehend the phenomenon of clientelism globally is to look at environmental characteristics. Vincent Lemieux has thus outlined "the conditions of political patronage."[11] Among the political conditions appears the existence of a real rivalry, such that no single actor could have a monopolistic control over political power. This rule seems to apply as well to traditional actors as to modern organizations, such as hegemonic parties with various factions. An egalitarian distribution of power would ruin the influence of the patron. For clientelism to arise, a certain concentration of power, rights, and capacities is necessary. We may say that the domination of the Christian Democratic party in Veneto or Basilicata creates a context more favorable to clientelism than the alternation in power of two parties in the Anglo-American style. On the other hand, by eliminating competition a situation of absolute concentration destroys one of the major incentives for actually "patronizing" clients. The history of feudal Europe, as well as that of the precolonial African kingdoms studied by Lemieux, attests that the lords behaved more as patrons the more they needed to compete with each other. The same observation has been made at the local level. Carl H. Lande has analyzed how local factions are structured in the Philippines around prestige rivalries; each family strives to enhance its position by regaling scores of supporters with entertainment and feasts.[12]

The most perceptive studies demonstrate that clientelism is a phenomenon that marks all social life. Its political aspects may be perceived as secondary by the local community, particularly when the political sphere is not really distinct from the social, and when central authorities seem extremely distant. But precisely in such contexts, clientelism is likely to lead to an effective structuring of the political game because it takes root in relationships colored by affectivity, and it offers a kind of reward for the participation of the village or ethnic group in the national political life.

To speak of favorable "administrative conditions"[13] means that clientelism can only really function in an environment where the structures of the central power are themselves accessible to personal influence. But to evoke this kind of condition reemphasizes that "the utility of the clientelist notion is not limited to personalist, primitive politics."[14]

Another essential point about the "social" and "cultural" conditions favorable to clientelism is that this kind of vertical structuring is most likely to take place in a historical context that is neither modern nor traditional, but typically "modernizing." John Duncan Powell has expressed this link between clientelism and a certain stage of national maturation very sharply: "Two underlying processes are largely responsible for the establishment of linkages: state centralization and market expansion."[15] Such a context is particularly favorable because it confers a crucial role on social mediators. The individual living in the periphery can no longer ignore the center; at the same time, he does not really have the means to accede to it. The functions of the patron will be "to relate community-oriented individuals who want to stabilize or improve their life chances, but who lack economic security and political connections, with nation-oriented individuals who operate primarily in terms of complex cultural forms standardized as national institutions, but whose success in these operations depends on the size and strength of their personal following."[16] At this stage, when vertical traditional ties are loosening but have not yet been replaced by others, participation in the developing national system may be greatly stimulated by clientelistic rewards. Ergun Ozbudun's book on Turkey[17] is partly written from this perspective.

These observations point out the fact that clientelism may be transitory. Indeed, the evolution of societies creates serious competitors to the patrons. With the development of transportation, schools, and media, interest articulation tends more and more to be carried out through organized groups such as unions, which represent horizontal structures. Social consciousness takes priority over vertical clientelistic chains. Increasingly, partisan mobilization over-comes ancient allegiances, which were determined not on the basis of ideologies or interests but according to the particular place occupied by the individual in the network of local relationships.

Where modernization does not entail the disappearance of clientelistic chains, it nevertheless leads to their transformation. The patronage of political machines does not represent the same personalization of political relations as that of the notables, and the role of ideology in political options renders more difficult the symbiosis between social strata favored by classic clientelism.

The clientelistic scheme normally implies a knot of reciprocal exchanges. In order to find a counterpart to certain advantages obtained at the "center," the client at the "periphery," social or regional, sustains the patron. But this ideal model may be altered in many ways. René Lemarchand thus compares the traditional patrimonial type with the repressive type of clientelism where the patron, far from providing paternalistic protection, in no way represents the interests of his flock and instead imposes himself by coercion. This degen-eration of the mediating function is characteristic of many colonial or neo-colonial situations. It often marks the early stages of political development. Luigi Graziano has shown that clientelism between two parties can be threatened by one party gaining too large an advantage. The successful party, expecting nothing more from the other, gives it nothing, and is easily perceived as a class enemy.

With the extension of universal suffrage, the clientelistic link may be mod-ified in another way. Armed with the right to vote, the client may be able to sell his help to the patron. In practice, voters sometimes penalize this or that political machine for not having rewarded them with sufficient subsidies and official favors.

In many states of Africa, Asia, and the Middle East, one can observe an atrophy of clientele relationships that is essentially due to a decline in participa-tion. The political arena is shrinking, and embryonic parties are oppressed by authoritarian rulers. In such a situation, clientelism operates only in bureaucratic or military spheres. It no longer penetrates the society and can thus no longer constitute a vertical counterweight to horizontal cleavages.

What are the consequences of clientelistic phenomena? Clearly the efficien-cy of clientelism depends considerably on the context in which it develops. Mario Caciagli has pointed out how the maturation of the political "subject" can be inhibited by the patron's influence.[18] Specialists on Latin America have made the same observation, showing that the semiprotection offered by the traditional landlord has generally impeded the development of class conscious-ness among exploited people in rural areas. At the same time, clientelism may also involve some sort of participation for social strata that are just awakening to politics. The "captive vote," to use an image proposed by Alvaro Ancisi,[19] may present the first step toward a nonmediated participation.

Clientelism usually acts in a conservative way, since it pushes the exploited person to reach an agreement with the exploiter and enhances the advantage of those who are already in a position of strength in the system. But situations arise, based either on ethnic background or class, where former patrons and clients find themselves in hostile camps. The work of David and Audrey Smock on Lebanon shows that it would be a mistake to overestimate the integrating capacity of clientelism.[20]

The example of clientelism illustrates how difficult but rewarding it is to formulate a concept that can be applied on a world scale. A study of clientelism, even in countries one knows well, can profit by observation of the situation, for instance, in Turkey or Mexico. The way the understanding of these phenomena has been expanded is an excellent example of how comparative analysis can contribute to the body of knowledge.[21]

NOTES

1. "Le rapport de clientèle," *Revue Française de Science Politique* 26, no. 1 (February 1976): 103.
2. "Peasant Society and Clientelist Politics," in *Political Development and Social Change,* ed. Jason L. Finkle and Richard W. Gable, 2nd ed. (New York: Wiley, 1971), pp. 519ff.
3. *Le patronage politique* (Québec: Presses de l'Université de Laval, 1977).
4. "Patronage and Community-Nation Relationships in Central Italy," in *Friends, Followers, and Factions,* ed. S.W. Schmidt, J.C. Scott, C.H. Lande, and L. Guasti (Berkeley: University of California Press, 1977), pp. 293ff.
5. Ibid., p. 299.
6. In *Interest Groups in Italian Politics* (Princeton: Princeton University Press, 1954), pp. 252ff.
7. "Le rapport de clientèle," p. 104.
8. Cf. Luigi Graziano, *Clientelismo e sistema politico: Il caso dell'Italia* (Milan: Angeli, 1980).
9. Carl Lande, "Introduction," in Schmidt et al., *Friends, Followers, and Factions,* p. 18.
10. "Comparative Political Clientelism and the Client State" (paper delivered at the IPSA World Congress, Moscow, August 1979).
11. *Le patronage politique,* pp. 179ff.

12. In *Leaders, Factions, and Parties* (New Haven: Yale University Press, 1964), pp. 14ff.

13. Lemieux, *Le patronage politique,* pp. 187ff.

14. Powell, "Peasant Society and Clientelist Politics," p. 525.

15. Ibid., p. 522.

16. Cf. Eric Wolf, "Aspects of Group Relations in a Complex Society: Mexico," in *Contemporary Cultures and Society of Latin America,* ed. D. Heath and R. Adams (New York: Random House, 1965), p. 97.

17. E. Ozbudun, *Social Change and Political Participation in Turkey* (Princeton: Princeton University Press, 1976).

18. *Democrazia Cristiana e potere nel mezzogiorno* (Florence: Guaraldi, 1977), esp. chap. 3.

19. *La cattura del voto: Sociologia del voto di preferenza* (Milan: Angeli, 1976).

20. *The Politics of Pluralism: A Comparative Study of Lebanon and Ghana* (New York: Elsevier, 1975).

21. See S.N. Eisenstadt and L. Roniger, "Patron-Client Relations as a Model of Structuring Social Exchange," *Comparative Study of Society and History* (1980): 42-77.

Chapter 11

CONSOCIATIONAL DEMOCRACY: AN ELITIST MODEL FOR FRAGMENTED SOCIETIES

The concept of consociational democracy was born directly from comparisons. It was internationalized within a few years, between 1967 and 1974, when several important books[1] and articles[2] were published about the Netherlands, Belgium, Austria, Switzerland, and Canada. Shortly thereafter, the concept was applied to developing countries such as Lebanon, Malaysia, Cyprus, Colombia, Uruguay, and Nigeria. Obviously, we here consider these countries only for the period when consociational democracy actually functioned.

A double phenomenon is common to all these experiences: (1) a vertical segmentation of the population into several religious, linguistic, ethnic, racial, or ideological communities; and (2) an institutionalization of the process of negotiation as it occurs at the level of these communities' elites.

The Dutch political scientist Arend Lijphart formulated the concept of consociational democracy in the most comprehensive fashion. In coining the word "consociational," he considered and discussed expressions used by several authors, finally adopting the word *consociatio*, which David Apter had resuscitated apropos of Nigeria. Val Lorwin analyzed the organization of "segmented pluralism,"[3] without attaching sufficient importance, however, to the phenomenon of cooperation between the elites of various segments. Gerhard Lehmbruch first used the word *Proporzdemokratie*, and later spoke of *Konkordanzdemokratie* with regard to Austria and Switzerland. G. Bingham Powell devoted his attention mainly to the phenomenon of "social fragmentation," while Jürg Steiner emphasized "amicable agreement," contrasting with majority rule. Eric Nordlinger extended the field of research by analyzing the process of conflict regulation in all "divided societies." The Dutch word *verzuiling* has been adopted in international literature. It suggests the division of society into pillars that support the vault of the state like pillars support the front of a Greek temple. At the top of this social building, accommodation and compromise between elites of pillar-communities occur.

Lijphart has stressed the comparative paternity of the concept. Empirical observations indeed led him to challenge the validity of Gabriel Almond's typology of political systems, which was based on the contrast, originally noted by

Bentley, Truman, and Lipset, between cleavages that cut across one another and those that are superimposed on one another. According to these theorists, crosscutting cleavages would favor the stability of a political regime, whereas the superimposition of several cleavages would badly divide society and consequently foster instability. Then, some scholars working separately in Austria, Belgium, Switzerland, and the Netherlands almost simultaneously discovered a new kind of democracy, one characterized at the same time by a striking governmental stability and a profound cultural segmentation. So Lijphart proposed a new typology,[4] based on the crossing of two dichotomies.

Political Culture

		Homogeneous	Fragmented
Coalescent		Depoliticized democracy	Consociational democracy
Competitive		Centripetal democracy	Centrifugal democracy

Elite Behavior (vertical axis label)

FIGURE 11.1
From Arend Lijphart, "Typologies of Democratic Systems,"
Comparative Political Studies 1 (April 1968).

All societies are culturally heterogeneous. But they are not equally divided. At what degree of heterogeneity are we entitled to speak of organized vertical segmentation? Quantitative criteria have been suggested,[5] which we will not review here. Better to take a careful look at the four "classic" examples of consociational democracy.

Until around 1967 to 1970, the Netherlands[6] was characterized by the existence of five "blocs": one Catholic, two Protestant, and two secular (socialist and liberal). Each bloc had its own political party, and each of the four main parties found about 90 percent of its electorate in its own community. To every party was attached a trade union, and union membership was based essentially on religious and cultural criteria. (In 1954 the Catholic bishops forbade their flocks to join socialist unions, under threat of being deprived of the sacraments.) Three business and three agricultural organizations functioned parallel to one another; all were based on religious criteria. There were three employers' associations: one Catholic, one Protestant, and one liberal; and three organizations of agricultural workers: one Catholic, one Protestant, and one liberal. Each bloc had its own newspapers. Time on radio and television was distributed between four associations — representing the Catholic, Calvinist, socialist, and liberal communities — proportional to the number of their members. Many cultural, sports, and charitable associations had developed in every bloc. But the school system was the main agent in the vertical division of the country. For 75 percent of the youth, socialization was performed in a closed universe from kindergarten to university. Under such conditions, as Lijphart pointed out, the citizen had very few chances of making friends outside his or her subculture. Mixed marriages were extremely rare. In 1960, 94.7 percent of Catholics were married to Catholics. The various communities lived side by side without meeting.

Before the war, Austria was divided into two camps that lived in a situation of latent civil war: the socialist *Lager* and the Catholic one. Many sociologists studied the deep split of this country where each camp succeeded in mobilizing a large part of the population. Indeed, around 40 percent of all Austrian adults were members in one or the other party. Both parties had spawned numerous satellite groups and parapolitical organizations, which penetrated all sectors of society: education, mass communication, unions, leisure, and even hospitals and cemeteries. Such an impermeability between blocs characterizes all consociational democracies.

A second distinctive feature is the vertical communication that links the mass with the elite within each subculture. A corollary to the impermeability between subcultures is the internal cohesion of each segment under the leadership of a unified elite. Indeed, we find the same persons at the head of various political, religious, cultural, or economic organizations in every community. For the Netherlands, Lijphart manages to establish a relatively short list of what he calls the "four elites" that hold strategic positions in each of four major blocs. This managerial concentration is also visible in Austria, and to a lesser degree in Belgium, where linguistic cleavages do not coincide with religious ones. In Switzerland, where decentralization is pronounced, elites are dispersed through several nuclei.

In a vertically segmented political system, a well-organized elite inevitably exists within each societal segment, and in each camp the followers show deference to their leaders. Necessarily, consociational democracy is more elitist than competitive democracy. Leaders of communities would not have sufficient authority in negotiation processes if their leadership was contested in their own camp. This prevailing attitude of deference-confidence has electoral consequences. Indeed, the stability of the electorate, which until recently was the rule in European consociational democracies, is striking.

The institutionalization of negotiation between elites of blocs is a third characteristic of consociational democracy. Certainly elites everywhere follow certain rules; but in a consociational democracy, the phenomenon is even more pronounced. It is related to the process of interest aggregation. Within each camp, the articulation of interests is performed in a very effective way. But since no camp is in a position to win a majority, the aggregation must be performed by an accommodation between elites. The more important and controversial the issue, the higher the level at which a compromise will be reached. Contrary to competitive democracy, which rests on the principle of majority rule, consociational democracy retains the principle of proportionality. Each camp is represented in institutions proportionally to its electoral strength. But as Lijphart stresses, the principle of proportionality turns ineffective as soon as the decisions to be reached are of a dichotomous nature — as soon as it is necessary to say yes or no. When unanimity is out of reach in parliament or other institutions, two strategies are recommended.

First, it is possible to link several problems together in order to try and solve them simultaneously by joint reciprocal concessions. This is what Austrians call *Junktim.*[7] The second method consists in delegating the responsibility for the most difficult decisions to the most influential leaders of each camp. Decisions are postponed and transferred to a higher level according to a system founded on proportionality. As a consequence of multipartism and because of the very small number of independent voters, elections are never really conclusive. Robert Dahl would say that they are not the "site of decision." They nevertheless translate votes into parliamentary seats. Parliament is the site of decision only for problems that are relatively easy to solve. Much of the time, parliament simply ratifies decisions reached at a higher and extraconstitutional level by a group of leaders; in Austria this group constitutes the *Koalitionsausschuss,* and in the Netherlands it forms the Social and Economic Council. In

Switzerland, decisions are made, if necessary, by the Federal Council, that is, by the government itself, which is composed of seven members. In Belgium, where the main cleavage is linguistic, a constitutional reform stated in 1970 that every government, no matter what its political color, would have to include an equal number of Francophone and Flemish people. In Belgium, as in the Netherlands, certain problems are resolved before the government is even constituted, thanks to the mediation of the *formateur,* who does not necessarily become the prime minister.

These two strategies can be combined, since negotiations in small committees, protected by secrecy, have more chance of resulting in an exchange of concessions, by *Junktim.*

For a consociational democracy to be established and maintained, several conditions are required. First, a certain equilibrium must exist between the different subcultures. In a fragmented society, if the various subcultures are of comparable strength, they will be more inclined to cooperate than they would be in a society where one subculture is dominant. The best illustrations of equilibrium are to be found in Switzerland and the Netherlands. In Belgium, on the contrary, where two big subcultures confront each other, each one fears domination by the other. Francophones worry about the numerical superiority of the Flemish, who in turn feel frustrated by the cultural domination of Francophones.

Another factor favorable to the establishment of a consociational democracy is the existence of well-established boundaries between subcultures. A clear separation has the advantage of limiting contacts and, so, antagonisms and occasions for conflict. As Lorwin stresses, if relations with people from other subcultures are rare, occasions for conflict are also rare.[8] In decentralized Switzerland the cantons, which are very much like small states, are relatively homogeneous, and it is at the canton level that cultural problems are settled. In Belgium, most conflicts occur at the frontier between the two communities. In Austria, on the contrary, the segmentation has no real geographical basis. This ecology of subcultures may partly explain the variety of consociational systems.

Besides proportionality, three aspects of consociational democracy deserve special attention: the principle of the great coalition, the veto right, and the relative autonomy of subcultures. Extending William Riker's theory on coalitions, Lijphart stresses the necessity of integrating as many subcultures as possible in the political game. Indeed, Switzerland since 1959 and Austria between 1945 and 1966 illustrate the practice of a great coalition. In the Netherlands, the four *Zuilen* never governed together during the fifty years that the consociational era lasted (1917-67) but changing coalitions made it possible, sometimes for one camp and sometimes for another, to be in government.

Participation in governmental coalitions certainly represents a guarantee of rights for cultural minorities; but it is not sufficient. To ensure the protection of different segments, it is necessary to grant them the veto right in domains of vital importance. In Belgium, for example, since 1970 a parliamentary decision on a linguistic issue is not considered valid unless it is adopted by a double majority: of Francophone deputies on the one hand and Flemish ones on the other.

Too frequent an exercise of the veto right could bring about immobility. To avoid such a paralysis of the decision-making processes, consociational democracy gives subcultures considerable autonomy in fields of direct concern to them. If the country's ecology makes it possible, this autonomy may take the form of federalism. But autonomy may be granted even if subcultures overlap geographically, for example, by a proportional redistribution of public money for parochial schools.

The consociational formula is not exclusively European. Some other countries have practiced it, in one form or another, and with greater or lesser success. Especially notable are Canada, Lebanon, Malaysia, Cyprus, Uruguay, and Nigeria.

The consociational model has been applied to Canada by several authors, especially Kenneth D. McRae.[9] In spite of its immensity, Canada presents some analogies with the small Swiss consociational democracy, if only because of the relative linguistic homogeneity of the provinces. But Canadian federalism differs greatly from Swiss federalism. The federated states do not necessarily constitute isolated subcultures in Canada, nor do their representatives in Parliament have a veto right. Rather, it is within parties that consociational formulas are practiced. For this reason, Lijphart believes that Canada only partially fits the consociational model.

Lebanon adopted a certain number of consociational principles between 1943 and 1975.[10] As we all know, the precarious equilibrium was destroyed from outside.

An incomplete consociational system was introduced in Malaysia in 1955. Not all the necessary conditions for such a system to work were present, particularly because the Malays became a majority (53 percent) after the separation from Singapore. The experiment resulted in a failure in 1969.[11]

Nigeria, whose population amounts to nearly one quarter of the entire African population, is characterized by a parceling into hundreds of geographically concentrated ethnic groups. In the consociational framework adopted in 1957, the boundaries of federated states did not coincide with ethnic cleavages. That situation generated a disequilibrium in favor of one state in the north of the country in which 60 percent of the population was concentrated. The fall of this first consociational experiment occurred in 1966. A new constitution, with real consociational features, was adopted in 1979.

Has Colombia experienced a consociational system? This may be hard to defend, since accommodation in Colombia involves elites only, never implying any structured organization of subcultures. Consociational democracy, as indicated in the word "democracy," means a participation of the citizens, even if they are divided into isolated communities. To speak of a consociational pattern in Colombia (1958-74) when the agreement between the two parties established only a monopolistic sharing of power between them by alternation in government after each election would be to dilute seriously the incisiveness of the concept.

The failure of many Third World countries in their efforts to adopt the British competitive pattern has led several authors to wonder whether the consociational formula would not be more appropriate for these countries, especially when society is deeply divided into cultural, racial, ethnic or religious segments. They have asked whether the quest for consensus would not have a greater chance of success if it were sought at the elite rather than mass level. Among these authors, the most famous is Sir Arthur Lewis. Speaking of West Africa,[12] Lewis diagnosed these culturally segmented countries as needing coalitions rather than a government-opposition polarization. His recommendation was founded on direct observations; according to Lijphart, it is unlikely that Lewis knew anything about the theory of consociational democracy.

Two pitfalls should be avoided by scholars eager to apply the consociational concept to developing countries: (1) the temptation to transform the theoretical model into a normative one; and (2) the risk of inflating the analytical category to a point where it might cover situations that have nothing to do with the original pattern.

Paradoxically, it is precisely at the moment when the first signs of decay in the consociational system have been perceived in Austria and the Netherlands that this kind of democracy has become fully recognized in comparative sociology and is inspiring increasing theoretical thought. As a matter of fact, the "great coalition" was abandoned in Austria in 1966 and was replaced by an alternation in power between the "black" and "red" parties. In the Netherlands, the *Verzuiling* began to break down in 1967. Since then, the five traditional parties have been losing part of their electoral support, as new, small parties have developed that have protested against the old political game; so much so that a few years later, the Protestant and Catholic parties have merged in a coalition, the "Christian union." In Belgium, linguistic conflicts are seriously endangering the equilibrium among Catholic, socialist, and liberal *familles spirituelles*. Only in Switzerland is the consociational structure still intact. But while consociational democracy dwindles in three of the four countries where it blossomed, it is an object of increased interest for some Third World countries, which find themselves in a situation similar in some respects to that of Belgium or the Netherlands three or four generations ago.

Are we to interpret the changes experienced by Austria, Belgium, and the Netherlands as a failure of consociational democracy? Or, on the contrary, do these transformations attest to the success of an experience that has fulfilled its historical mission? A parallel examination of factors that favor the establishment of a consociational democracy and factors that contribute to its decline would help us answer this essential question. Most of the time, at a moment of great danger, the consociational mortar hardens under an external threat. In the Netherlands the consociational protocol was sealed during the First World War, in 1917; in Austria it was concluded when the national territory was occupied by four foreign armies, among them the Red Army, and at the time when the national economy had to be entirely rebuilt. In Switzerland the consociational framework was perfected in 1943 by the cooptation of socialists into the Federal Council, at a time when the country was surrounded by German armies. In Belgium consociational practices were strengthened, first, during the fight for national independence, and later, during World War I. In the same way, the consociational principle was adopted in Lebanon at the very moment of national independence in 1943, and in Malaysia in similar circumstances in 1957. Except in the case of Lebanon, this coagulating factor had long ceased to be operative when the consociational pattern began to decline.

Historically, religion was the main source of conflict and tension. But religious practice has been diminishing all over Europe for the last quarter of the century. Meanwhile, the consociational system has fully succeeded in establishing a religious peace in Belgium, Austria, and the Netherlands. Historical mission accomplished! From that moment, the consociational system can weaken without endangering the institutions, especially the school network, it has helped form.[13] Societies, mentalities, and behaviors have evolved, in large part, due to consociational practices; the structure of the state may now be fashioned to the requirements of a new social and cultural context.

Simultaneously, the technological development of mass media, particularly the spread of television, has profoundly changed the channels of social communication. The religious ceremony or the local newspaper now have to compete with waves that easily cross the walls that insulate subcultures. The Calvinist is exposed to socialist messages, and the faithful Catholic is confronted by nonconformist liberalism. A new cleavage develops, which separates generations within each camp. Technological changes thus accelerate the decline, or rather the transformation, of the consociational system.

In addition, as old problems are progressively solved, others get more and more important; we think of demands for increased social protection or a more equal share in national income. A double movement occurs, implying the weakening of vertical cleavages on the one hand and an increasing significance of horizontal stratifications on the other. Society itself generates these new political issues. And this is possible precisely because the consociational system has already resolved religious and ethnic conflicts.

Consociational democracy in Europe corresponds to a historical phase in the development of pluralist segmented societies. And it is its very success that permits its replacement, rapidly or slowly, by a more competitive model.

This historical stage, now over in the Netherlands and other advanced countries, at present characterizes scores of Third World countries. Consociational democracy was not exported during the colonial period because the two great colonial powers, France and Great Britain, practiced other forms of government. Attempts at implementation in the former Belgian and Dutch colonies did not succeed, for various reasons analyzed by Lijphart.[14] But the consociational system is recommended today for a great number of countries in Southeast Asia and Africa, including South Africa. And some of them will probably experiment with it.

NOTES

1. Arend Lijphart, *The Politics of Accommodation: Pluralism and Democracy in The Netherlands,* 2nd ed. (Berkeley: University of California Press, 1974); Gerhard Lehmbruch, *Proporzdemokratie: Politisches System und Politische Kultur in der Schweiz und in Österreich* (Tübingen: Mohr, 1967); Jürg Steiner, *Amicable Agreement versus Majority Rule: Conflict Resolution in Switzerland* (Chapel Hill: University of North Carolina Press, 1974); Kurt Steiner, *Politics in Austria* (Boston: Little, Brown, 1972); Eric A. Nordlinger, *Conflict Regulation in Divided Societies* (Cambridge, Mass.: Center for International Affairs, Harvard University, 1972); G. Bingham Powell, *Social Fragmentation and Political Hostility: An Austrian Case Study* (Stanford: Stanford University Press, 1970). The most encompassing book is Arend Lijphart, *Democracy in Plural Societies: A Comparative Exploration* (New Haven: Yale University Press, 1977).

2. Most of these articles are to be found in Kenneth McRae, ed., *Consociational Democracy: Political Accommodation in Segmented Societies* (Ottawa: Carleton Library, 1974).

3. Val R. Lorwin, "Segmented Pluralism," *Comparative Politics* 3 (1971): 141-75.

4. Arend Lijphart, "Typologies of Democratic Systems," *Comparative Political Studies* 1, no. 1 (April 1968).

5. See, for example, Bruce Russett et al., *World Handbook of Political and Social Indicators* (New Haven: Yale University Press, 1964), which lists 66 countries in order of decreasing linguistic homogeneity.

6. Lijphart, *Politics of Accommodation,* chap. 2.

7. Steiner, *Politics in Austria.*

8. Lorwin, "Segmented Pluralism."

9. Kenneth D. McRae, "Consociationalism and the Canadian Political System," in *Consociational Democracy,* pp. 238-61.

10. Michael W. Suleiman, "Elections in a Confessional Democracy," *Journal of Politics* 29, no. 1 (1967): 109-28; Michael C. Hudson, "Democracy and Social Mobilization in Lebanese Politics," *Comparative Politics* 1, no. 2 (January 1969).

11. J.A. Nagata, *Pluralism in Malaysia: Myth and Reality* (Leiden: Brill, 1975).

12. *Politics in West Africa* (London: Allen & Unwin, 1965).

13. In Austria, for instance, the principle of proportionality in the allocation of positions and public funds is still practiced, despite the end of the great Coalition, which occurred in 1966.

14. *Democracy in Plural Societies,* chap. 5.

CHAPTER 12

POLITICAL CRISES:
HISTORICAL EVENTS OR
STAGES OF DEVELOPMENT

When social scientists analyze the social, economic, and political transformations related to the process of historical development, they generally shed light on causal factors rather than sequences. It is indeed easier to find generalizations at the level of structures than at the level of events, which are by definition unique and incomparable. Thus a division of tasks is tacitly practiced between historians and sociologists: the former focus on abrupt events, eruptions, and depressions; the latter consider the crisis as an epiphenomenon, as a stage in the maturation of underground forces.

This orientation appears clearly if we consider the few attempts made at studying historical events from a sociological point of view. The point is not so much to inquire about the nature or the consequences of the crisis as to look for its causes. The question is seldom "which" crisis, or the crisis "with what effect"; rather, it is "why" the crisis.

To that question, many answers have been proposed. Aristotle already saw the uprising as resulting from a quest for equality, the majority rebelling against a minority that holds the wealth, enjoys the honors, and exercises the power. By relating class struggle to the concept of exploitation, Karl Marx modernized this fundamental approach. But by emphasizing the importance of "consciousness" in class alignment, he seemed to admit that psychological frustration may nourish tensions and disorders as much as real injustice does. Alexis de Tocqueville was aware of this possibility; he noted that, on the eve of their revolution, the French had begun to feel their situation insupportable, even though the reign of Louis XVI had been the most prosperous of the old monarchy. Tocqueville explained in *L'ancien régime et la révolution* that revolutions do not necessarily erupt following an aggravation in the situation; in fact, the misfortune that is patiently accepted when it looks inevitable becomes intolerable as soon as it seems possible to overcome it.

Elaborating his theory of revolution, James C. Davies[1] proposes a model that takes into account these subjective and objective elements. A particularly unstable period is one in which an intolerable gap exists between what people expect and what they actually get from government. The author thus gives a central place in his explanation to the "revolution of rising expectations." The gap existing between what is expected from the system and what the system is capable of offering engenders tensions and explosions. This approach could help explain the frequency and violence of crises in developing countries, which often suffer from the weight of prematurely "imported" demands.

In an earlier book, Crane Brinton undertook an "anatomy of revolution" and as a true comparativist, he tried to shed light on what different revolutionary situations—in Puritan England, Washington's America, France of 1789, and Russia of 1917—had in common.[2] His conclusions noted several general causes that modern analyses often stress. What he labeled the incompetence of the elite, or institutional blockage, would be categorized today as "inefficiency"; the desertion of intellectuals would be approached under the broader perspective of a decline in "legitimacy."

But these explanations, in truth, do not help us understand the meaning and nature of historical drama. They do not tell us what the fundamental difference is between the American uprising against the mother country and the revolution in Paris or the insurrection in Saint Petersburg. They do not help us make the distinction, or lay stress on the analogies, between old and recent crises, between obvious events and subtle trends.

Only recently have scholars felt the need of a systematic approach. The multiplicity of crises in developing countries has stimulated a theoretical debate in which Edward Shils, Samuel Huntington, Seymour Martin Lipset, Lucian Pye, and Leonard Binder have participated on the front line. Adopting the functionalist perspective, these scholars have found, at a median level of conceptualization, a few handy "operational" categories.

Their point of view has led them to consider crisis, not so much a result of, but rather a challenge to, the political and social systems. They have proposed generalizations that shed light on the profound historical meaning of events more than their causes. For all these authors, crises correspond to the emergence of fundamental problems in the development of a nation. Now it remains to determine what these fundamental problems are.

It is a difficult task, for the theoretical *a priori* may well condition and bias the empirical analysis. Those who have undertaken a general study of critical situations have not always detected the same categories of significant crises. For the authors of *Crises and Sequences in Political Development,*[3] several evolutions characterize the process of development: a differentiation of structures, an evolution toward greater equality, and a growth in the capacity for adaptation and integration of the political system. These developments often lead to crises that are inherent in the nature of "modern" or "modernizing" systems. "While traditional social orders might not be spared internal tensions and contradictions, the very essence of modernization is a dynamic state based on the need to manage and ameliorate the inescapable tensions inherent in the development syndrome."[4] This perspective, Lucian Pye explains further, has made it possible "to see the problems of the currently developing countries of Africa and Asia as being closer to the persisting problems of the advanced industrial societies than to the state of affairs associated with traditional orders."

Because development is a process that never ends, the inclusion of Third World countries in the category "modern" gives a universal profile to an analysis of crises. The United States as well as Nigeria, and France as well as Indonesia, are submitted to the pressures of these profound movements. The difference comes from the fact that a highly developed society can more easily mobilize more resources in replying to the tensions it experiences.

Considering these pressures, the authors of *Crises and Sequences in Political Development* have identified five crises: crises of identification, legitimation, penetration, distribution, and participation. An analysis of the crises experienced by every country in the course of its history would certainly permit the recognition of universal trends that imply a transition from local or clannish allegiances to a national consciousness, the replacement of divine right by a more rational legitimacy, expanding demands for a more egalitarian distribution of goods, a growing aspiration to participate, and so on.

One could naturally contest the validity of such a conceptual scheme. To place in the same analytical category the military penetration of peripheral territories with institutional penetration could lead to confusion about very different kinds of performance. There are also some overlappings, such as between the crises of identity and participation. Myron Weiner, for example, sees secessionist movements as expressing demands for an increased participation,[5] which is not altogether obvious.

These categories could thus be accepted as hypotheses, provided we add one more, which played a crucial role in Europe and could be called the "crisis of secularization." Seymour Martin Lipset points out its importance. "In modern times, three major issues have emerged in Western nations: first, the place of the church and/or various religions within the nation; second, the admission of the lower strata, particularly the workers, to full political and economic 'citizenship' through universal suffrage and the right to bargain collectively; and third, the continuing struggle over the distribution of the national income."[6]

Interest in such categories is obvious to the comparativist. They can undoubtedly help him understand history; help him link the noisy event with the silent underground processes, relate different situations that shed light on one another. The "crisis of democracy," as it has been perceived, shows that the so-called overdeveloped countries are in fact probably less developed than some believe. They are not sheltered against the profound contradictions existing between demands for participation or distribution on the one side and the means to satisfy them on the other. The crisis of efficiency is cyclical, and the crisis of legitimacy always remains in the background. Research by Juan Linz and Alfred Stepan[7] on the breakdown of democratic regimes would attest to this.

It would be artificial to draw a distinction between crises that are "solvable" once and for all and those that reappear cyclically. It is clear that some tensions manifest themselves in a more visible way than others. But no legitimacy is definitely anchored, no national identity is so profoundly rooted that, one day or another, it could not be threatened. The resurgence of autonomy movements in old Europe is an eloquent testimony to this.

The global comprehension of crises should permit us to distinguish between several kinds of solutions — from pacific resolutions to revolutions — without forgetting the possibility of simply postponing decisions. When new demands give rise to more appropriate institutions, the vitality of a system and its capacity for adaptation is reaffirmed. Postponing could become a factor of instability, itself symptomatic of more fundamental inadequacies. The incapacity of the French Fourth Republic to resolve the problem of its colonies has been rightly considered as one of the causes of its fall.

When it occurs, the explosion can take several forms. Revolt or revolution, says Jacques Ellul,[8] depends on whether or not the explosion leads to change. But change itself may go in the direction of progress or regression. For the comparativist, it is certainly a fascinating problem to ask which elements, at a certain moment, make a political system overly or insufficiently "advanced."

History tells us that crises tend to propagate themselves as epidemics do. We need only think of the Reformation at the end of the Middle Ages, of the Revolution of 1848 that embraced all of Europe, of the awakening of nationalities in the second half of the nineteenth century, of the fascist explosions in Europe in the 1930s, of the national liberation movements that developed simultaneously in forty countries in the 1950s, of the student unrest that broke out in twelve industrialized countries in 1967-68, of the sudden awakening of Islam, and so on. These phenomena, which spread with the force of a real contagion, lead the comparativist, skeptical about explanations in terms of "microbes," to inquire about the genesis and mechanics of the crisis.

The two notions that impress themselves on the analyst are, first, the existence of an appropriate soil, and second, the presence of a ferment. How many situations, apparently mature for the onset of crisis, do not develop because the model or the agitator is missing? How many cases, conversely, of ferment dissipate into nothing because the soil was not appropriate? The independence movement in the United States in the eighteenth century and the ideas of the Young Turks at the beginning of the twentieth were not disseminated because the potential receptors were immature. We must stress also that the soil may prove sterile for reasons that are not social or economic but strictly political. A police or military control administered in large doses can prevent the propagation of the crisis, even if such a drastic remedy appears worse than the sickness itself. The manner in which crises in Eastern Europe blow up in a discontinuous fashion—now in Berlin, now in Warsaw, now in Budapest, now in Prague, Poznan, or Gdansk—illustrates the power of these blocking mechanisms.

We could also stress the positive role played by political factors in the emergence of a crisis. Let us think, for example, of the Chinese Cultural Revolution, an eruption provoked from the summit in order to purge the system. Revolutions engender rites, but rituals, even if totalitarian, sometimes prove impotent in regulating the course of social life. It would be an interesting dimension of comparative research to inquire about the role of the state as producer of crises: territorial expansion, wars, purges, and so on.

The manner in which each country experiences crises provides another fertile field of investigation. The nation that progresses from crisis to crisis has long been contrasted with one that resolves tensions in a more peaceful way. An interesting question could be to ask whether all systems have the same capacity to solve crises, or whether capacities vary according to the kind of crisis. Michel Foucault noted the incredible faculty for resistance and adaptation of the "bourgeois power" by contrast with the feudal one.[9] In a somewhat different way, well-meaning journalists, and even political scientists, have been known to ask whether, for some developing countries, a strong regime, which might be expected to resist crises of identity or participation better, might not be more appropriate than a liberal pluralistic system.[10]

Another interesting dimension of this comparative research consists in identifying various sequences in the succession of crises, which would help a dynamic approach to the maturation processes. It is important to know, as Seymour Martin Lipset stresses,[11] whether it is possible for a nation to resolve problems one at a time or whether old causes of conflicts amalgamate with new sources of tension. Are crises staggered so that they can be progressively eliminated, or do unresolved crises accumulate, creating an explosive situation? Most European nations faced successively the problems posed by nation building, the consolidation of the state, the political integration of less privileged social strata, and the fiscal redistribution of wealth. On the contrary, the new nations of Africa or Asia must face all these problems at once, in the space of a single generation. Countries in which a national identity and the legitimacy of institutions were strongly rooted when, for example, the working class began to demand the extension of the voting right have had an experience totally different from countries in which participation was granted before legitimacy of the regime or national integration had been fully established. The simultaneity of crises, their accumulation, is a fundamental explanation of the political instability in many countries of the Third World.

NOTES

1. James C. Davies, "Toward a Theory of Revolution," *American Sociological Review* 27, no. 1 (February 1962): 5-19. The reader interested in the theories developed on political violence will find an adequate guidebook in James C. Davies, ed., *When Men Revolt and Why: A Reader in Political Violence and Revolution* (New York: Free Press, 1971).
2. Crane Brinton, *The Anatomy of Revolution,* rev. ed. (New York: Vintage Books, 1965).
3. Princeton: Princeton University Press, 1971.
4. Lucian Pye in Leonard Binder et al., *Crises and Sequences in Political Development* (Princeton: Princeton University Press, 1971), foreword.
5. Myron Weiner, "Political Participation: Crises of the Political Process," in ibid.
6. Seymour Martin Lipset, *Political Man: The Social Bases of Politics,* new expanded ed. (Baltimore: Johns Hopkins University Press, 1981).
7. Juan Linz and Alfred Stepan, *The Breakdown of Democratic Regimes* (Baltimore: Johns Hopkins University Press, 1978).
8. Jacques Ellul, *De la révolution aux révoltes* (Paris: Calmann-Lévy, 1972).
9. Michel Foucault, "L'oeil du pouvoir," introduction to Jeremy Bentham, *Le panoptique* (Paris: Belfont, 1977), p. 26.
10. See the critical point of view of Charles C. Moskos and Wendell Bell, "Emerging Nations and Ideologies of American Social Scientists," *American Sociologist* 2, no. 2 (May 1967).
11. *Political Man,* p. 71.

PART 3

THE CHOICE OF COUNTRIES

ACCORDING TO the dictionary, to compare means to recognize similarities and differences. But scientific comparisons are designed not only to acquire this relative knowledge but also to infer general laws from a multiplicity of specific cases. This process of induction is at the heart of the comparative method; and it may be greatly facilitated by a judicious choice of the field of inquiry.

Confronted with social bodies whose elements are inextricably intertwined, the comparativist must determine the angle that will allow him to perceive the variables he wants to study with great clarity. He must find a way to take the optimal view that will permit him to draw reliable and rigorous conclusions. In a word, he must select a field of research that will enhance the significance of his prospecting.

When we speak of the "field" of the analysis, we are in reality speaking of two dimensions. On the one hand, there is that part of the social and political system that is to be compared. The operation we refer to as "segmentation," and with which we deal first, corresponds to this dimension. On the other hand, there are the number and kind of countries to be included in the analysis. Some authors have discussed this issue. Gabriel Almond has recommended the regional approach, later challenged by Dankwart A. Rustow. Harry Eckstein has drawn up a list of the advantages and disadvantages connected with case study. Adam Przeworski and Henry Teune have proposed two research designs, one for the "most similar systems" and one for the "most different systems." What is missing from the literature, however, is an overview of the different possibilities offered to the researcher who has to delineate the area of analysis and choose the countries to be included in the comparison.

Our design here is precisely to distinguish the various strategies that are open to the comparativist and discuss their respective advantages and weaknesses. We successively consider the case study in comparative perspective, the binary analysis, the comparison of rather similar countries, the comparison of rather contrasting countries, and the conceptual homogenization of a heterogeneous field.

Decisions made by comparativists in determining the field of inquiry will naturally influence the choices they make regarding the methods of analysis or the conceptual tools to be used. Quantification may certainly be useful both in a comparison dealing with rather similar countries and in an analysis encompassing most different systems. But it is clear that the indicators of interest for comparing France and Brazil will not be the same as for comparing France and West Germany. If socioeconomic data are given so much importance in certain very broad comparative studies, it is precisely because these data are the only ones that have a relatively homogeneous meaning all over the world. The significance of birthrates, mileages of railroad, or energy consumption remains more or less constant when one passes from Japan to China or Angola. The same could not be said of rates of unionization or levels of electoral participation. But the comparativist interested in Western Europe will certainly find that hard data on urbanization, literacy, or infant mortality are not significantly differentiated. The discriminatory power of certain variables decreases as the observer, instead of taking a general view, considers a more limited and homogeneous field.

The choice of countries also determines the abstraction level of the concepts utilized. It is not necessary to fly very high to take a comparative view of communist votes in France, Italy, Spain, and Portugal. Even at this level, naturally, notions such as "alienation behaviors" or "protest attitudes" may prove useful. But to take an abstract view becomes a real necessity when highly contrasting systems are compared. In the Poland of 1980, the communist vote could be interpreted as a conformity vote, while membership in Solidarity probably meant protest behavior. To go to Mass has not the same political meaning in Cardinal Segura's Spain and Rakosi's Hungary; the mosque has not the same significance in Iran and in Turkey. To approach comparatively and appreciate the significance of such religious practices, it is necessary to climb up the ladder of abstractions; it is indispensable if one is to carve concepts capable of summing up apparently different phenomena.

CHAPTER 13

ON THE NEED TO SEGMENT
BEFORE COMPARING

In a sense, all comparative studies deal with segments, with parts of a society. Overall analyses in the tradition of Montesquieu, Spencer, or Weber are becoming increasingly rare; first, because the social sciences today are more analytical and functional; and second, because the progress of knowledge leads sociologists increasingly to define and limit their field of investigation. A similar specification of research is to be found in physics. The intellectual profile of Nicolaus Copernicus, Leonardo da Vinci, or Isaac Newton no longer corresponds to that of the leading scientists of today. The distance that separates a Curie or a Fleming from these earlier profiles can be "compared" to the distance separating the expert in comparative studies from the political philosopher. The discipline matures by dividing the social reality it studies.

This is not to say that the holistic perspective has been abandoned. Indeed, even great comparativists have contributed to keep it alive—we think of Gabriel Almond, Karl Deutsch, Seymour Martin Lipset, or Daniel Bell. But one has only to consult the best bibliographies devoted to comparative analysis, such as that of Robert M. Marsh[1] (listing 1146 studies) or the more specialized one by Stein Rokkan, Jean Viet, Sidney Verba, and Elina Almasy[2] (comprising 982 titles), to note the overwhelming predominance of sectorial comparisons. Very few studies attempt to compare, in their entirety, vast political and social structures. The division of the system into segments is the normal course of the comparative approach. Confronted with the complexity of the political system, unless he opts for pure theory, the researcher is led to make a choice, to divide, to select the phenomenon on which to center comparison.

We must also state at the outset that the distinction between segmentation and the global approach is a matter of degree. Between the restrictive sectorial study and the global approach that loses itself in abstract theory, there lies a progression from the particular to the general. In contrasting these two facets, it is the overall method that we wish to emphasize. Comparing always involves extracting a small or large sector from a society or political system. But there is a considerable distance between, say, an analysis of the political behavior of farm workers in two countries and a study of the aggregative functions of parties in twenty or thirty countries.

Comparison has helped in approaching all the domains of interest to the political scientist. "Compared institutions" have long constituted a privileged field, especially in countries such as France and Germany. But sectorial comparison rapidly began to cope with domains more difficult to identify than parliaments or governments. As political science developed beyond its early and exclusive concern with formal institutions, it investigated new fields and segments. One could even say that it actively contributed to their discovery, as though the distance cultivated by the comparativist allowed him to perceive better the key agents of the political process. A good illustration to that positive contribution can be found in the pioneering book in which David Truman first explained *The Governmental Process*[3] in terms of exchange and interaction between diversely structured groups. Later on, functionalists adopted this approach, which led them to recognize the political game as resulting from a multiplicity of actions that were performed by actors with different goals and means.

Broadly speaking, comparativists have developed their investigations in three directions. First, they have considered the politically relevant groupings. Pressure groups, parties, and trade unions, as well as bureaucracies and armies, have attracted the attention of many scholars and inspired a lot of comparative works. At a higher level of conceptualization, studies have even been conceived on phenomena more difficult to define, such as "oppositions." Robert Dahl inspired this kind of comparative study. In *Political Oppositions in Western Democracies,*[4] he combined the sectorial delimitation with a geopolitical one; in *Regimes and Oppositions,*[5] on the other hand, the comparison included Latin America as well as India, and Japan as well as tropical Africa. But the indisputable dilution of the argument that resulted from this extension makes clear that it is generally useful to couple segmentation with a rigorous and consistent selection of the countries being compared.

Political processes have constituted a second important field investigated by the comparativists. The processes of opinion formation, socialization, communication, decision making, implementation, legitimization, and the like, have been studied with increasing care. Here again, a spatial delimitation has often proved to be an indispensable corollary of segmentation. It is clear that issues such as the political role of the military, the decay of parliaments, or even the growth of the state take on a different meaning according to whether we consider Black Africa or North America, the Soviet bloc or Western Europe. To decide whether the philosophy of the leaders influences the content of governmental output, it is of course necessary to limit the analysis to countries situated at a rather similar level of development and characterized by the same kinds of ideological cleavages.[6]

Comparativists have considered various social categories. They have contrasted women with men, young people with adults, Protestants with Catholics, white-collar workers with blue-collar workers, and so on. Special attention has been devoted to political elites and, generally speaking, to sections of the population reputed to be important in the decision-making process. A comparative study of their social origins often makes it easier to understand their behavior. The role played by the army in Portugal, for example, becomes clearer when one considers that the majority of its officers came from the lower middle class and not from upper social strata. The same remark could apply to Nasser's Egypt. Some analysts have explained the course taken by the Iranian revolution by the rural origin of the bulk of Islamic students. Others have clarified some major contrasts existing between European socialist parties by the different proportions of trade unionists or intellectuals among their activists.

Our purpose is certainly not to review the many segments on which the analysis may focus. Rather, what we intend to do is to emphasize that the comparativist is very much at liberty to choose his own way of approaching reality. The "political system" is an abstract whole that covers a multiplicity of institutions, processes, behaviors, and groups. As a function of the segments he selects and according to the geographical field he considers, the comparativist will orient his efforts toward extremely different analyses — some ambitious and some more specific, some broadly significant and some more limited in scope and meaning. The choice of a limited segment seems to make possible imaginative and valuable comparisons between widely differing polities. But it is not an absolute guarantee of relevance. When the parts extracted from the political systems function in highly contrasted environments, they have nothing in common but their name. To compare municipalities in India and Sweden, for example, has proven artificial and finally uninteresting.

Many books could be mentioned, the results of which have proven disappointing because the segments were extracted from such different political systems that their comparability is very low. The book by Jean Blondel on *World Leaders,*[7] which considers all "heads of government in the postwar period," has such weaknesses; the chapter devoted to "routes to leadership," for example, raises problems due to its lack of consistency. What sense is there in comparing the "regular ministerial career" in the Middle East and in the Atlantic and communist worlds? Aren't we here misled simply by verbal similarities? What is the meaning of comparatively studying the "duration of leadership" when the nature of the leadership is so different? It is true that the book has the merit of raising such questions.

The book by Kay Lawson devoted to *The Comparative Study of Political Parties* in France, Guinea, and the United States[8] does not escape serious problems either. The intention of the author was to complement a theoretical approach to political parties with the richness and specificity of three case studies. As Lawson states, "no political institutions operate in a vacuum, political parties least of all."[9] But the shift from abstract theory to more empirical comparison brings about the paradoxical result that one doubts whether it makes sense to ask the same questions of such strikingly different situations.

The practice of segmentation indeed raises the important strategic problem of how to control the impact of the national context on the sector analyzed. The risk is obviously that of going too far in erasing the overarching context wherein each sector of social life takes root. What, for example, is the meaning of a comparison of parliaments if it neglects the impact of the environment on these institutions? One knows full well that the efficiency of the same "worthy" institutions can falter according to the social context. This is particularly apparent when one tries to "export" them without taking into account the psychological and social structures on which they are based. As Roy Macridis[10] and Henry Ehrmann[11] stress, those who study interest groups always end by reaching a point beyond which the explanation of the differences moves outside the framework of any "theory of groups"; the contrasts must then be attributed to some element buried in the cultures, social structures, or political systems considered in their entirety.

The number of political parties and the nature of the electoral rules have no automatic consequences for the functioning of a system. Their significance and impact depend on the specific attitudes of members of those political parties, or on the attitudes of citizens voting according to legal regulations. As Richard Pride points out, a "stable democracy" coincides with certain party structures *only* in countries where democratic institutions, creeds, and practices were long established and preceded the multiplication of parties and the development of mass parties.[12]

In carrying out relatively restrictive sectorial division, the researcher naturally runs the risk of neglecting history, an error denounced by Georges Balandier.[13] The facts, institutions, and events are infused with a subjective dimension that disappears if one considers these facts, institutions, or events out of context. One cannot isolate a segment of social life without reducing its profound "meaning." In this spirit Georges Lavau reproaches Maurice Duverger for explaining political phenomena in exclusively political terms. What is lacking from Duverger's theory of political parties, Lavau claims, is not only the study of their doctrine and their social composition "but also the study of the types of societies in which the parties move and of the economic conditions and historical circumstances in which they evolve."[14] This is an obvious shortcoming. But how could such an exhaustive framework of analysis as that proposed by La-

vau have advanced our knowledge of the political party? The study of diges-
tion *in vitro* constituted a fundamental stage in physiology. The configurative
study cannot produce the same results as the sectorial analysis.

One must stress the fertility of the sectorial approach. Paradoxically, it
is often by "eliminating," insofar as possible, the contextual data that the analyst
manages to bring out the causal relationship, the interaction between factors
that can be observed and their cumulative effect.[15] To isolate artificially certain social strata from their sociological context in order to make a comparative
study of the behavior of the working class, or women, or the younger generations can be even a means of weighing the importance of cultural variables.

Some comparativists have argued that the practice of segmentation is possible and fruitful even when the countries under consideration are very different.
They have proposed to overcome the difficulties related to great contextual variations by undertaking what Stein Rokkan called "second order" comparisons.
What they compare is not a determined variable, isolated from its context—
say, the propensity to vote in France and in the United States—but rather hierarchies, patterns of interconnection between a cluster of variables—say, whether
women or uneducated people in France and the United States tend to the same
degree to vote less than men or women with higher education. As Sidney Verba writes, "from the point of view of the achievement of equivalence in measures, this type of comparison controls for many of the contextual differences."[16]
Verba himself, with Ahmed Bhatt, later proposed a study where the attitudes
of the lowest stratum in India and the United States were compared, although
there exists a great objective distance between the situation of American blacks
and that of Harijans.[17]

Once the comparativist has decided which part of the political system or
sector of society he wishes to study, he has another decision to make. He has
to choose the countries to be included in his analysis.

NOTES

1. "Comparative Sociology 1950-1963," *Current Sociology* 14, no. 2 (1966).
2. *Comparative Survey Analysis* (Paris: Mouton, 1969). See too, J. Delatte and
   E. Almasy, *Comparative Survey Analysis: A Bibliographical Follow-
   Up* (International Social Science Council 1972). One excellent review
   of current comparative studies is to be found in a specialized periodi-
   cal, *Comparative Research* (International Studies Association), which
   gives critical appraisal, not only of books but also of articles. A very
   substantial review of systematic and explicit comparative studies that
   have been published since 1965 is to be found in two special issues

edited by J. Michael Armer and Robert M. Marsh of the *International Journal of Comparative Sociology* 22, nos. 1-2 and 3-4 (1981).

3. David Truman, *The Governmental Process* (New York: Knopf, 1951).

4. New Haven: Yale University Press, 1963.

5. New Haven: Yale University Press, 1973.

6. On that wide issue, see the contradictory findings of Frank Parkin, *Class, Inequality and Political Power* (New York: Praeger, 1971); R.W. Jackman, "Socialist Parties and Income Inequalities in Western Industrial Societies," *Journal of Politics* 42, no. 1 (February 1980); and John D. Stephens, *The Transition from Capitalism to Socialism* (New York: Macmillan, 1979), esp. chap. 4.

7. Beverly Hills, Calif.: Sage, 1980.

8. New York: St. Martin's Press, 1976.

9. Ibid., p. 27.

10. "Interest Groups in Comparative Analysis," *Journal of Politics* 23, no. 1 (1961): 36 et passim.

11. "The Comparative Study of Interest Groups," preface to *Interest Groups in Four Continents* (Pittsburgh: University of Pittsburgh Press, 1958).

12. "Origins of Democracy: A Cross-National Study of Mobilization, Party Systems and Democratic Stability," in *Comparative Politics,* ed. Leon Epstein and Ted Gurr (Beverly Hills, Calif.: Sage, 1970).

13. *Sens et Puissance* (Paris: Presses Universitaires de France, 1971).

14. *Partis Politiques et Réalités Sociales* (Paris: Colin, 1953), p. 8.

15. See Mattei Dogan and Stein Rokkan, eds., *Quantitative Ecological Analysis in the Social Sciences* (Cambridge, Mass.: MIT Press, 1969), especially the introduction and the chapters by Erwin Scheuch, Juan Linz, and Erik Allardt.

16. "Cross-National Survey Research: The Problem of Credibility," in *Comparative Methods in Sociology,* ed. Ivan Vallier (Berkeley: University of California Press, 1971), p. 328.

17. Sidney Verba and Ahmed Bhatt, *Caste, Race and Politics: A Comparison of India and the United States* (Beverly Hills, Calif.: Sage, 1971).

Chapter 14

THE CASE STUDY IN COMPARATIVE PERSPECTIVE

It may look paradoxical to include the case study among the strategies open to the comparativist. However, many comparativists make use of this strategy, relying not only on monographs written by others but often doing the research personally. They may concentrate on a country they know particularly well, or even go in search of multiple confirmations of their hypotheses. This is what Barrington Moore[1] did, for example, with a series of analyses centered on India, Japan, and the Chinese Empire. Reinhard Bendix's *Kings or People*[2] is another good illustration of this strategy of selecting a limited series of historical cases—here Great Britain, France, Germany, Russia, and Japan—to inspire and sustain a general reflection. In such studies the author asks the same questions of the different countries he considers; Bendix, for example, systematically tries to evaluate the role of wars in nation building or how intellectuals contribute to mobilize people. And that set of issues gives consistency to the work. The comparativist may also sponsor collective endeavors designed to shed light on a precise issue through the contributions of various experts.

However, most monographs cannot be integrated into the comparative discipline. Very often, a study limited to one country emphasizes the uniqueness of the situation considered. The researcher tends then to concentrate his interest on the *Gestalt,* the way in which different parts of the system combine to make up a unique whole. The role of intuition can be large in these analyses, which accounts for the fact that they sometimes diverge so widely from one author to another. When faced with a series of explanations of equal plausibility, the comparativist hesitates. The heterogeneity or absence of evaluative criteria makes the choice difficult, and often makes impossible a theoretical integration of the accumulated knowledge.

In this sense, Sidney Verba is right to say that one can validly explain a particular case only on the basis of general hypotheses.[3] All the rest is uncontrollable, and so is of no use. Alfred Grosser puts it differently: "In a certain sense, no monograph is scientific. There is science only if the analysis of a specific subject is conceived straightaway as a case study: that is to say if one asks the subject questions deduced from a comparative, even though brief, view of similar subjects."[4]

The nature of the problem thus is an important factor for deciding whether a case study will be of value for the comparativist. Studies focused on structural or systemic data have rather good prospects because the political system already provides a universal matrix; that is, it exhibits a generally relevant set of issues and alows a translation from one particular experience to another. This translation may become more difficult when the field considered in the monograph implies the kind of intimate approach that only history can provide. Case studies dealing with segments of the political system, such as parties or parliaments, generally are more relevant to a comparative perspective than, say, analyses devoted to ideologies. The problems in this field could be illustrated by *The European Right*,[5] edited by two leading historians, Hans Rogger and Eugen Weber. Here, eleven specialists studied rightist ideologies in as many countries. Although they focused on the same main issues, which were clearly defined in the introduction, the monographs did not really lead to a comparative synthesis.

One cannot hope to approach a psychological reality without going down to a level where universal scientific categories lose most of their sharpness. Fabian ideology or Russian nihilism are clearly very specific trends, not to be evaluated with objective measures; nor could one easily find anything like "orleanism" outside of France. This is not to say that comparison is of little interest in gaining an understanding of such matters. The comparative perspective is facilitated when, like Weber in his classic study of religious ethics, the analyst emphasizes how political ideology affects political behaviors or processes.

Recent works by Giovanni Sartori and Giacomo Sani,[6] Jean Laponce,[7] and Samuel H. Barnes and Max Kaase[8] open new perspectives, thanks to survey techniques that complement the historical approach. They shed light on the functions, rather than on the nature of ideological phenomena. Research on political culture shows that it may be interesting to take a comparative view of different configurations of values. But such research has also demonstrated how difficult it is to objectively measure subjective beliefs and representations. Intuition is always a better guide in approaching this kind of reality. But then translating the knowledge into general terms becomes much more difficult.[9]

The case study results from confrontation and aims at generalization. Naturally this generalization can be found at different levels. To view Morocco in the perspective of the Arab world, to consider the Nazi experience within the framework of the totalitarian model, or to study recent Turkish history in the light of problems raised by development means including the monograph in a series of comparative studies. Sometimes the general perspective is clearly stated, and sometimes it is implicit. But it must be present for the monograph to become a real case study.

The case study is normally conceived within a theoretical perspective. It is meant to illustrate constant features of certain broadly significant situations or processes. When the French historian Paul Veyne analyzes ancient Rome in the light of cultural pluralism in general,[10] he produces a work of interest to all sociologists or political scientists. In the same way, any study on nation building has to take into account the *The First New Nation* by Seymour Martin Lipset.

This generalizing trend is even clearer when the monograph is written by a comparativist. As a matter of fact, many researchers have tested or developed general models within the framework of a single country. We think here of the works of David Apter on Ghana, James Coleman on Nigeria, Fred Riggs on Thailand, Michael Hudson on Lebanon, and Lucian Pye on Burma. If we consider this last case, we see how, by pondering the problems of this new Asian country, Pye made certain theoretical observations[11] that have since been widely recognized and discussed in studies on political development and communication. No modern society can take shape unless complex and efficient large organizations develop; but the case of Burma makes it clear that such organizations cannot be established in the absence of informal communication between citizens, that is, in the absence of an adequate social context. The French "bureaucratic phenomenon," as described by Michel Crozier,[12] also shows that cultural models may be important elements in the dynamics of organizations. These works exemplify how a case study may bring to light significant factors and variables neglected in more inclusive comparisons. Limiting the analysis to a single country has the advantage of allowing the researcher to study the subject in depth.

The case study becomes "heuristic," as Harry Eckstein would say,[13] when it contributes to the refinement of a theory. To study Malaysia as a consociational democracy means distinguishing explanatory elements that become integrated into the cumulative knowledge of this type of democracy. To note, for example, how little resistance the consociational model offers to excessive governmental responsibilities, as in Lebanon, leads to a better understanding of the rules of the game in such a system. These examples illustrate how the case study, far from passively depicting sociological rules, contributes actively to their depiction.

This appears even more clearly when the case considered is "clinical" or "deviant," and thus focuses on a critical or exceptional situation rather than an average or illustrative one. By studying the end of the German democracy, Karl D. Bracher identified which weaknesses may be decisive in such critical, even if fortunately rare, situations.[14] Juan Linz[15] considered the case of Spain in the same perspective. The radical rejection of an imported culture and the complete dislocation of a nation-state may be phenomena of special interest to those studying Iran or Pakistan. The absence of socialism in the United States has long constituted an enigma. Considering the causes of that relative "anomaly," Werner Sombart at the beginning of the century ventured to say that socialism would cetainly soon develop in America.[16] In a more recent work, John H.M. Laslett and Seymour Martin Lipset explained why this prospect proved to be a mere "dream."[17] Here, the specificity of the American "case" appears all the more clearly since it constantly referred to the European general model.

An analysis of deviant cases is of great interest because it may disclose new causes and oblige the observer to develop or reformulate his theory.[18] Holt and Richardson rightly stated[19] that all scientific disciplines advance by progressively solving a certain number of puzzles or unanswered questions. It is clear that political science also progresses by clarifying enigmas—by explaining, for example, why underdeveloped India has managed to keep a democratic regime. The analysis of deviant cases is at the heart of the comparative method. Indeed, comparison is at the forefront because it directs the researcher to cases worthy of interest; and at the same time it in turn calls for new explanations to be included in the theoretical model.

We need not consider case studies only in terms of their contribution to general knowledge. One could give many examples of research techniques or methodological approaches that derived from monographic studies and have since been used in comparisons. Thus, "tree" analysis, which consists of selecting a series of dichotomous variables according to their explanatory potential, has been elaborated for one country and then used for many comparative studies.[20] Few scales of "attitude," "authoritarianism," "nationalism," or "alienation" have been directly drafted on a comparative basis. Nevertheless, the best ones are naturally meant to be used in this extensive manner.

While devoting our attention to the case study, we have not forgotten that comparison normally implies the confrontation of several units. At a minimum there will be two countries; at a maximum, there will be all the nations on earth, considered historically.

NOTES

1. *Social Origins of Dictatorship and Democracy* (Boston: Beacon Press, 1966).
2. *Kings or People: Power and the Mandate to Rule* (Berkeley: University of California Press, 1978).
3. Sidney Verba, "Some Dilemmas in Comparative Research," *World Politics* 20, no. 1 (1967): 114.
4. *L'Explication Politique* (Paris: Colin, 1970).

5. *The European Right: An Historical Profile* (London: Weidenfeld and Nicholson, 1965).

6. Giacomo Sani and Giovanni Sartori, "Polarization, Fragmentation and Competition in Western Democracies" (report to the World Sociology Congress, Uppsala, 1978), reprinted in Hans Daalder and Peter Mair, eds., *Western European Party Systems* (Beverly Hills, Calif.: Sage, 1983).

7. J.A. Laponce, "In Search of the Stable Elements of the Left-Right Landscape," *Comparative Politics* 4, no. 4 (July 1972): 455-75.

8. Samuel H. Barnes and Max Kaase, eds., *Political Action, Mass Participation in Five Western Democracies* (Beverly Hills, Calif.: Sage, 1979).

9. An interesting discussion of different possible issues in comparative ideology has been made by Robert Wuthnow, "Comparative Ideology," *International Journal of Comparative Sociology* 22, nos. 3-4 (1981): 121ff.

10. Cf. *Le pain et le cirque: Sociologie historique d'un pluralisme historique* (Paris: Seuil, 1976).

11. *Politics, Personality and Nation Building: Burma's Search for Identity* (New Haven: Yale University Press, 1962).

12. *The Bureaucratic Phenomenon* (Chicago: University of Chicago Press, 1964).

13. "Case Study and Theory in Political Science," in *Handbook of Political Science,* ed. Fred I. Greenstein and Nelson W. Polsby (Reading, Mass.: Addison-Wesley, 1975), vol. 7.

14. See Karl D. Bracher, *Deutschland zwischen Demokratie und Diktatur* (Bern: Scherz, 1964).

15. See Juan Linz and Alfred Stepan, *The Breakdown of Democratic Regimes* (Baltimore: Johns Hopkins University Press, 1975).

16. *Why Is There No Socialism in the United States?* (New York: Macmillan, 1976).

17. *Failure of a Dream: Essays in the History of American Socialism* (Garden City, N.Y.: Anchor Books, 1974).

18. See Bruce M. Russett, Hayward R. Alker, Karl M. Deutsch, and Harold D. Lasswell, *World Handbook of Political and Social Indicators* (New Haven: Yale University Press, 1964), pp. 302-3 et passim.

19. "Competing Paradigms in Comparative Politics," in Robert T. Holt and John E. Turner, eds. *The Methodology of Comparative Research* (New York: Free Press, 1970), p. 26.

20. For example, in Richard Rose, ed., *Electoral Behavior: A Comparative Handbook* (New York: Free Press, 1974).

CHAPTER 15

THE BINARY ANALYSIS

A binary analysis is a comparison limited to two countries that have been carefully selected according to the subject. Although it is the most natural method, the binary analysis is not necessarily the easiest. We can distinguish two kinds of binary comparison: implicit and explicit.

Binary comparison is implicit in the perception of any "other," thought of as different, continually seen in relation to the observer's own culture. This implicit system of reference can throw light on our knowledge of a subject in a remarkable way. By a kind of dialectical process, the view from afar strengthens our reflections on ourselves, our own culture, and our own society. One knows one's own country better when one knows other countries too. Perhaps Ralf Dahrendorf's penetrating look at German society owes something to his having lived in England. By going abroad intellectually, one acquires points of reference. It is possible that certain specific features of French culture appeared clearly to Tocqueville only after he could see them in the light of his intimate knowledge of another culture, the American in this case.

We could list several reference books on such and such a country that are the work of "foreigners." Written from a distance, they allow a more perceptive survey. Tocqueville's is one of the best studies of American society. Elie Halévy's contribution to the knowledge of nineteenth-century England is well known. Louis Dumont's work on India, as well as Jacques Berque's on the Arab world, are famous in the very countries they describe. So are the study on Norway by Harry Eckstein, on England by Richard Rose, on Italy by Joseph La-Palombara, on Germany by Lewis Edinger, on Japan by Bradley Richardson and Edwin O. Reischauer—to exemplify how the American perspective has contributed to a better understanding of some countries. "There are people born to observe from outside," stated Stanley Hoffmann. "The distance they enjoy . . . tends to positively compensate for exile and uprooting."[1]

Explicit binary comparison is on a different level of systematization. Frequently it makes use of the historical method, no doubt because this approach enables one most easily to find out what determines the uniqueness of each nation. As a matter of fact, binary comparison permits a kind of detailed confrontation that is almost impossible when the analysis encompasses too many cases. Thus its prime interest lies in that it makes possible a study in depth.

Binary comparison sometimes seems the best way to undertake a study that leaves out neither the specific nor the general. Comparing two countries naturally enhances one's interest in each one; in particular, it stresses the main characteristics and the originality of each situation. But binary comparison can be used not only for increasing, through contrast, our knowledge of two different systems. In the best cases, it can also contribute to an understanding of general phenomena. In such cases, the two countries considered are thought of as contrasted illustrations for a broad, encompassing theoretical reflection. When Charles Kindleberger compares the British and French industrial revolutions,[2] he proposes an analysis worthy of consideration not only for those interested in France or Great Britain but also for those who study the dynamic of industrialization.

Why did the Samurai in Japan become agents of the central power and modernization, whereas in Germany the Junkers became a conservative force? In attempting to answer this question, Reinhard Bendix[3] was able to bring to light some phenomena of general significance. It was partly because Japan had withdrawn into itself that its aristocracy, unlike that of Germany, did not feel threatened; it was partly because the Samurai had been deprived of private lands that they so easily adapted to city and administrative life. Structural factors such as the openness of a country and the connections people have with the land can have important effects on the behavior of members of a society. In such cases, binary comparison may provide general illustrations of the way in which development, modernization, or national integration come about.

Binary comparison is often used for countries that show contextual similarities, even if the aim of the analysis is to bring out differences in one or more specific fields. To analyze comparatively the recruitment and tenure of Cabinet ministers in France and Britain, considered as opposing systems, might show some analogies between the two countries, for instance in the stability of a "governmental nucleus."[4] Conversely, a study of political cleavages in France and Italy, in contexts considered similar, might demonstrate that various social strata do not distribute themselves similarly between political parties in the two countries.[5] It is more attractive to use pairs of countries like France and Italy, Morocco and Tunisia, Norway and Sweden, or Uruguay and Costa Rica than to compare Finland and Bolivia or Brazil and Pakistan. Some pairs will produce a great deal of interest, while others will give only meager results. A comparison of England and Japan, as two insular nations or two shipping powers, might be meaningful, but an attempt to compare Switzerland and Chad, as two countries having no direct access to the sea, would be of little interest.

Of course, the comparativist has the liberty to establish original pairs based on his own conception of relevance. It would be relevant to compare India and

China in the framework of a study of the choices available to overpopulated Asian countries as they try to solve problems connected with demography, underemployment, and famine. On the other hand, someone interested in power structures or mobilization of the masses would no doubt find it more meaningful to compare China and the USSR. A comparison between Germany and Japan could be justified by the various institutions these two countries have in common, by historical period, by type of industrialization, by role of civil servants and the army, and so on. For those interested in European fascism, Germany could pair with Italy. With England, Germany forms a pair often used by those studying the industrial revolution. Germany and France can be studied together in the framework of an analysis of unstable democracies. These examples show the breadth of possibilities open to comparative studies.

One specific advantage of binary analysis is the possibility of covering political life as a whole, including institutions, structures, cultures, socialization, and recruitment processes. There are few studies of such magnitude, but they are feasible. A book on Japan and Turkey edited by Robert E. Ward and Dankwart A. Rustow[6] is a good example of the results that can be obtained by this kind of endeavor. At the same time it illustrates the almost inevitable fragmentary nature of these many-sided comparisons. One cannot see at a glance just what makes Turkish and Japanese experiences unique. Only gradually, while reading chapters dealing with various aspects of development in each of the two countries, is the reader able to assemble the parts of a global knowledge and to reflect on it.

One pitfall of such broad studies is that they normally imply contributions by a series of experts. To undertake research on the similarities and differences between Soviet and Chinese communism[7] is no small task, and it is understandable that experts in one of these immense and hermetic worlds may not be specialists in the other. But there is always the danger that collaboration among many authors of different sensibilities may result in some loss of homogeneity in the collective work. Many books purporting to be comparative studies are in fact unintegrated series of monographs put side by side.

Another serious risk attached to binary strategy is that the comparison may be based on a subject that is clearly more appropriate to one country than to the other, or at least expressed in a way that is difficult to apply to both cases. We can refer here to a book on the role of local administration in France and Italy, *Tra centro e periferia,* edited by Sidney Tarrow.[8] It is interesting in detail but not very convincing in its synthesis. Its weaknesses are probably due to the diffuseness and equivocity of the concept used. In fact, the periphery is considerably more unwieldly and more isolated from the center in Italy than it is in France.

Binary comparison may often throw light on certain key sectors of the political system. This appears clearly in *The First New Nation*.[9] Here, Lipset was interested not only in the configuration of fundamental values in the United States and Great Britain, he also asked questions about the impact made by these values. His results, based on a historical analysis, have recently been contested; and it is interesting to consider that the argument was triggered by another binary comparison, this time based on surveys. By undertaking in-depth surveys on samples of English and American citizens, Wendell Bell and Robert V. Robinson[10] were able to confirm the doubts of certain sociologists concerning the egalitarian nature of American society, which is rather frequently shown as being in opposition to the elitist British model. Differences in perception and judgment appear to be more striking between groups of different status within the same country than between the two countries.

Opposing two strongly contrasting countries is often perceived as a way of more surely appreciating the relations existing between systemic variables; if the same factor produces the same effects in two very different situations, its influence tends to be confirmed. Such a strategy is of relatively low cost because the researcher takes only two countries into account. If social mobility tends to have common effects on partisan preferences in two contrasted countries, there is a chance that social mobility can be effectively considered as an autonomous factor. In comparing the English situation and the Italian situation, Paul R. Abramson has thus been able to state the importance of vertical social mobility on political behavior and to contradict the idea that such mobility essentially benefits the right wing.[11] What is common to two particular situations should not be the result of the context, which is by definition different.

Despite its merits, the binary strategy is often powerless to make a distinction between what reflects the cultural context, the political system, or a particular variable. The boldest theoretical attempts to isolate what seems to be a result of the context have not met with great success. Henry Teune and Krzysztof Ostrowski tried this in studying local American and Polish communities.[12] "The central problem of comparative analysis is to succeed in extracting what is true in a general way, from data influenced by the context," they stated. At the same time, they admitted they had reached a semi-deadlock. To eliminate variables affected by the context when almost all variables are affected leaves the research with a somewhat meager utility for understanding local American and Polish communities. Its interest for the comparativists' strategy is nonetheless certain.

In a binary comparison the two countries can be relatively similar or relatively contrasting. If they are contrasting, they can sometimes be considered prototypes of two series of countries. If they are relatively similar, the propensity of the researcher, at a certain moment, is to expand the analysis to other similar countries.

NOTES

1. *Essais sur la France* (Paris: Seuil, 1974), p. 14.
2. *Economic Growth in France and Great Britain, 1851-1950* (Cambridge, Mass.: Harvard University Press, 1964); see also, on a similar issue, J.H. Clapham, *Economic Development of France and Germany, 1815-1914* (Cambridge: Cambridge University Press, 1963).
3. *Nation-Building and Citizenship* (New York: Wiley, 1964), pp. 177-213.
4. M. Dogan and P. Campbell, "Le personnel ministeriel en France et en Grande Bretagne (1945-1957)," *Revue Française de Science Politique* 7, no. 2 (April 1957) and 7, no. 4 (October 1957): 313-45 and 793-824.
5. Mattei Dogan, "Political Cleavage and Social Stratification in France and Italy," in *Party Systems and Voter Alignments,* ed. Seymour Martin Lipset and Stein Rokkan (New York: Free Press, 1967), pp. 129-95.
6. *Political Modernization in Japan and Turkey* (Princeton: Princeton University Press, 1964).
7. Cf. Donald W. Treadgold, ed., *Soviet and Chinese Communism: Similarities and Differences* (Seattle: University of Washington Press, 1967).
8. Bologna: Il Mulino, 1979.
9. New York: Basic Books, 1963.
10. "Equality, Success and Social Justice in England and the United States," *American Sociological Review* 53 (April 1978): 125-43.
11. "Intergenerational Social Mobility and Partisan Preference in Britain and Italy," *Comparative Political Studies* 6, no. 2 (July 1973): 221-34.
12. "Political Systems as Residual Variables: Explaining Differences Within Systems," *Comparative Political Studies* 6, no. 1 (April 1973): 3-21.

CHAPTER 16

COMPARING
SIMILAR COUNTRIES

Binary comparison sufficiently highlights each national case for the specificity of each to be noted, no matter what separates them. The full originality of each country paired stands out whether one compares France with distant Japan or with nearby Italy. It is clear that the comparative exercise cannot be the same when the political entities compared show many similarities or extreme contrasts.

This distinction takes on its full meaning as soon as the study is extended to a large number of cases. One does not compare trade unions within Western Europe in the same way as one highlights the differences between political processes in developed and developing countries. The significance of the research, its methods, its viewpoint, and its results will vary according to whether the analyst considers relatively similar or contrasting countries.

We must insist on the word "relatively." Indeed, neither similarities nor differences are absolute. They are clearly a matter of viewpoint and perspective. If you look at a chain of high mountains, the landscape will change according to the position of the sun in the morning, at noon, and in the evening. Viewed from afar, South American countries present a series of analogies that become much less evident when one crosses the ocean to look at them more closely, allowing the contrasts to appear. A comparison between relatively similar countries may aim at noting similarities or differences. For example, some researchers may concentrate on rural unemployment in order to bring out the common features peculiar to Latin American countries; others may consider the communist nations to stress the contrasts existing within this relatively homogeneous world.[1] When we draw a distinction between the comparison of similar countries and the comparison of contrasting countries, we do not refer to the objective distance that separates the nations under study; our purpose is to make clear two strategies. Although both strategies intend to give weight to the comparison through the selection of a consistent field, they imply very different approaches. The comparativist may try to shed light by contrast on the main features of different societies, or may intend to benefit by a certain homogeneity to appreciate better causal relationships and evaluate marginal differences. In the first case, the choice of countries to be included is based on significant recognized differences; in the second, the starting point is a relative similarity.

A comparison between "relatively similar" countries sets out to neutralize certain differences in order to permit a better analysis of others. This strategy is at the heart of the comparative method. As John Stuart Mill once stated, it is by reducing, insofar as possible, the number of interacting variables that one has the means to observe the influence of factors one wishes to study. It is easier to test the weight of certain institutional rules on political behaviors by choosing democracies that have common roots than by incorporating authoritarian regimes or pseudo democracies into the analysis. We know that the comparativist, unlike the chemist, can never eliminate the impact of the environment. No two nations in the world would enable the researcher to measure the influence of the Protestant religion or certain rules of ownership "all things being equal in other respects." What the researcher can do is to increase the pertinence of his conclusions by carefully choosing the political and social entities he decides to compare.

For the researcher who studies political systems, analogies are to be sought either in the sociocultural environment of those systems or in their structures and features of operation. The homogeneity will be more a cultural one if, for example, Anglo-Saxon countries are chosen, and more a structural one if the researcher decides to study single-party regimes.

Similarity is not necessarily linked to proximity. Nevertheless, in the search for analogy the most natural approach is to limit the analysis to a geographical area that, in effect, delineates a homogeneous milieu in more than one respect: history, culture, level of development—so many dimensions can be used as elements of control. Today, all the major universities in advanced countries possess specialized centers on Latin America, Africa, Southeast Asia, and the Middle East.

The regional approach presents both advantages and risks. The advantages are evident. First, this strategy ensures in the most natural way a control over those variables that the observer would like to keep constant so as to better analyze variables of interest. The area study, then, normally gives more insight and penetration to the analysis. It is often the relative similarity of situations that enables the marginal difference and its causes to be appreciated.[2] By focusing on a relatively homogeneous field, the comparativist increases his or her capacity to do in-depth analyses. Finally, limiting the study to a consistent group of countries makes it possible to clarify the issue. Many questions take on their true dimension within a particular area. There would certainly be little interest in analyzing parliamentary government on a world scale, although a parliament, be it a real one or a puppet, exists in the great majority of independent nations. The questions asked by Klaus von Beyme[2] on the role of political parties in the constitution of coalitions, on the move toward more consensus, and on the "volatility" of electors flowing from one party to another are obviously of interest only for competitive democratic systems. As a matter of fact, all experts in political parties know that identical questions are not to be asked even when comparing Europe to the United States.

Electoral participation or party membership is not mechanically comparable from one universe to another. But one merit of the regional approach may be precisely to stimulate discussion on the meaning of certain phenomena or factors by shedding a new light on them. One will not necessarily go so far as to say, as Ruth Schachter Morgenthau[4] suggests, that the single mass party represents, in a context such as Africa, a step toward democracy. But it will be admitted that in states where the national political scene is not yet a fully experienced reality, "democracy" is not automatically assessed according to the number of parties.

The main pitfall associated with a "regional" strategy is tied up with the risks of confinement it conceals. Limited to a certain part of the globe, it favors an interdisciplinary approach because one can define "context" only if one is familiar with its multiple facets. But each time the regional approach leads to notions such as "culture" or "personality," be they North African, South American, or Latin, one must ask oneself what the real contribution of this culture or personality is, and what scientific interest lies in referring to a new "specificity" that cannot be broken down simply because we fail to explain the phenomenon under study.

One way of avoiding the pitfall of descriptive studies or those obscure explanations that explain nothing is to try to throw light on the structural data associated with the phenomena analyzed. The works of Jacques Lambert[5] or Gino Germani and Kalman Silvert[6] on Latin America show the advantage to comparative political science of analyses that are limited in space. But it is worth separating which particularities are linked to the specific history of this subcontinent and which are of a more universal character. The presence of strong democratic ideologies is a feature that may distinguish this part of the world from others; the numerical weakness of the middle class is, on the contrary, an element that could be identified, compared, and measured for all developing countries.

The regional approach contributes to scientific knowledge all the more when it does not set out to be an end in itself but involves reflection on a general problem. James S. Coleman and Carl G. Rosberg's book on political parties in tropical Africa illustrates the mechanism of this extension.[7] The subcontinent appears to the authors as "an ideal laboratory for development analysis."

A multitude of nations have experienced the same shock of colonization, have reached independence together, and have found themselves confronted with the same ethnic divisions. In this situation there are many elements that call for an in-depth analysis of the ways in which groups and parties crystallize and the ways in which vertical structures succeed in accelerating national integration and filling the institutional vacuum at the center.

Of course, neither problems pertaining to the construction of nations nor structures of the "single-party" type, such as they develop south of the Sahara, are the sole prerogative of Africa. In this sense, research of this kind naturally challenges those who are interested in political development in another context. But the choice of a relatively homogeneous field also enables theoretical results to be gone into more deeply in order to break up categories that have become insufficiently discriminating. The single-party concept, applied to Black Africa, turns out to be too loose to make a clear distinction between situations in Guinea, Senegal, and Cameroon. This is why Coleman and Rosberg choose to contrast the "pragmatic-pluralist" model with the "revolutionary-centralizing" model.

The selection of "relatively similar" countries normally leads one to situate the analysis at a median level of generalization. By limiting the analysis to Africa, or even to the Maghreb or the Sahel, the comparativist will no doubt be in a position to test theoretical explanations—to appreciate, for example, the role of social class or religion as factors of history. But he or she will not overlook the fact that paths of development, historical actors, and opposing forces are not the same in Africa, Latin America, and Southeast Asia.

When the hypotheses to be tested are clearly formulated, however, comparative analysis can embrace worlds larger than one well-defined region. Many comparativists have thus attempted wide sector-based subjects such as the role of the armed forces,[8] bureaucracy,[9] mass communication,[10] religious forces,[11] and political oppositions.[12] Irving Louis Horowitz has tried somewhat ambitiously to connect the African and Latin American situations by examining the mixture of bureaucracy and charisma, of extralegal power and rationalization, that affect a number of single parties in the Third World.[13] His study is sufficiently abstract to allow this kind of comparison. But it would be more difficult to envisage an overall comparative analysis that would consider the African and Latin American political systems in their entirety. No author, to our knowledge, has attempted an undertaking of this scope. Its pitfalls would doubtless be on the same scale as the enormous differences existing between the two continents.

Some areas lend themselves well to a coordinated study, and others do not. Latin America, as we have seen, has abundantly nurtured the regional approach; it has stimulated the formulation of coherent development models such as those of Robert D. Putnam[14] or Martin Needler.[15] Black Africa has aroused the same kind of interest. Other regions of the world lend themselves less easily to comparison because contiguity does not involve enough significant analogies. There are, of course, demographic and economic similarities between Thailand and the Philippines, Indonesia and Burma, and Vietnam and Malaysia. But from the political, social, and cultural points of view, there is so great a diversity that comparison cannot yield a cumulative knowledge. An enormous book that attempts to cover nine countries of Southeast Asia does not contain a single synthetic conclusion. "South-East Asia," the authors simply state, "that corner of the continent flanked by China and India, forms one of the most heterogeneous regions. . . ."[16] Most studies devoted to the Southeast Asian mosaic, even if they make an attempt at coordination, cannot proceed otherwise than by a series of monographs.

The Mediterranean remains an area of choice for geographers and historians such as Fernand Braudel. But a political scientist is soon at a standstill in making a comparative study of the northern and southern countries of this "sea in the middle of the world" unless he or she has limited the study to a few elements, such as the importance of parental relationships or clientelism. Indeed, all the exchanges of civilizations have not overcome the sharp divisions between the Arab and Greco-Latin worlds. Furthermore, in spite of a thousand-year history, the southern shores attained independence only one or two generations ago.

In spite of their diversity, the countries of Western Europe display substantial similarities. Nevertheless, the comparative literature on Western Europe, as a continent, is less impressive than one would expect.[17] Is this because proximity makes one more aware of differences? Some of the best studies that look at Europe from an integrating point of view have been written by scholars from the other side of the Atlantic. This is no doubt because salient features stand out more clearly from a distance. Many European authors tend to see the trees —and to note that no two are identical—while American authors are better placed to look at the whole forest.[18]

Considered from a distance, high rates of electoral participation and the large membership in political parties are remarkable features of the European political systems. At first glance, so are the mediated character of the political game, the recruitment of elites through cooptation, and the somewhat authoritarian aspect of power.[19] The place of the state in European societies is perceived as unique by one who considers it from the other side of the Atlantic. The depth of political antagonisms also appears with particular clarity when considered from a long distance.

The American Leon Epstein[20] stressed the existence in Europe of strong mass parties and the political significance of social cleavages. Otto Kirchheimer, from the United States, first noted the evolution of Western European parties toward broad undifferentiated catchall parties.[21] More recently, Peter Merkl's *Western European Party Systems*[22] proposed an all-embracing view of the forces of change at work, and cited the significance of *Verdrossenheit,* signaling that more and more people are dissatisfied with the classical political forces in Europe. Stephen R. Graubard's *A New Europe*[23] represents another interesting attempt at portraying Europe. Even the European scholars who contributed to this book made clear efforts to consider their own continent from a certain distance. The same remark could apply to Gordon Smith's *Politics in Western Europe*[24] in which the author, although an Englishman, managed to achieve a comprehensive view of the whole continent.

Nevertheless, we find more wide-ranging works on "developed" countries, "advanced" or "postindustrial" societies, "pluralist" or "Western" democracies, and parliamentary regimes than on Europe as a continent. By a numerical logic the Europe continent is represented more than any other in these researches. Lawrence C. Dodd's *Coalitions in Parliamentary Government,*[25] for example, covers seventeen countries, only two of which (Australia and New Zealand) are not in Europe. Robert Dahl's *Political Oppositions in Western Democracies*[26] examines ten countries, nine of which are European. Douglas W. Rae, analyzing *The Political Consequences of Electoral Laws,*[27] studies twenty countries, only four of which are not European. Although all these authors shed an interesting light on European countries, they do not define their field according to sociocultural criteria peculiar to the old Continent, but according to systemic features. In these thematic studies, the Atlantic becomes a river, Australia moves into the boreal hemisphere, and Japan marks the Far West.

The background of a common configuration of characteristics gives meaning and substance to comparisons between similar countries. The regional approach, states Lijphart, "should not be used indiscriminately, but only when it enables the control of a maximum number of variables. In this regard, certain small regions can offer more possibilities than large regions."[28] The four Scandinavian countries have been one of the favored fields of comparison;[29] it is true also that the number of sociologists per square kilometer is greater in Scandinavia than anywhere else in the world.

But countries of relatively similar cultures exist that are not neighbors. James A. Bill and Carl Leiden have studied the processes of modernization in a Middle East that extends from Morocco to Pakistan, passing through Sudan, Turkey, and Iran. In reality, Islam defines the relative homogeneity of the field considered,[30] as one chapter of their book testifies. Michael Hudson, studying the "Arab world," has chosen a more limited field to analyze problems of identity and legitimacy.[31] His criteria too are not geographical, but cultural: Arabism depends as much on a conscience and a will as on factors such as language or religion. The presence of this *Umma al arabiya,* the supranational entity of all "Arab brothers," renders the maturation of nation-states in this part of the world difficult, and studies of them valuable.

Anglo-Saxon nations are a good example of a discontinuous series of countries united by a common political culture. An abundant literature has been devoted to them. One can ask if what they have in common weighs heavier in the balance than what differentiates them. Thus geographical proximity is neither the sole nor necessarily the best way of defining a relatively homogeneous world. Some countries can be in different continents and yet present striking similarities. Cultural kinship or historical heritage can have more weight than proximity. But other characteristics can enable comparisons between countries that are at the four corners of the earth. One could thus choose France, the USSR, Japan, and Austria for a study on state centralism; or Hong Kong, Singapore, Uruguay, and Luxembourg to form a series of ministates; or Canada, Malaysia, and Yugoslavia as multiethnic entities. If the "tropical Africa" of Coleman and Rosberg includes the Congo, for example, it is because the definition is more a political than a climatic one. Unlike the geographer, the political scientist naturally gives priority to factors that concern the functions of political systems.

It is not always easy to make a distinction between sociocultural context and political structure as the two intercommunicate, and an analogy at one of these levels generally leads to an analogy at the other. But the emphasis may be either on culture or on structure. When Karl Dietrich Bracher analyzes the persistence or even the new spreading of ideologies within the Western World,[32] contesting the thesis of their decline, he values cultural criteria of homogeneity. When Klaus von Beyme, on the contrary,[33] studies interest groups in "democracies," he highlights systemic analogies. The influence of pressure groups, their methods, and their insertion into different parliamentary, governmental, administrative, and party organs is analyzed against a background of pluralist structures and institutional mechanisms that are largely similar. Certainly it makes more sense to explore attitudes of elites and their relationships within a relatively homogeneous field than in very different systems. Indeed, the international research designed to study these issues,[34] and projected to include countries like Morocco and Jamaica, gave birth to a comparative synthesis devoted to *Bureaucrats and Politicians* in Western democracies.[35] The work by Samuel Eldersveld, Jan Kooiman, and Theo van der Tak on Dutch elites,[36] which shows the relative isolation and subordination of higher civil servants vis-à-vis parliamentary elites, brings to light features remarkable only in reference to situations where deputies or partisan elites exist. The book on Sweden by Thomas J. Anton,[37] in the same way traces a high-level bureaucracy that proves original only in comparison to rather similar countries.

William A. Welsh's introduction to *Comparative Communist Political Leadership*,[38] also shows how the choice of a clearly defined area improves the pertinence of the questions the comparativist poses of the political reality. It is by isolating the communist world that one succeeds in grasping its specific characteristics, as well as the singularity of each country. Under observation, the balance that each communist state finds between classical *apparatchiki* and experts, ideological or instrumental orientation, or open recruitment or cooptation often proves to be original. Nevertheless, the features of the communist system define the homogeneity of the field considered.

Comparison between relatively similar countries is carried out against the background of few or many characteristics that are more or less deep-seated. When the heterogeneity of the field is very great, however, the loose and weak analogy often makes it impossible to reach any significant conclusion. At the point where the analogy becomes too loose, another strategy can be effective.

NOTES

1. See Gilles Martinet, *Les cinq communismes* (Paris: Seuil, 1971).
2. See Mattei Dogan, "Les attitudes politiques des femmes en Europe et aux Etats-Unis," in *Le vocabulaire des sciences sociales,* ed. R. Boudon and P. Lazarsfeld (Paris: Mouton, 1965); as well as "Le vote ouvrier en Europe Occidentale," *Revue Française de Sociologie,* no. 1 (1960).
3. Klaus von Beyme, *Parteien in Westlichen Demokratien* (Munich: Piper, 1982).
4. "Single Party Systems in West Africa," *American Political Science Review* 55, no. 2 (June 1961): 294-306.
5. Jacques Lambert, *L'Amerique Latine: Structures Sociales et Institutions Politiques* (Paris: PUF, 1968).
6. Gino Germani and Kalman Silvert, "Politics, Social Structure and Military Intervention in Latin America," in *Garrisons and Government: Politics and Military in New States,* ed. Wilson Carey McWilliams (San Francisco: Chandler, 1967).
7. *Political Parties and National Integration in Tropical Africa* (Berkeley: University of California Press, 1966).
8. See the pioneering work of Morris Janowitz, *Military Institutions and Coercion in Developing Nations,* expanded ed. (Chicago: University of Chicago Press, 1977).

9. Cf. Joseph LaPalombara, *Bureaucracy and Political Development* (Princeton: Princeton University Press, 1963).

10. See Lucian W. Pye, ed., *Communications and Political Development* (Princeton: Princeton University Press, 1963); and Wilbur Schramm, *Mass Media and National Development* (Stanford: Stanford University Press, 1964).

11. Donald E. Smith, *Religion and Political Development* (Boston: Little, Brown, 1970).

12. Robert A. Dahl, *Regimes and Oppositions* (New Haven: Yale University Press, 1973).

13. *Three Worlds of Development* (New York: Oxford University Press, 1972).

14. Robert Putnam, "Toward Explaining Military Intervention in Latin American Politics," *World Politics* 20, no. 1 (October 1967).

15. Martin Needler, *Political Development in Latin America: Instability, Violence, and Evolutionary Change* (New York: Random House, 1968).

16. George McT. Kahin, ed., *Governments and Politics of Southeast Asia,* new ed. (Ithaca: Cornell University Press, 1969).

17. See D.W. Urwin, "Political Parties, Societies and Regimes in Europe: Some Reflections in the Literature," *European Journal of Political Research* 1 (1973); and D.W. Urwin and K. Eliassen, "In Search of a Continent: The Quest of Comparative European Politics," ibid., 1975.

18. The preponderance of American scholars in the field of comparative politics could be explained by several factors (seven at least); see Mattei Dogan and Dominique Pelassy, *La comparaison internationale en sociologie politique* (Paris: LITEC, 1980), pp. 14-17. On a list of 60 important American comparativists in political science or sociology born before 1930, we found that more than half of them were either born or raised in Europe or at least have European family ties. See also Donald Fleming and Bernard Bailyn, *The Intellectual Migration: Europe and America, 1930-1960* (Cambridge, Mass.: Harvard University Press, 1969).

19. Cf. Martin O. Heisler, ed., *Politics in Europe* (New York: McKay, 1974).

20. *Political Parties in Western Democracies,* new ed. (New Brunswick, N.J.: Transaction Books, 1980).

21. "The Transformation of Western European Party Systems," in *Political Parties and Political Development,* ed. Joseph LaPalombara and Myron Weiner (Princeton: Princeton University Press, 1966), pp. 177ff.

22. New York: Free Press, 1980.

23. Boston: Houghton Mifflin, 1964.

24. New ed. New York: Holmes & Meier, 1980.

25. Princeton: Princeton University Press, 1976.
26. New Haven: Yale University Press, 1967.
27. New Haven: Yale University Press, 1963.
28. Arend Lijphart, "Comparative Politics and the Comparative Method," *American Political Science Review* 65, no. 3 (September 1971).
29. See studies by S. Rokkan, E. Allardt, M. Pedersen, H. Valen, P. Pesonen, E. Damgaard, S. Kuhnle, K. Eliassen, G. Sjöblom, W. Lafferty, U. Torgersen, and others.
30. *The Middle East: Politics and Power* (Boston: Allyn and Bacon, 1974).
31. *Arab Politics: The Search for Legitimacy* (New Haven: Yale University Press, 1977).
32. *Zeit der Ideologien. Eine Geschichte politischen Denkens im 20. Jahrhundert* (Stuttgart: Deutsche Verlags-Anstalt, 1982).
33. *Interessengruppen in der Demokratie* (Munich: Piper, 1969).
34. Associated with that project were S.J. Eldersveld, J.D. Aberbach, T.J. Anton, R.F. Inglehart, R.D. Putnam, A. Singham, and J. Waterbury.
35. Robert Putnam, Joel Aberbach, Bert Rockman, with the collaboration of Thomas Anton et al. (Cambridge, Mass.: Harvard University Press, 1981).
36. *Elite Images of Dutch Politics: Accommodation and Conflict* (Ann Arbor: University of Michigan Press, 1981).
37. *Administered Politics: Elite Political Culture in Sweden* (Boston: Martinus Nijhoff, 1980).
38. New York: McKay, 1973.

CHAPTER 17

COMPARING
CONTRASTING COUNTRIES

"Analogy" and "contrast" are obviously relative notions. In one sense, no comparison is possible unless there are both analogies and contrasts. One does not compare identical objects; nor does one compare objects that are unique or mutually exclusive. No two countries are identical; two countries always have something in common.

Depending on their objective, at times comparativists will emphasize similarities, at times differences. They will tend to look for differences in contexts that are roughly similar or, on the contrary, will try to find analogies in contrasting political systems. But comparison will always be made at the point where the analogy cuts across the contrast. All comparisons are based on analogies; all comparisons are also contrasting in a sense. This is true no matter how many countries are considered—two, fifteen, or one hundred fifty.

A comparison between contrasting countries, in the sense we refer to here, is a comparison implying (1) that attention is fixed on phenomena presenting a maximum of contrasts, and (2) that these contrasts are of broad significance and delineate political areas defined by systemic features. "Contrast," in this perspective, is not synonymous with trivial difference. It is of a general character; that is, it implies that the situations under consideration have been chosen for their exemplarity. In this perspective, a comparison between France and Great Britain will imply that the two situations are considered profoundly different. The differences that will be registered will not be attributable to history or to some irrepressible national character, but will emphasize elements that, in a general way, could bring into contrast systems that are stable or unstable, centripetal or centrifugal, two-party or multiparty, or Anglo-Saxon or continental. For such a comparison to be fruitful, each country must be representative of a type, a class, a conceptualized category.

To compare the Soviet Union and the United States with the idea that they represent opposing political worlds, and with the underlying conviction that such a study can throw light on certain features that generally differentiate two types of society, is to carry out a contrasting comparison. Such a strategy does not aim at highlighting processes that are more or less analogous or common; on the contrary, it seeks to identify specific areas characterized by unique features or rules. At this stage, we must distinguish between a comparison that opposes contrasting worlds and a comparison of specific situations to exemplify a general reflection on a single process, a single phenomenon. Samuel Huntington[1] and Reinhard Bendix[2] have found it fruitful to contrast the process of modernization or national construction in America and Europe. In such studies, the contrast enables the comparativist to understand better the essence of the process, to render its definition clearer, to discern its components, and to establish connections between certain contextual variables and its particular manifestation. But comparison here is not designed to enlighten, through contrast, the specificity of two worlds.

As in the North America versus Europe example, the contrasting comparison is frequently based on two sets of similar countries. One can thus contrast a few Mediterranean countries with a few from northern Europe, or industrialized countries with nonindustrialized ones, or traditional societies with secularized ones, or modern nations with developing ones. All these major dichotomies can nourish, and have nourished, comparisons between contrasting countries.

In the harsh light of contrast, the heterogeneity of the groups thus constituted suddenly becomes indistinct. Only the prominent features that characterize these groups remain, at a high degree of abstraction and generalization. Comparisons between strongly contrasting countries try to find through deliberate simplification the key to knowledge that would otherwise be unattainable. This process of "stylization" is all the more necessary as the internal heterogeneity of each of the two sets of contrasting countries increases.

The idea of making a frontal contrast between democracies and totalitarian regimes is almost as old as the emergence of totalitarianism. It was developed first by Hans Kohn,[3] then by Zevedei Barbu,[4] Hannah Arendt,[5] Robert Tucker,[6] Carl Friedrich and Zbigniew Brzezinski,[7] among others. Many critics have stressed that a fundamental contrast between pluralist democracies and modern dictatorships is obtained only by making a questionable amalgam of all forms of totalitarianism, in particular fascist and Stalinist forms. In fact, this approach eliminates a whole series of differences that are irrelevant to the central contrast. But such a proceeding certainly helps us to better appreciate the core of essential features. Concepts of totalitarianism and democracy take on meaning only in a comparative way. For this reason, definition of such systems may appear excessive. But the force of such definition also stems from this same simplifying power.

The so-called developing world is clearly multiform. Those who have made close studies of it have emphasized how difficult it is to distinguish its general features amid the profusion of political and social forms. Characteristically this is an undertaking that meets with greater success when one studies this world from a certain distance and considers it, as Lucian Pye did,[8] in counterpoint to the Western experience. The "non-Western political process," to take the significant title chosen by the author, then seems to contain a certain number of constants—characteristic features: the personalized forms of allegiances, the considerable freedom of maneuver of the national elites, the gap between central institutions and the periphery, the confusion of roles, the stress laid on the emotional and symbolic aspects of politics, the absence of intermediary structures, and so on. Some of these "features" could be criticized. Those who are familiar with African or Arab countries could question the overgeneralized aspect of these "rules of the game." Again, certain specialists on Europe have questioned the supposed similarities of the Western experiences that serve as an implicit model; by their account, many of the features evoked by Pye to characterize non-Western political processes are applicable, in watered-down form, to certain fragmented and centrifugal Western systems. Obviously, the pertinence of the contrast studied is a function of the internal coherence of series, and the potential for generalization of such comparisons is linked to the consistency of the types proposed.

Even if one admits that "stylization" implies a reduction, one perceives the at times decisive advantages of such an approach. To recapitulate conceptually the characteristics of the political game in the Third World is a difficult exercise and one that is full of pitfalls. Just such an exercise, however, has enabled the extremely interesting contemporary proliferation of explicit or implicit comparisons between developed and developing worlds. It is always in the light of an antithesis present in the analysis, either explicitly or just beneath the surface, that the perception of the particularity of a world is structured.

This method of comprehension presents certain weaknesses. A comparison between contrasting countries often tends to concentrate on extreme, almost "abnormal" types. It is to be regretted that, in this perspective, a "type" can even become a means of distorting the reality, instead of representing it.

Sometimes too, the contrast leads to an exaggeration of differences. To state the antithesis between "under-development and over-power" on the one hand and "over-development and under-power" on the other is to reproduce in a figurative way the deadlocks connected with each kind of society.[9] At the same time, one would have no difficulty in showing how deceptive, for example, the concept of "over-power" is in new states. Indeed, it is not necessary to go far in depth to realize that a political vacuum gapes beneath the feet of the omnipresent and omniscient leader. The same weakness of intermediary structures that reveals the majesty of his position decisively reduces his means of action. Praetorianism may be only "the revelation that, in spite of appearances, African societies are not in reality governed, that they suffer not from an excess of power, but from a lack of power partly due to the weakness, even the absence of a party. The African state is, in fact, a feeble state."[10] At the other extreme, to evoke the "under-power" of developed states is at the same time to stress the inefficiency of decision mechanisms obstructed by too many demands; that is, victims of the excessive pressure exerted on political organs that have become incapable of meeting rising expectations.

The radical nature of the comparison between contrasting systems may cloud the reality of change. Evoking primitive societies, Pierre Clastres was right to stress how ethnocentric our conception of state and our religion of work are. In fact, the originality of primitive societies is so great that, by reference to them, all modern societies, Western and Eastern, belong to the same "macroclass." But it is certainly regrettable not to explore also possible signs of congruence between those contrasting social types; Clastres himself appears somewhat aware that embryonic elements of a nascent power exist even in the most primitive village.[11]

One might expect that the concept of functional equivalence would play an important part in comparisons between contrasting countries. In fact, those who study contrasting worlds tend to stress the specificity of each type. Scholars who oppose the totalitarian and the democratic worlds do not talk of "participation"; they know the difference between participation and mobilization. Those who have contrasted traditional societies with developed societies, or new states with old ones, have perceived the many differences in their means and even their aims. Of course, concepts such as articulation of interests or aggregation of interests are indispensable to the comparativist for creating a bridge between situations felt to be radically different. The functional equivalences guide the approach. But they disappear as soon as the analysis becomes a little more detailed. Often all that remains is the label, the thread that enables comparativists to "visualize" the difference.

The contrasting strategy does not consist in stressing merely the more evident or seemingly vivid contrasts. Like the mountaineer who, on reaching a summit, discovers other heights behind it, so the expert in comparative studies proceeds by fits and starts. The contrast between democracy and totalitarianism appeared originally as a statement of the obvious. But it did not take long to perceive to what extent these concepts are in fact superficial. To amalgamate Nazism and Stalinism goes against common sense. The most contemporary political research tends to stress to what extent a concept such as that of totalitarianism is a reducing agent. Even authors such as K.D. Bracher,[12] who sees some value in this simplification, stress that the concept really applies only to the three decades 1922-53. Bracher questions, at the same time, the pertinence of another general label, that of "fascism," which could lead to underestimating the specificity of each experience and particularly to overshadowing the differences between movements that are, to a greater or lesser extent, revolutionary or reactionary. Nazism is to be distinguished, if Bracher is to be believed, particularly by the emphasis placed on "socialism" and racism, the mythical glorification of the land and country people, and the predominance of the matrix concept of *Volk* over that of *Stato,* as cultivated by Mussolini. Thus a new contrast can come to light behind the first, and often tends to supersede it. Even while our perceptions progress and become sharper, they continue to feed on contrasts: new contrasts, which spring into view, like those mountains that appear only after the hiker has reached the first summit. The concept of dictatorship does not convey the variety of regimes to be found under this label. But within this "nondemocratic" world, comparative knowledge often advances along with new contrasts.

One must go beyond the difference between polyarchy and hegemony, to borrow the conceptual categories carved by Robert Dahl, so that the value of other contrasts comes to the fore. It is in closely analyzing "nondemocratic regimes," which predominate in the contemporary world, that Juan Linz was able to bring out what differentiates authoritarian regimes from totalitarian regimes. His approach is exemplary, as he defines the nondemocratic world by referring to the positive aspects of democracies, and authoritarian regimes by opposing them to totalitarian regimes. The definition he gives to these authoritarian systems retains a set of negative criteria: limited pluralism, absence of elaborated ideology, and absence of intensive political mobilization.[13]

The incisiveness of the comparative analysis can increase as the field under consideration narrows. It can be more significant to study contrasts arising from the existence of federal structures or from a strong ethnic fractionalization inside Europe than to study the same contrasts on a world scale.

The contrasting strategy may become sharper when the analyst renounces the bipolar model and defines more than two categories—sociological types that will remain clearly delimited and very different. All typologies, in a way, can inspire contrasting comparisons of this kind. One can contrast the Third World with the Western world in an overall (i.e., simple) way or tackle the same problem by contrasting a whole range of stages on the road leading to economic development, cultural secularization or the differentiation of structures. D.A. Rustow has distinguished some stages that could represent just as many categories, depending on whether the emerging nation is at the "preparatory" phase, the "decisive" stage, or the stage of "consolidation."[14] In a more empirical way, Bruce Russett and his colleagues[15] have "divided" mankind into five slices representing different levels of economic, social, and cultural growth. These categories are not watertight, but it is nevertheless an extremely fruitful exercise to identify, at each phase of a process, determinant variables, in what manner political structures evolve, and how they are affected by or themselves affect the changing of infrastructures.

But the notion of contrast tends to get lost as the analyst differentiates a greater number of less contrasted categories. At the end of this process, the comparison may retain nothing of the contrasting strategy. The comparativist who tries to embrace a very large field, but renounces the identification of broad contrasting types, must look for a universal empirical key in order to arrange the nations of the world: some measure that has similar significance for all the countries studied. Such a standard instrument is not easy to find.

NOTES

1. *Political Order in Changing Societies* (New Haven: Yale University Press, 1969), chap. 2.
2. *Nation-Building and Citizenship* (New York: Wiley, 1964).
3. *Revolutions and Dictatorships* (Cambridge: Harvard University Press, 1939).
4. *Democracy and Dictatorship* (New York: Grove Press, 1956).
5. *The Totalitarian System* (Paris: Seuil, 1972).
6. "Toward a Comparative Politics of Movement-Regimes," *American Political Science Review* 55, no. 2 (June 1961): 281-93.
7. *Totalitarian Dictatorship and Plutocracy* (Cambridge, Mass.: Harvard University Press, 1965).
8. "The Non-Western Political Process," *Journal of Politics* 20, no. 3 (August 1958).
9. See R.G. Schwartzenberg, *Sociologie Politique* (Paris: Montchrestien, 1974), pp. 248-49.
10. P.F. Gonidec, *Les systèmes politiques africains* (Paris: LGDJ, 1978).
11. See the analysis of the role played by the sorcerer in *La société contre l'Etat* (Paris: Eds. de Minuit, 1974), chap. 11.
12. K.D. Bracher, *Zeitgeschichtliche Kontroversen um Faschismus, Totalitarismus, Demokratie* (Munich: Piper, 1976), pp. 71ff.
13. Juan Linz, "Totalitarian and Authoritarian Regimes," in *Handbook of Political Science*, vol. 3, ed. Fred I. Greenstein and Nelson W. Polsby (Reading, Mass.: Addison-Wesley, 1975).
14. *A World of Nations* (Washington, D.C.: Brookings Institution, 1967).
15. *World Handbook of Political and Social Indicators* (New Haven: Yale University Press, 1964), pp. 293-303.

CHAPTER 18

THE CONCEPTUAL HOMOGENIZATION OF A HETEROGENEOUS FIELD

In comparative studies there is never a totally "homogeneous" field. Thus it is always the observer's viewpoint that gives a certain unity to the corpus studied, and it is the analyst who decides which elements constitute factors of homogeneity.

According to Ferdinand de Saussure, "the point of view creates the object." The most diverse scholars, from Oswald Spengler to Raymond Aron, when considering the Western world as an entity, all make a conceptual synthesis, whether it be of a historical or a political nature. Certainly there is no Western world without the elements of which it is composed, but neither is there a Western world without the analyst's integrating viewpoint. This integration inevitably implies a certain simplification of reality, but all abstractions entail such reduction. Roy Macridis pointed this out when he said: "Comparison involves abstraction; concrete situations or processes can never be compared as such. Every phenomenon is unique, every manifestation is unique, every process, every nation like every individual is in a sense unique. To compare them means to select certain types or concepts, and in so doing we have to distort the unique and the concrete."[1]

All comparativists conceptually homogenize their field even when they base their selection on purely physical criteria. No series of nations is chosen mechanically. When Robert A. Dahl and Edward R. Tufte decide to examine the small-sized democracies[2] to identify their main features, they are not inspired by the atlas. They are guided by structured hypotheses. They expect to find out that a relationship exists between the size of the nation and the propensity of individuals to organize in groups, the capacity of minorities to defend themselves, the freedom of the citizen, and the efficiency of the state.

To concentrate on one region of the world is to highlight historical or cultural elements of continuity, whereas to study military dictatorships as a significant group is to establish more systemic elements as criteria. But the field of comparison always results from an active selection. Dankwart A. Rustow was right when he emphasized that "comparability is not an inherent characteristic of every given series of objects. It is rather a quality which is attributed by the point of view of the observer."[3] Homogeneity never appears automatically. The researcher detects it in the structural or cultural elements that seem relevant; in this sense, the homogenization process is always the result of an intellectual process.

Obviously, however, the conceptualization may be greater or lesser. It appears to be less when the field is determined by spatial criteria and to be somewhat more elaborate when its boundaries follow cultural outlines that do not coincide with continents or subcontinents. It also seems to be relatively simple when the elements held to be important can be observed directly. The prudent comparativist does not choose countries by chance; he is guided by pertinent criteria. The presence of coalition governments can lead to a comparison between Belgium, Norway, and Italy. In such a case the "homogeneity" appears to be almost factual; it seems that the field presents itself naturally, not that the researcher invents it. The mechanism of conceptual homogenization is much more apparent when the researcher has to manufacture a key; that is, has to develop an analysis that enables him to extrapolate further than the countries initially taken into consideration so as to include other countries that function according to the rules he is studying in the comparison.

This conceptual modeling, the fundamental procedure of comparative studies, merits special attention. The more heterogeneous the field of analysis, the clearer is the effort to make it homogeneous. Some specific examples of comparative research will serve to illustrate the mechanism of this approach.

Consociational democracy exists only insofar as it is perceived by the analyst. In a sense, it does not exist before the concept is formulated. The comparativist determines the elements that will be for him factors of homogeneity. An analogy between Belgium, Canada, Switzerland, Holland, Austria, or even Malaysia and Nigeria is the result of an intellectual process.[4] The explanatory hypothesis necessarily exists before any selection of countries to be studied.

The "bureaucratic empires" studied by S.N. Eisenstadt are presented as a series of intermittent points in time and space, for the author studies the Roman and Ottoman Empires as well as those of the Habsburgs and Incas. In order to formulate the conceptual framework, Eisenstadt proposes to consider particularly "the place of the political system in the social structure and the major interrelations between the polity and other subsystems or spheres of the society."[5] His "centralized bureaucratic empires" are defined notably by a certain degree of differentiation in their structures, by the existence of autonomous political aims, and by a sort of legitimacy. Thus these are hybrid regimes that only an analysis of this type could manage to define in a systematic way. It is no longer to factual history that one looks to find the key to the disruption or decline of these empires, but to the fundamental relationships between certain political and social structures. Similarly, Juan Linz, Samuel Huntington, and Clement H. Moore analyzed authoritarian situations, particularly studying how different categories of regimes could evolve, whether they were regimes of a military nature or not, revolutionary or not, ideological or pragmatic, populist or bureaucratic, oligarchic or popular, and so on. Within the group outlined at the outset, several lines of research then appear, in obedience to laws that may vary. Here are some of the best examples of the conceptual homogenization of a heterogeneous field.

In their analysis of authoritarian systems, Guy Hermet and Alain Rouquié[6] delineate the heterogeneous field of what they term "bastard regimes," those that are somewhere between totalitarianism and democracy. They emphasize that the formulation of a hypothetical model must precede a concrete analysis. This hypothetical model enables them to define their area of study and choose, in particular, the most pertinent cases, as the basis of their analysis. Three elements are contained in the definition of the "semi-competitive" system: the conciliatory power of the bureaucracy, the absence of totalitarianism in the strictest sense of the term, and the will to integrate the working classes formally into the project of statehood by mobilizing them in a noncoercive way. These structural features of the semi-competitive system lead the comparativist to assemble "a large variety of 'eccentric,' 'baroque' or simply disconcerting regimes." Thus, Hermet and Rouquié follow the same procedure as did Eisenstadt or Lijphart: the formulation of the integrating concept comes before the determination of the apparently heterogeneous universe they intend to study.

Knowledge will be increased through such organization of an apparently heterogeneous field, as the preliminary step toward an analysis of the concrete operation of a power system. The conceptual framework, more than anything else, helps the scientific knowledge of social or political phenomena to advance. It is notable that a historian like Paul Veyne defends this strategy, arguing that facts are emphasized by their place in an intellectual construction. "The spatio-temporal continuum is only a didactic framework that perpetuates the lazily narrative tradition. Historical facts are not organized by period or people, but by notion; they do not need to be replaced in their time, but grouped under their concepts. . . . History does not study man in time; it studies human materials subsumed under concepts."[7]

Any comparison that leads to a typology may result in different homogenizing processes. When studying single-party regimes, one moves from the specifiic to the general; the sectorial analysis then serves to define a field that is no longer studied partially, but in an overall way. The whole of the political system is reintegrated around the chosen variable: here the number of parties, elsewhere the role of parliament, the structure of power elites, or the level of political development. It is the whole of a political system that is studied comparatively.

Where do the possibilities for homogenization end? For the political scientist, they end where the homogeneity of situations is not particularly obvious on the political level. The prominent political role of the military,[8] or factionalism,[9] may be good inductors of conceptual homogenization because they have direct and observable consequences on political life. On the contrary, one of the main reproaches that can be leveled at theories of "convergence," for example as they were formulated in the 1960s, is to have underestimated the fundamental political heterogeneity of the capitalist and socialist systems compared. That industrial societies share common problems and perspectives is indisputable; and it is certainly true also that the logic of industrial organization cannot remain without consequences for politics. Today, mobilization appears to be less important than in the past in the Soviet Union; parallel to this is that the role of the state has increased in all pluralist democracies. But are we entitled to detect a trend toward "democratization" in the move toward bureaucratic rationalization that is developing in Soviet Russia? And what about the resistance of the creeds, beliefs, and values that cement two highly self-conscious systems? Zbigniew Brzezinski and Samuel Huntington implicitly condemn any excessive homogenization; it would be simplistic to imagine that human history might someday enter a single socioeconomic or political mold.[10]

The five strategies set out here analytically, as concurrent ones, are seen in practice to be complementary. They correspond to different points of view as well as to different degrees of abstraction and conceptualization. All phenomena can be submitted to these approaches and can gain effectively from being examined from these different angles. Through case studies, comparativists have brought out the importance of certain variables. Comparison between relatively homogeneous countries enabled theories, models, and typologies devised on the basis of comparisons between contrasting countries to be perfected or revised. On the other hand, these same comparisons between contrasting countries have led to the formulation of general laws that would not have appeared in a binary comparison.

It may be inferred that approaching a field of research by a single path gives only a partial view of reality. The qualitative progress represented by the passage from one strategy to the other enables an advance in knowledge, a revision of theories, and the perfection of concepts.

Let us consider, for example, the field of bureaucracy. The case studies of Lucian Pye on Burma, Fred Riggs on Thailand, and Michel Crozier on France have contributed a sophistication that was out of reach for any theory of organization. Meanwhile, in contrasting several phases of development, Reinhard Bendix has stressed that bureaucracy is not defined in the same way and does not correspond to the same functions in countries where it is just appearing and in countries that have been industrialized for a long time. On the other hand, one needs to study a relatively homogeneous area, such as Western Europe, to see features that do not interest the expert dealing with problems of bureaucratization in African countries. In another context, that of countries in the process of modernization, B.F. Hozelitz has examined the relationships that exist between the structure of bureaucracy and the system's performance. Using yet a different approach, S. Eisenstadt has homogenized the field of bureaucratic empires. Each approach is characterized by a different way of looking at things, and each fosters a cumulative progress.

The same remarks are applicable to many other domains. Whether it is political parties, electoral behavior, or the role of the armed forces, a list of complementary works springs easily to mind when one considers these five strategies. The generalization that the concept of totalitarianism has made possible has led to the establishment of invaluable analogies between totalitarian regimes of the extreme left and those of the extreme right. These comparisons, although sometimes considered hasty, have encouraged specialists in comparative studies to analyze both communist and fascist countries with a greater sophistication. By a kind of dialectic movement, a rereading of the Hitlerian experience in the light of these discussions enriches the ambitious syntheses dealing with totalitarianism. A problem matures as the research develops, inviting, in an almost natural way, researchers to direct their investigations in such or such a direction, depending on the gap to be filled and the progress registered.

Those who consider the problem of governmental stability at a worldwide level may be attracted by Tocqueville's hypothesis: the more equal the distribution of wealth, the greater the stability. Bruce M. Russett[11] and Tatu Vanhanen[12] have tried to test it by taking into account a large number of countries. But when a more limited and homogeneous field is considered, other variables take on a particular meaning. Party systems, electoral behaviors, and institutional rules become important subjects of interest. Considering a single nation, Harry Eckstein[13] has oriented his research toward still different variables, such as the attitudes of the elite.

Comparativists are also evidently guided in their choices by their tastes, their knowledge, and the material possibilities open to them. It is unlikely that two researchers, studying the same problem at exactly the same time, will choose the same countries. The same researcher, at different stages in his career, can be led to consider different fields. Michael Hudson, for example, has studied development problems by concentrating on just one country, Lebanon, and then by examining a large number of countries as co-editor of the *World Hand-*

book of Political and Social Indicators, and then again by limiting his focus of analysis to Arab countries.

In reality, a researcher's freedom of choice is great unless, of course, the problem is too closely linked to a determined context. It is evident that the countries to be considered in the framework of a study on consociational democracy stand out with a certain compelling force; the fact remains that even for such a study, the five strategies are open—a comparison between contrasting countries implying the choice of an exterior pole of reference, such as centrifugal democracies or homogeneous societies.

The comparativist can therefore give his preference sufficiently freely to any one of the five strategies, but his choice will have consequences for the method he adopts, particularly insofar as statistical data are concerned. He will not rely on the same kind of quantified information if he studies similar countries or contrasting ones. The same remarks could be made at the level of the concepts and theoretical frameworks utilized. Functional equivalences are more valuable for comparisons between contrasting countries than between similar countries. But by focusing on contrasts, the comparativist will be led to refine categories that, as Giovanni Sartori stressed, as they become overstrained run the risk of losing in intensity and clarity what they gain in "extension." Indeed, the choice of countries, the formulation of concepts, and the adoption of a method are not independent, successive decisions; they are inextricably linked.

NOTES

1. Roy Macridis, *The Study of Comparative Government* (Garden City, N.Y.: Doubleday, 1955), p. 18.
2. *Size and Democracy* (Stanford: Stanford University Press, 1973).
3. "Modernization and Comparative Politics," *Comparative Politics* 1, no. 1 (October 1968): 45-47.
4. See Arend Lijphart, *Democracy in Plural Societies: A Comparative Exploration* (New Haven: Yale University Press, 1977).
5. *The Political Systems of Empires* (New York: Free Press, 1963), pp. 8ff.
6. Alain Rouquié, "L'hypothèse bonapartiste et l'émergence des systèmes politiques semicompétitifs," *Revue Française de Science Politique* 25, no. 6 (December 1975); and Guy Hermet, "Dictature bourgeoise et modernisation conservatrice: problèmes méthodologiques de l'analyse de situations autoritaires," ibid.
7. P. Veyne, *L'inventaire des differences* (Paris: Seuil, 1976), pp. 49-50.
8. See, for example, Claude E. Welch and Arthur K. Smith, *Military Role and*

Rule (Belmont, Calif.: Wadsworth, 1974).

9. Cf. the possible comparison between India, Japan, Italy, and Mexico suggested in M. Dogan, "La sélection des ministres dans divers régimes politiques," *Revue Internationale de Science Politique,* no. 2 (1981); or the chapter devoted by Giovanni Sartori to "Italy and Japan: Factions within Parties," in his *Parties and Party Systems* (Cambridge: Cambridge University Press, 1976).

10. See *Political Power: USA/USSR* (New York: Viking Press, 1963).

11. "Inequality and Instability: The Relation of Land Tenure to Politics," *World Politics* 16 (April 1964): 442-54.

12. "Political and Social Structures"; pt. 1: American Countries, 1850-1973; pt. 2: European Countries, 1850-1974 (Tampere, Institute of Political Science, 1976).

13. *Division and Cohesion in Democracy* (Princeton: Princeton University Press, 1966).

PART 4

HOW TO STRUCTURE THE RESULTS
OF THE COMPARISON

As WE have seen in preceding chapters, two conditions contribute to the quality of comparative studies: (1) the accuracy of the conceptual tools, and (2) the consistency of the fields selected. To be a good cameraman, it is not sufficient to have a good camera. It is also necessary to determine the proper distance and the best angle of sight, to use the most appropriate background, and to decide whether to choose a soft-focus or a wide-angle lens. In the same way, even the most sophisticated computers do not automatically produce interesting comparisons. At each stage of the scientific process, the analysts must rely on their creative imagination to approach their subject adequately, discover the right techniques and methods, and single out a pertinent field from the social reality.

The next stage is to assemble the accumulated findings in a meaningful way. Indeed, the scientific spirit will never be content with conclusions stating, for example, that the Italian society is more prone to conflict than the English one. It will always be important to understand the reasons for the differences listed—to establish constant relationships between the variables, to find a logical order, to detect the causes, to imagine the future. The results of international comparisons must be articulated because the progress of scientific knowledge implies at the same time analysis and synthesis, a quest for empirical evidence and the expression of concepts. We all know that comparison is not simply a matter of observation. We see what we are looking for, what we are conceptually prepared to perceive. But conversely, all conclusions drawn from empirical observation transform our perspective, throwing a new light on the area to be explored.

When concluding a comparative study, the researcher may opt for one of several kinds of formal construction, arranging the pieces of knowledge collected in order to grasp their scientific meaning. These formal syntheses are essentially different, with specific advantages and disadvantages, which we propose to identify here.

In considering the dichotomy, we shall point out the clarifying but somewhat distorting function of this bipolar structure. Shifting to more complex typologies, we shall oppose frameworks that organize segments or parts of the social system to typologies that deal with whole regimes.

While dichotomies and typologies are static constructions, models and theories promise a causal exploration. Models can be defined as dynamic structures, aiming at partial explanations. Theoretical syntheses, which exist at a higher level of generalization and articulation, represent more comprehensive conclusions to comparisons. Of course, the word "conclusion" suggests here only one aspect of the scientific process. As noted, all conceptual frameworks guide the research as much as they are nourished by it. But it must be stressed also that even the most abstract theories are syntheses, induced from empirical findings. We shall argue that point before examining how international comparison may help predict the future.

CHAPTER 19

THE DICHOTOMY
AS CLARIFICATION

Classification is an old undertaking in all sciences. Like chemistry, geology, zoology, and botany, political science and sociology have been marked from their origins by a sustained effort to make inventories and to rank. At the first level, intellectual order seems to be tied to this classificatory undertaking.

A simple dichotomy, conceived as an opposition of two classes, is apparently the most immediate and easy classification. It is a natural step in thinking. Claude Lévi-Strauss has shown that it is universal and nourishes even the primitive mind. Applied by scientists, dichotomization can be more or less ambitious and can produce results of unequal value. It is possible to measure its benefits by pointing out its intrinsic limits. Dichotomization can be done on a complex basis or a relatively simple one; it can synthesize a comparative analysis or just trace the perspective of a study that remains to be done.

Thus one could divide the world into two categories, starting with such a rudimentary criterion as GNP per capita, and analyze how rich and poor nations contrast with one another. Such a division constitutes an outline of a true classification, "exclusive and exhaustive," as Stanislav Andreski stresses,[1] since it considers the totality of the universe and permits the ranking of all existing cases into one of the two classes considered.

Dichotomization as an approach does not necessarily result in a formal dichotomy. It is also essential that the considered categories represent a complete inventory of existing cases. The antagonistic social classes identified by some theorists do not cover the entire social spectrum. Marx in particular was aware of this, and questioned the historical place of the peasantry in France, for example. In this sense, the opposition between proletariat and bourgeoisie is not a real dichotomy. Only some simplistic views later have tended to cast all social categories into the mold of these two classes.

Dichotomization helps in the comparison between contrasting countries when attention is concentrated on extreme cases; but whereas the dichotomous classification encompasses the totality of the field studied, the contrasting analysis may be more or less representative, according to whether the cases selected are median or marginal. Because the dichotomy presents itself as an opposition, it may lead the social scientist to concentrate on extreme cases, where the contrast exists in the starkest light. Thus, one can arrive at the paradoxical result of a classification that is not a true one because, instead of ranking the totality of known cases, it focuses on two atypical cases in the series of nations, systems, societies, and so on.

A dichotomy can be based on such a simple criterion as size, wealth, or age. Such an approach, which values raw data, is useful in many disciplines, for example biology. Economists and demographers often rely on these dichotomies at first glance. In the field of politics, however, dichotomization is more ambitious, searching for criteria less in immediately perceptible forms than in functioning modalities. One could say, paradoxically, that the ideal character of each type, in the Weberian sense, appears with utmost clarity when the classification is refined in this exemplary opposition.

Since the dichotomy consists in the identification of conceptual categories abstracted from reality, it constitutes a precious initial ordering. It guides the study. The classical opposition between rural and urban or between the sacred and the profane has long contributed to orient the investigation. Today the implicit contrast between modern and modernizing, or between developed and developing countries, often helps focus even the questions asked about one or the other world. Simplification aids perception, that is obvious. One poses in opposing. The caricature helps one to see what is essential. Gino Germani noted the extent to which the dichotomous typology is a necessary, maybe inevitable, point of departure.[2] If we are to believe him, any progress in understanding what development really means will require the outlining of two contrasted types, each of which is broad enough to cover a wide array of systems and forms. Thus the opposition between traditional and modern societies will be misleading if the researcher is unaware of the diversity of empirical cases that have been reduced into these two categories.

For a dichotomy reduces everything. Never can two classes be as precise in their discriminating power as seven, nine, or twenty classes. It is clear that categories like *Gemeinschaft* and *Gesellschaft* (Ferdinand Tönnies), folk culture and urban culture (Robert Redfield), mechanic and organic solidarity (Émile Durkheim), and sacred and secular society (Bronislaw Malinowski), are representations that excessively refashion the reality they pretend to account for. This is also true for more recent distinctions, opposing, for instance, particularism and universalism or ascription and achievement.

Very useful in designing a field for comparative research, a dichotomy may, when prematurely presented as a conclusion, induce detrimental simplifications or nourish a kind of "manicheanism," far distant from what is expected in a sociological analysis. As Gabriel Almond and G. Bingham Powell have stated, "in the discussion of cultural patterns, too sharp a line is often drawn between societies characterized by traditional cultures and those characterized by modern culture. . . . Modern social science research has demonstrated the continuing significance of primary groups and informal organizations in the social processes of Western societies. . . . All political systems have mixed political cultures. The most primitive societies have threads of instrumental rationality in their structure and culture. The most modern are permeated by ascriptive, particularistic, and informal relationships and attitudes. They differ in the relative dominance of one against the other and in the pattern of mixture of these components. Secularization is a matter of degree."[3]

In the same way, Joseph R. Gusfield has pointed out how the opposition between tradition and modernity, when used without precautions, may be contestable[4] because the terms coexist, obviously in different proportion, in every country, advanced or developing. Reinhard Bendix has expressed his reservations in the same manner, saying that each modern society is in fact "partially developed," an amalgam between modernity and residues of tradition.[5]

Reality does not easily enter the mold of dichotomies. And it resists all the more when conceptual categories are inaccurate. Most of the criticisms that can be formulated about dichotomies are justified by the inadequacy of these categories. To reduce the planet to two ideal types makes no sense if each type does not include a substantial part of reality. Is there still a meaning in the old opposition between traditional and modern societies when in practice today few societies correspond entirely to the definition of traditional?

One could also question the pertinence of the dichotomy democracy versus totalitarianism, for statistically the first category represents only 25 to 30 countries and the second only 10 to 12 in today's world of over 150 nations. Here is the weakness of a dichotomy inherited from a recent but already outdated past. Applied to the heterogeneous reality of today, this dichotomy has no substance. It does not help us to understand the diversity of nations; on the contrary, it irons out differences in gross categories that are in fact situated at the two poles. There are not just political regimes that elect their representatives and other regimes that do not; rather, between these two extremes, there is a graduated series of countries with *Elections without Choice;*[6] a new category thus appears between democratic regimes and totalitarian regimes. The analyst rapidly perceives the roughness of these labels. Under the category of dictatorship, G.W. Hallgarten distinguishes classical, ultrarevolutionary, counterrevolutionary, and pseudorevolutionary models.[7] Samuel P. Huntington and Clement H. Moore,[8] for their part, have no difficulty in showing, under the façade of the single-party system, the great diversity of authoritarian regimes, which could together be opposed to all forms of political pluralism. In domains as subtle as this, dichotomization is somewhat forced. Its simple criteria badly substitute for the scales needed: the degree of participation, the degree of oppression, and other gradations.

Here it is not so much the obsolescence of conceptual schemes that should be indicted but the incapacity of a polarized opposition to measure a progression. This could appear almost as a paradox, for it is true that in most cases the paternity of these constructions belongs to authors who are sensitive to social change. In effect, ambitious dichotomies frequently carry an evolutionary vision, regardless of whether the author, like Tönnies, regrets seeing the structure of the community weakening, or whether, like many American social scientists, he is unconsciously pleased to discover "rational trends." If it is true that any dichotomy tends to freeze the distinctions in exaggerated contrasts, it remains nevertheless true that too much severity concerning the dichotomous approach would lead to misunderstanding its capacity to clarify, initially at least, the prolific realities.

The compared nations are almost always situated somewhere between the two extremes: from underdeveloped societies to postindustrial societies, from strict liberalism to collectivism, and so forth. The dichotomy naturally nourishes the idea of a continuum, but it is incapable of capturing it because it *de facto* ignores the conceptual axis linking one category to the other. In its effort at clarification, it does not provide itself with any choices other than stringent alternatives. It is for this reason that we contrast the dichotomy with the typology.

Dichotomization is necessarily unidimensional, whatever its complexity and the variables used for identifying the two terms. It can retain only one perspective. This is another limit that can be illustrated by many examples. Considered from the point of view of their foreign policy, political regimes can be distinguished according to their ideological orientation. But Raymond Aron has shown that other groupings are possible if one looks to the workings of the systems. In 1939, only the totalitarian nature of the Soviet and Nazi regimes rendered possible the German-Soviet pact: "Obliged to persuade public opinion, to represent its allies as good and its enemies as bad, the diplomacy of Western parliamentary states is modest in its long-range goals, with a limited margin of maneuver. Only regimes whose leaders are at great liberty in face of public opinion can abruptly burn what they worshipped and worship what they burned, without even puzzling the masses."[9]

Depending on the choice of classificatory axes, the two extremes opposed in one scheme could find themselves together along other classificatory axes. The social structure is certainly not the same in the United States and the Soviet Union. But Stanislaw Ossowski noted the strange similarities that one could find in the dominant values in these two countries: the same meritocratic content in the political culture, the same advocacy of mobility, the same tendency to oppose a society without classes to the insupportable hierarchies of the old world, and the same "religious" faith in an indefinite progress toward a better future.[10] An analysis of myths shows the same ambiguities. History knows of spectacular conversions of extremists. Those who analyze utopias well know how sometimes *le grand soir* of a certain Left could resemble the millennium of a certain Right. These paradoxes are not ignored by those studying political behavior.

NOTES

1. "Classifications et terminologies: des outils à manier avec circonspection," *Revue Internationale des Sciences Sociales,* no. 3 (1974): 225.
2. *Politique, Société et Modernisation* (Gembloux: Duculot, 1972), pp. 57ff; see, in English, *The Sociology of Modernization.*
3. Gabriel Almond and G. Bingham Powell, *Comparative Politics* (Boston: Little, Brown, 1966), pp. 32-33.
4. "Tradition and Modernity: Misplaced Polarities in the Study of Social Change" in *Political Development and Social Change,* ed. Jason Finkle and Richard Gable (New York: Wiley, 1971).
5. *Nation Building and Citizenship* (New York: Wiley, 1964), pp. 181-82.
6. Guy Hermet, Richard Rose, and Alain Rouquié, eds., *Elections without Choice* (London: Macmillan, 1978).
7. *Why Dictators? The Causes and Forms of Tyrannical Rule from 600 B.C.* (New York: Macmillan, 1954).
8. *Authoritarian Politics in Modern Society* (New York: Basic Books, 1970).
9. *Paix et guerre entre les nations* (Paris: Calmann-Lévy, 1962), p. 285; see, in English, *Peace and War: A Theory of International Relations* (Garden City, N.Y.: Doubleday, 1966).
10. *La structure de classes dans la conscience sociale* (Paris: Anthropos, 1971), esp. pp. 190-94. See, in English, *Class Structure in the Social Consciousness,* rev. ed. (London: Routledge & Kegan Paul, 1979).

CHAPTER 20

CROSS-NATIONAL TYPOLOGIES
OF SOCIAL ACTORS

There is no rigid barrier between dichotomies and typologies. Sometimes typologies "decant" so much as to allow the showing of a bipolar skeleton. The analyst may deliberately concentrate his attention on two polar types at the expense of middle or mixed categories whose existence the research has demonstrated. Conversely, and this is a point we want to stress, a simple opposition between two terms often constitutes a preliminary stage in working toward more complex distinctions.

This opening may be accomplished in two ways. First, the analyst is often led to introduce gradations and middle-range categories between the two poles of his scheme. On the political left-right axis, for example, he may rank a series of ideological configurations, some of them radical, some of them combining in varying degrees the desire for order with a preoccupation with social justice. But the analyst may wish to cross this first perspective with another one to consider not only the content of political ideology but also the rigidity of behavior.

Ideological Left	Pragmatic Left	Eclectic Center	Pragmatic Right	Ideological Right
∟_____	___|___	___|___	___|___	_____⌐

FIGURE 20.1
Elongating the Single Axis

The crossing of two dichotomous variables provides the sketch of a quadripolar scheme that it will be possible to develop at a second stage by adding further axes. One would consider, then, not only left and right but also pragmatic left and ideological left, pragmatic right and ideological right. Thus the dichotomization develops into a typology not by the elongation of one dimension but by the crosscutting of two axes.

In fact, the two procedures of crosscutting and elongation operate jointly to sustain the passage from a dichotomy to a more elaborate typological construction. Paul Lazarsfeld clarified the mechanism of these constructions, show-

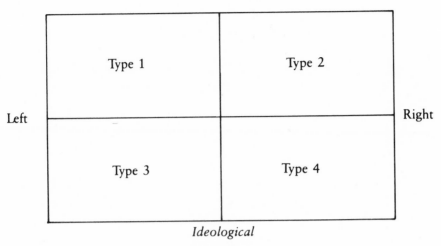

Pragmatic

Type 1   Type 2

Left   Right

Type 3   Type 4

Ideological

FIGURE 20.2
Crossing of Two Dichotomies

ing how their complexity progressively increases as the dimensions are no longer dichotomized, but graduated or serialized. It is possible, for instance, to take an inventory of a population based on relatively simple criteria like adults or minors and city dwellers or villagers. But if the analysis is not to be oversimplified, the binary opposition must give way to gradations when variables like age and education are taken into consideration. Let us now suppose that we want to include motivations and attitudes in the analysis. Then the hierarchy could be built only on a comparative basis, the intervals appearing on the attitude scale being directly determined by the way in which the attitudes of members of the society are actually distributed. That is, the hypothesis of the researcher largely preconditions the form of the survey and the typologies finally elaborated.

One sometimes distinguishes between typologies resting on broad intellectual categories, which are essentially irreconcilable, and typologies based on measurable variables, which permit an evaluation of degrees. In fact, all typologies combine a subtle mix of induction and deduction. Even the classic typologies are partly based on empirical observations. Conversely, and in spite of their appearances, most of the typologies induced from empirical research are largely based on a deductive approach. One cannot establish a typology of voters, pressure groups, or political parties without being guided by hypotheses, which shape the perception of reality. If there is an evolution here, it may be that today typologies are increasingly formulated in an inductive manner. This tendency is related to a greater availability of empirical data.

All the categories retained nevertheless should have an internal coherence. P. de Bruyne, J. Herman, and M. de Schoutheete correctly emphasized that it is rarely the "natural" type, the spontaneously perceived, that interests the sociologist; rather, it is the constructed type, the abstract combination of attributes judged pertinent. "The notion of type is not identical to the notion of category."[1]

Although some confusion exists within sociological literature, it seems that one could establish this distinction: The class is an empirical category, whereas the type is a conceptual category. One could walk down the street and see young and old, men and women, tall people and short. But one will not so easily pick out the introvert and the extrovert, the optimist and the pessimist, the individual who makes decisions according to his conscience and the one who internalizes social pressures. Even if the sociologist bases his reasoning on statistics, he himself discovers types and elaborates them intellectually. Distributing cities according to their size is to classify them according to a numerical criterion, which may be useful; but such classification does not identify significant conceptual categories. Just as a dichotomy does not mechanically result from the operation of scission, in the same way a typology does not necessarily result from all kinds of classificatory operation.

Establishing a series of attributes defined, for instance, by the dimension "occupation," dichotomized into manual and nonmanual, and by the dimension of political attitudes trichotomized into right, center, and left, results in the separation of six boxes. Within them, however, not all types are necessarily coherent. In order to build typologies, it is not enough to crosscut variables. It is further necessary that the invented categories have a sociological meaning in relation to the problem being analyzed.

A definition of typology proceeds from that of type. But it is not sufficient to make an inventory of a few types to construct a typology. It is indispensable to try to rank all the objects considered in such a way so that each is located in just one category. The task of intellectual construction does not end with the polishing of types. It is also essential to order them in a coherent fashion.

Nor should the typology be confused with a series of different analytical categories. One could distinguish several types of social movements or parties, but one would not speak of typologies in discussing their various functions or actions. The typology does not respond to the question, "How does it work?" or "For what purpose?" but to the question, "How is reality ordered?"

Here appear the advantages and limits of an approach that aims at integrating logically the elements of accumulated knowledge on a particular subject. Because the typology proposes an abstract organization, it leaves room for the researcher's subjectivity. This is certainly one reason for the impressive number of typologies found in the literature and the fact that they do not necessarily communicate between themselves.

Numerous studies have been devoted to the role of the army in the Third World, and practically all of them propose an inventory of types of military intervention in politics. An examinaton of these constructions shows that they rarely coincide. Most frequently, the multiplicity of constructed types corresponds more to a difference in perspective than to an actual dispersion of categories. Researchers do not pose the same questions to reality. Whereas some look to the psychological profile of the military, others give priority to behavior in power, and others to the content of military policies. The latitude of the researcher at this level is very great, and is not necessarily conditioned by the data he possesses. For instance, Robert Lane,[2] working on data collected for *The Civic Culture,* managed to identify types of teenagers having little in common with the types of citizens portrayed by Almond and Verba.

A typology is fashioned by the perspective of the sociologist. It is organized at the crossroads of his or her creative imagination and data. Hence the diversity of possible constructions. In order to characterize different models of political behavior, Max Kaase and Alan Marsh[3] chose two dimensions: the intensity of political activity, high or low, and the nature of the means of action, either conformist or nonconformist (e.g., wildcat strikes, sit-ins at the factory, blockages of highways, refusals to pay income taxes). Logically, a diagram based on the intersection of these two axes should result in four categories of citizens. But as the interest of researchers was focused on the modalities of participation, all inactive citizens were grouped in one category. "Activists," for their part, could have been treated in two classes, conventionals and nonconventionals. The other possibilities were to multiply these categories either according to the intensity of commitment—as the authors did—or according to diverse means of action, or else by considering gradations along these two axes. Here, total freedom is left to the researcher. This freedom, limited only by the inventiveness of researchers, certainly constitutes an advantage of the typology. A symmetric disadvantage also appears to the extent that this active creativity may result in an excessively abstract construction that is inconsistent and disconnected from reality. It would take too long to enumerate here the stillborn constructions that sleep in the cemeteries of libraries.

This is not the case with the best typologies, which take on a function of promoting scholarly communication and exchange. There are typologies around which no dialogue takes place; others, more rare, more precious, become the bearers of collective memory. The latter help in the accumulation of knowledge. They become inventories, periodically updated. Comparativists have a natural vocation to participate in this reshuffling. They need these concrete keys that facilitate analysis across various social contexts. At the same time their strategic position allows them to select the most incisive typologies.

What is the meaning of "incisiveness" for the comparativist? We may first remark, perhaps paradoxically, that interest in the typology is not bound to the context for which it was initially elaborated. Some typologies that were conceived from the outset to be comparative have had short lives, whereas others that "grew up" in a single country have had international careers. This internationalization seems inhibited when the typology is overly conditioned to the particular context for which it was formulated: when it is rooted in too particular a context and reflects so specific a reality that any extension to other countries becomes difficult or impossible. A good example of a typology that is difficult to extrapolate is that formulated by Eric A. Nordlinger,[4] Robert McKenzie, and Allan Silver.[5] Accepted by most British political scientists, it distinguishes two types of conservative workers: the Tory worker, characterized as deferential toward traditional values and hierarchies; and the secularized worker, whose behavior depends on the perception he has of his own interests. To say that such a typology could not be "exported" does not imply the denial of its interest for the comparativist. To know that the Tory worker exists in Great Britain and not elsewhere in Europe is to find a significant contrast. It only means that the typology cannot serve to integrate the comparative analysis.

Other typologies have proven useful for the comparativist even if they were developed within a relatively limited field. A series of surveys conducted in France and Italy attested to the existence of six types of workers, labeled "revolutionary," "protester," "reformist," "Catholic," "conservative," and "indifferent."[6] A later inquiry showed that such types are also to be found in Spain.

One could find many examples of typologies built in and for a single country that were later taken up by political scientists who tested their validity in other contexts. Typologies conceived for one national context are thus utilized as outlines for enlarged studies. The construction then passes from hand to hand, being refined with each new application. Richard Peterson proposed a typology of American students, partly inspired by the works of Martin Trow and Burton Clark and partly developed on the basis of survey analyses. Later, Seymour Martin Lipset turned this typology into a canvas for international comparison.[7] Of course, one could argue that the eight profiles detected in the United States are not to be found in a similar way in Paris or Buenos Aires, in Tokyo or Bangkok. The sociological features characterizing "careerists" or "activists" are certainly different from one continent to another. The proportion of "hippies," characterized by their pessimism and political abstinence, or "collegiates," those eager for entertainment, is undoubtedly higher in countries where education has been expanded. But because students everywhere constitute a group in the same relatively privileged position, because they generally carry with them the same secularized and meritocratic values, such a typology could well be extended beyond the limits of the United States. A hypothesis that has been tested and proved, it demands to be applied to a second, third, and fourth country. Here the typology is not the product of comparison; it is its lever.

Such internationalization of typologies has been possible in many fields, particularly when the study focuses on segments of the political system that are relatively little influenced by contextual variables. For instance, the typology of parliamentarians proposed by Heinz Eulau[8] has proven widely useful, without doubt because parliaments are somewhat similar structures in most democracies. The same could be said for typologies of higher civil servants, union leaders, clergymen, or military chiefs.

Political opinions and electoral behavior have stimulated many typological constructions. Here again, one could distinguish those that were intially conceived in a comparative framework and those "imported" from a particular context, as, for instance, H.J. Eysenck's and Herbert McClosky's typologies of liberals and conservatives.

To say that the types considered are generalizable does not mean that each type can be found in the same proportion in different contexts. When used in comparisons, the typology serves not only to increase the knowledge of structures and actors but also to compare one nation to another. It is in this way that the typology becomes a valuable instrument for international comparison. Paradoxically, the typology often results from comparison and formalizes its results; but at the same time, it serves as a guide because it invents the necessary concepts and provides direction to investigations. To contrast the modernizing mentality and the traditional mentality, as do Alex Inkeles and David H. Smith[9] is not only to oppose two psychocultural types. It is also—or it could have been, had their study not been limited to relatively similar countries—the means to differentiate between nations in which the "modern man" represents 90 percent of the population, 50 percent, 20 percent, or 5 percent. It might measure social differences among, for example, Canada, Argentina, Tunisia, and Afghanistan.

Since the value of a typology depends on its inventiveness, its explanatory role is not necessarily related to its formal perfection. It is rare that all categories in an abstract framework are found in reality or that they have an equal sociological or political relevance. This is why sociologists are frequently led to skip some boxes, to neglect some improbable situations, or to combine neighboring cases under the same rubric. Some typologies are aesthetically constructed; others, less sophisticated, nevertheless prove more stimulating. Max Weber's typologies are of the latter nature.

Indeed the art of constructing a typology is not the art of classifying; it is the art of finding axes that logically account for the relative positon of the nations or segments submitted to comparison. A typology, in its most accomplished form, should consequently be not only an inventory but also incisive and explanatory; it should recapitulate previous discoveries in order to seek further; it should provide the researcher with a conceptual tool. It was the classification of Carl von Linné, responding to the criteria of formal logic, that permitted Charles Darwin to build the theory of evolution. Stanislav Andreski saw in this filiation "a magnificent example of the primacy of the logical order in the progress of knowledge."[10] The same could be said for the classification of Dmitri Mendeleev.

Paul Lazarsfeld has eloquently shown that the typology borrows from the empirical order and the logical order at the same time. And this dialogue increases our knowledge. Studies are often stimulated by the presence of categories unclassifiable in the conceptual scheme. Conversely, the device of logical deduction often leads to the detection of types that are not so easy to recognize empirically. Lazarsfeld has underlined the advantages of this strategy. In a study on the family sponsored by the International Council of Social Research, Erich Fromm had identified four types of relationships between parents and children: complete authority, simple authority, lack of authority, and rebellion. In an article published a few years later, Paul Lazarsfeld showed that recourse to logic would have disclosed a fifth type, one that was certainly worthy of consideration. Indeed, by crossing the two axes of parental authority on the one side and children's acceptance on the other, one found the possibility of potentially great obedience combined with an actual lack of authority. "The substruction," noted Lazarsfeld, "may be used as a tool for discovery. It disclosed the possibility that children might long for an authority which no one offers them. These discovered combinations suggest further research."[11] In a much broader way, it would be easy to show how the typological reasoning of the last twenty years or so has come increasingly to shed light on types of behaviors and structures that today provide the bases for most comparative studies.

Some debatable and contested typologies are still alive. The distinction between associational interest groups (like unions), institutional ones (like armies or churches), nonassociational (like linguistic, racial, or communal groupings) and of anomic groups (spontaneously created in a situation of frustration) was originally formulated by George I. Blanksten in a study dealing with Latin America.[12] The distinction was later adopted and sharpened by Gabriel

Almond.[13] In *Politics Within Nations,* Joseph LaPalombara also makes critical use of it.[14]

The typology proposed in 1951 by Maurice Duverger illustrates in the same way how a living typology may engender discussion and stimulate controversy, thus improving the understanding of the phenomena being analyzed.[15] The typology, precisely because it is an abstraction, resists becoming outdated better than the empirical analysis does. The frontiers traced by Almond and Verba between participant, passive, and parochial behaviors have stimulated many discussions and critical comments. But their concepts of participant culture or civic culture have had sufficient impact to inspire new research. A good example may be found in the book edited by Samuel H. Barnes and Max Kaase on the modalities of political participation in five democracies.[16] Dealing with the Netherlands, Britain, the United States, Germany, and Austria, the authors arrive at conclusions partly inspired by Almond and Verba's typologies. Participation today does not necessarily take the ideal "civic" route. More and more individuals who are active political participants in a conventional manner tend to use, in a parallel fashion, other methods that are not at all conventional. "Activists" who combine methods tend to be more numerous than "reformists" who limit themselves to conventional means or than protesters who totally reject electoral or organized participation. For the authors of *Political Action,* as well as for Samuel Huntington,[17] this evolution must be attributed to the inability of old institutions to answer citizens' increasing demands and capacities to participate in politics. Ronald Inglehart further developed these ideas, calling this growing propensity to play an active role in city life a "silent revolution."[18] Whatever these explanations and hypotheses, what is clear from the Barnes and Kaase book is a recognized debt to *The Civic Culture.* The "participant" cultural type is still alive. It has simply taken a new path.

NOTES

1. *Dynamique de la recherche en sciences sociales* (Paris: PUF, 1974), p. 169f.
2. Robert Lane, "La maturation politique de l'adolescent aux Etats-Unis et en Allemagne," *Revue Française de Sociologie,* Supplement (1966): 598-618.
3. Max Kaase and Alan Marsh in *Political Action: Mass Participation in Five Democracies,* ed. Samuel H. Barnes and Max Kaase (Beverly Hills, Calif.: Sage, 1979), p. 57.
4. Eric A. Nordlinger, *The Working Class Tories* (London: Macgibbon & Kee, 1967).
5. R. McKenzie and A. Silver, *Angels in Marble* (London: Heinemann, 1968).

6. Mattei Dogan, "Political Cleavages and Social Stratification in France and Italy," in *Party Systems and Voter Alignments,* ed. Seymour Martin Lipset and Stein Rokkan (New York: Free Press, 1967), pp. 175-79.

7. Seymour Martin Lipset, "Students and Politics in Comparative Perspective," (Report to a conference on Students and Politics, San Juan, Puerto Rico, 1967).

8. Heinz Eulau, "Four Legislative Roles," in *The Legislative System,* ed. John C. Wahlke, Heinz Eulau, William Buchanan, LeRoy C. Ferguson (New York: Wiley, 1962), p. 259.

9. Alex Inkeles and David H. Smith, *Becoming Modern: Individual Change in Six Developing Countries* (Cambridge, Mass.: Harvard University Press, 1974).

10. Stanislav Andreski, "Classifications and Terminologies," *International Social Science,* no. 3 (1974): 525.

11. *Zeitschrift für Sozialforschung* 6 (1937).

12. George I. Blanksten, "Political Groups in Latin America," *American Political Science Review* 53, no. 1 (March 1959).

13. Cf. Introduction to *The Politics of the Developing Areas,* ed. Gabriel Almond and James S. Coleman (Princeton: Princeton University Press, 1960).

14. Englewood Cliffs, N.J.: Prentice-Hall, 1974, pp. 326ff.

15. Maurice Duverger, *Les partis politiques* (Paris: Colin, 1951). Also in English, *Political Parties* (New York: Wiley, 1963).

16. Barnes and Kaase, *Political Action.*

17. Samuel Huntington, "Post-Industrial Politics: How Benign Will It Be," *Comparative Politics* 6, no. 2 (January 1974): 163-91.

18. Ronald F. Inglehart, *The Silent Revolution: Changing Values and Political Style among Western Publics* (Princeton: Princeton University Press, 1977).

Chapter 21

TYPOLOGIES OF
POLITICAL REGIMES

Typologies of social actors are often elaborated in a single national context, whereas typologies concerning systems, regimes, and societies are from the outset conceived of in an international framework. Someone who observes individuals or groups can compare them without looking beyond national frontiers. He can do a noninternational comparison. Thus it is possible to build a typology of leaders or voters considering just a single country, or even one city. This becomes difficult, if not impossible, when the analysis deals with classes, groups, institutions, structures, and so forth. International comparisons become more valuable when the objects of analysis are classes or parties than when the study deals with families or individuals; they are more useful for understanding pressure groups and unions than for distinguishing among the leaders of these groups. Typologies require an extension of the field across national boundaries when the number of cases is insufficient within one nation. The typology of political systems falls naturally into the hands of the comparativist.

Like typologies of social actors, typologies of regimes can be valued according to the amount of debate they generate. It is essential that a certain consensus mature in order to see the typology become a real instrument for national comparisons. The dichotomy democracy-totalitarianism lost most of its analytical interest from the moment the number of "hybrid" countries increased. As so many countries of the Third World became independent, comparativists studying these new countries rapidly found that the concept of totalitarianism was inefficient. In these countries, undoubtedly because of the absence of a technical infrastructure permitting the control of individuals, there was little real analogy between this or that African or Asian country and Stalinist or Nazi regimes. Leo Strauss has rightly defined totalitarianism by two elements. Contrary to the classical tyranny, he wrote, the tyranny of today possesses technology and ideology.[1] This means that the will to mobilize the population totally—the ideological factor—is not sufficient to transform the new state into a totalitarian state. For that, the development of the country must be at a level that permits the penetration of the political apparatus deep within the society. It is necessary that the central government be in possession of the channels, means, and mechanisms represented by the media, educational system, planning, employment, taxation, travel, and violent repression (as magnified by propaganda and important military or police forces). Idi Amin, Batista, Bokassa—even Nkrumah, Sukarno, or Sekou Touré, to mention leaders whose revolutionary commitment is beyond doubt—clearly did not possess such means.

To these technical weaknesses are added ethnic, religious, linguistic, and cultural cleavages that sustain an embryonic pluralism. These countries often manifest the wish, more or less sincere, to imitate the institutions of Western democracies. The new leaders who have assimilated the pluralistic models in London, Paris, Brussels, the Hague, and more recently in American universities have tried to adapt such institutions. At the same time, leaders who have chosen to follow the socialist model have insisted that their "socialism" is specific. Kenyatta as well as Nyerere argued that there were no social classes in Black Africa; they pretended to find in traditional clan or family solidarities the inspiration of original new political forms. Looking toward South America, comparativists observed that urbanization and education were developing new social forces..

At first, the concepts of charisma and populism were used to fill the void left by the inadequacy of the concept of totalitarianism. But these explanations rapidly became unsatisfactory. The persistent void soon gave rise to many field investigations that resulted in the elaboration of numerous new typologies. Nothing is more stimulating than the empty space on a table. We all know that the lacunae in a classification are not less significant than the full boxes. The multiplication of studies on these previously nonexplored areas eloquently attests to this.

The great diversity of newly independent states engendered many typologies that often overlapped. What is remarkable is the consensus that has been finally reached among the greatest comparativists. The typology elaborated by Edward Shils[2] marked a pioneering stage in this clarifying direction. Shils distinguished two intermediary types between the extreme poles of democratic and totalitarian regimes—the tutelary democracies characterized by the hypertrophy of the executive, and the modernizing oligarchies marked by the domination of a military or bureaucratic group unconcerned with democratizing the country. To these four types, Shils added a fifth, which is rapidly disappearing: the traditional oligarchy. In 1960 James S. Coleman distinguished between three types of developing countries: competitive, semi-competitive, and authoritarian; the orientation toward modernization introduced a second axis that permitted the elaboration of five types. Finally, the typology was refined by an in-depth analysis that took into consideration the roles of the army, bureaucracy, party, religion, and so on.[3]

In the following years, many studies were published that covered one continent or even the entire range of Third World countries and that culminated in various typologies. We could mention one proposed by Almond and Powell in 1966.[4] It was based on two classificatory axes concerning the structural differentiation of roles and cultural secularization. A third axis, borrowed from Robert Dahl and considering the autonomy of subsystems, came into view. The relatively complex typology that resulted from these crossed perspectives distinguished between three types of authoritarian regimes: premobilized, conservative, and modernizing. A consensus was slowly engendered around the concept of authoritarianism, which Juan Linz later refined in the Weberian tradition.

Confronted with the problem of finding an analytical axis to distinguish among the different forms of authoritarianism, Linz rejected the content of ideology as not really significant. He gave priority to the structural forms of what he called "limited pluralism." The participation of groups in political power, he said, is controlled by certain social forces and channeled by various organizations. Along this line of the different groups' acceding to power, he identified eight types of authoritarian regimes.[5]

In a similar way, prominent analysts of one-party systems have arrived at the common conclusion that it is necessary to stress the diversity of those regimes. It was interesting to see how three great comparativists—Giovanni Sartori, Juan Linz, and Jerzy Wiatr—finally agreed to distinguish between real one-party systems and systems charactrized by a dominant or hegemonic party.[6] Socialist Poland in the 1960s was not Franco's Spain.

Other comparativists sought to introduce new distinctions between one-party systems according to whether or not they were dominated by the military. Thus, Samuel Huntington proposed a distinction between revolutionary single-party systems and exclusionary single-party systems (a term designating political regimes that exclude from the political arena entire segments of the population, such as ethnic minorities).[7] He also proposed distinguishing between revolutionary and established parties according to whether the revolutionary power is institutionalized or not.

The establishment of typologies dealing with political regimes requires the introduction of numerous variables into the analysis. Maurice Duverger has already shown that the number of parties is not enough to characterize a political system and that it is necessary to take into account the structure of parties (rigid or supple) and their nature (mass parties or cadre parties). Naturally, the configuration is more difficult to capture than its diverse elements. This is visible when one passes from the identification of types of parties to the formalization of a typology of party systems.

Giovanni Sartori holds also that numerical criteria will never suffice to differentiate political systems. There are everywhere parties that are so small that they are politically insignificant. But no universal threshold could permit the separation of those that should be retained from those that should be excluded. To know the number of parties is not sufficient for deciding whether a regime belongs to a two-party system. Austria, for instance, divided between "blacks" and "reds," functioned until 1966 according to a model that had nothing in common with the classical alternation, since populists and socialists shared power.

Political systems cannot be analyzed according to simple criteria. To elaborate his typology, Sartori added an ideological dimension (doctrinal rigidity) to the numerical dimension. This crossing permitted him to reveal the essential differences behind misleading "identities"; within the broad category of one-party systems, he contrasted the totalitarian, authoritarian, and pragmatic types.[8] The ideological-pragmatic dimension had been used already by Myron Weiner and Joseph LaPalombara.[9] But Sartori extended its significance from competitive to noncompetitive contexts. Whatever the parliamentary representation of Liberals or Welsh or Scottish nationalists, Great Britain more accurately illustrates what a two-party system is than does West Germany, where coalitions have nearly always proved indispensable. This is not to say that the situation could not be very different in a few years. It is not impossible that the Social Democrats in Great Britain tomorrow may manage to constitute a strong third party, while the Liberal party might well vanish from the German political scene. What remains indisputable is that strategic and cultural elements always contribute in deciding the real significance and importance of little parties.

It would be easy to illustrate the way in which a typology of political regimes is constructed by the crosscutting of two variables. Consider here again Lijphart's typology of democratic systems. As we have seen (supra chapter 11) by retaining on one axis the political culture and on the other the behavior of the elite, Lijphart identifies four types, which he labels "centripetal," "centrifugal," "depoliticized," and "consociational." What we must stress here is the key role played by the classificatory scheme. The logical pattern clearly contributes to stress important differences that might otherwise have been neglected. The category "depoliticized democracy" invites Lijphart to throw a new light on the experience of the Austrian "great coalition," for example. "There are crucial differences between depoliticized and consociational democracy, . . . the two types may be fruitfully compared. The abandonment of strictly competitive politics in consociational democracies is a deliberate response to the tensions of a fragmented society, whereas the adoption of grand coalition politics in depoliticized democracies is in response to the convergence of ideologies. In the latter, depoliticization occurs as a natural consequence of growing consensus, whereas it has to be imposed on an inherently highly politicized system in the former. An even more important, though closely related, difference is that grand coalition patterns in consociational democracies typically occur at the highest level; the party leaders are the pivotal actors. In the depoliticized type of democracy, on the other hand, decision-making takes place in grand coalitions at lower levels: interest group representatives and bureaucrats are now the principal actors."[10]

It may also happen that an author, in trying to refine his analysis, retains more than two dimensions. Samuel E. Finer, for example, proposes to distinguish political regimes along three axes: "*(a)* how far the mass of the public are involved in or excluded from this governing process—this is the *participation-exclusion* dimension; *(b)* how far the mass of the public obey their rulers out of commitment or how far out of fear—what may be called the *coercion-persuasion* dimension; and *(c)* how far the arrangements are designed to cause the rulers to reflect the actual and current values of the mass of the public or how far they may disregard these for the sake of continuity and future values—what may be called the *order-representativeness* dimension."[11]

Each dimension retained permits the author to design a series of possibilities: going from the greatest submission of a subject-individual to an active control by the citizen, from physical coercion to emotional manipulation or even rational persuasion, from an absolute rule of the majority to a system of checks and balances granting the minority a certain autonomy. In progression along the main coercion-persuasion axis, Finer distinguishes five types of regimes. Besides liberal democracies and totalitarian systems, they include *military regimes* based on fear rather than regimentation, *façade democracies* where the oligarchy retains the reality of power, and *quasi democracies* that rely on a sentimental involvement of the masses.

More complex, more ambitious, and more abstract than typologies of actors, the global typologies have a crucial place in comparative research. From Aristotle to Max Weber, history has been marked by these constructions, the best of which were true tools in the progress of sociological knowledge. It is because the analyst tries to fill the voids left by conceptual instruments that he is led to formulate new ones. There is no better generator of concepts than a good typology.

NOTES

1. *De la tyrannie* (Paris: Gallimard, 1954), p. 42.
2. *Political Development in the New States* (The Hague: Mouton, 1960).
3. "The Political Systems of the Developing Areas," in *The Politics of the Developing Areas,* ed. Gabriel Almond and James S. Coleman (Princeton: Princeton University Press, 1960).
4. *Comparative Politics,* 2nd ed. (Boston: Little, Brown, 1978), pp. 72ff.
5. Juan Linz, "Totalitarian and Authoritarian Regimes," in Fred I. Greenstein and Nelson W. Polsby, *Handbook of Political Science* (Reading, Mass.: Addison-Wesley, 1975), 3:174-411.
6. Giovanni Sartori, "The Typology of Party Systems"; Jerzy Wiatr, "The Hegemonic Party System in Poland"; and Juan Linz, "An Authoritarian Regime, Spain"; in *Mass Politics: Studies in Political Sociology,* ed. Erik Allardt and Stein Rokkan (New York: Free Press, 1970).
7. "Social and Institutional Dynamics of One-Party Systems," in *Authoritarian Politics in Modern Society,* ed. Samuel P. Huntington and Clement H. Moore (New York: Basic Books, 1970), pp. 3-47.
8. Seymour Martin Lipset and Stein Rokkan, eds., *Party and Party Systems* (New York: Free Press, 1967).
9. Joseph LaPalombara and Myron Weiner, eds., *Political Parties and Political Development* (Princeton: Princeton University Press, 1966), p. 36.
10. Arend Lijphart, "Typologies of Democratic Systems," *Comparative Political Studies* 1, no. 1 (April 1968): 39.
11. Samuel E. Finer, *Comparative Government* (Baltimore: Penguin, 1970), pp. 39ff.

CHAPTER 22

THE DYNAMICS OF MODELS

Like the typology, the model is a synthesis, capable of taking an inventory in order to clarify and systematize the results of a comparison. To define the originality of models we have chosen to contrast them with typologies.

The typology orders the universe, the model tends to explain it. In a way, the model is more incisive than the typology. The typology can rank all political systems; the model can clarify the movement from one system to another, in the sense of a progression or a regression. According to Jean Baechler, the role of the typology consists in constructing ideal types "by unilaterally developing one or more distinctive features. Such a proceeding will never explain the causes of the identified phenomena. It will just—but this is also important—present the objects for further inquiry."[1]

In fact, the distinction proposed here is not always that clear. It happens that the dynamic of processes appears in the typology. All types get older or deformed. We have known this since Aristotle. It is a very current exercise for constitutionalists to determine the possible evolutions attached to each type of political regime. Jean Blondel, for example, stresses that pluralist democracies, under the constant pressure of their electorate, could prove unable to elaborate long-term policies. The communist systems experience other specific difficulties and are often confronted with a dramatic choice between liberalization on the one hand and some "cultural revolution" on the other.[2] The typology may also evoke the idea of a filiation. For instance, when Fred Riggs contrasts regimes that have only an executive to those that have a bureaucracy as well, and also to those that have a legislature, and again to those with political parties, he notes that a kind of progression exists among these types. He supposes that "there is no polity with a bureaucracy that does not have an executive, no polity with a legislature that lacks a bureaucracy, and no polity with political parties that lacks a legislature."[3]

This means that he includes the idea of development in his scheme. Edward Shils and Gabriel Almond do the same, since they classify the regimes precisely as a function of the place they occupy on a certain number of significant axes. It has been said that typologies represent an insufficiently developed stage in a scientific discipline; this would correspond to the elaboration of a descriptive framework, with limited capacity for generalization. But one need only consider the best typologies in order to see their capacity to synthesize. The typology is also inventive. The typology will not explain the diversity of military regimes or why civil servants play different roles in France and Belgium, but it will make an inventory of possible behaviors, in the absence of which no statements about causality would be possible.

The model orients itself specifically toward an analysis of causality. For this reason, it often implies a rigorous methodology based on mathematical analysis.[4] It brings to light movements of linear, curvilinear, or cybernetic causalities. A recourse to quantified data is thus more necessary for the elaboration of models than for that of typologies. Nevertheless, it should be stressed that this "rule" tolerates exceptions. Most typologies of social actors are formulated on the basis of survey results and use sophisticated methods of analysis. Conversely, some of the models do not rely on quantification. For instance, Dankwart Rustow,[5] Samuel P. Huntington, [6] and Reinhard Bendix,[7] studying the processes of nation building, have utilized relatively few quantified data. It is in history that Stein Rokkan has found the significant "faultages" that explain political cleavages in Europe today: National integration has not met the same peripheral resistance everywhere, the rising state has not encountered the same defiance toward secularization, and the industrial revolution has not induced everywhere an equal decline of territorial disputes. Rokkan's model furnishes sociologists with a sophisticated tool, but it is in the meanderings of history that it was found.[8]

Model building normally tends to provide explanations. That is, sequences described in an analysis of development or modernization have no real interest if they are not related to the evolution of a few variables, which are considered essential by hypothesis or deduction. This exercise is difficult, as can be shown by the great number of models that slip into overly abstract theory. We think, for example, of the theory developed by Cyril E. Black,[9] who philosophically explains "modernization" by the increased control men manage to take over nature, and the resulting growing interdependence between individuals and groups.

On the other hand, when the researcher tries a rigorous analysis of empirical data, his results are often hardly worth the effort, for the new information provided is often meager and deceiving. Examining the causes of civil unrest, Ted Gurr has shown that violence is related to social structures and to the degree of the population's discontent.[10] But we would be disappointed by the vagueness of the model as soon as we tried to locate hierarchies, significant thresholds, and so on. Donald J. McCrone and Charles F. Cnudde[11] did a study very similar to that of Daniel Lerner, tracing a relationship between urbanization and education, the diffusion of which would spread participation through the media, thus contributing to democratic development. But their model is atemporal; it ignores historical experiences and social contexts, and it does not question the link between the new media and the form of "democracy" that could evolve.

Because one can more easily measure electricity consumption or infant mortality than political violence or participation, the temptation is great to rely on an analysis in which political life becomes a dependent variable. A curious result for a science that calls itself political! Quantification permits a rigorous analysis of significant relationships that for centuries were supposed or presumed, but it would certainly be an error to orient research according to the hard data at our disposal.

The precision of decimals does not substitute for the rigor of thought, especially when sophisticated models are elaborated on the basis of weak statistical data or when the correlation coefficients are not very significant. Unfortunately, there are many examples to illustrate the slipping from a legitimate search for causes toward a sophisticated search for models that are removed from reality.

The typology is more static, the model more dynamic. It is difficult to allow for change and maturation in a typology because types are exclusive. On the contrary, the model can include movement. David Apter has rightly invited comparativists to step away from formal structures to focus on the comprehension of dynamic processes.[12] Whereas the typology tends to freeze the reality it wants to synthesize, the model tends to perceive processes over time. The typology contrasts several stages of social and political develpment whereas the model attempts to film social change itself.

A very interesting dimension from this point of view is the use of longitudinal analysis. One has a better chance of discovering priorities and significant phases by taking into consideration quantified data over a long period. Several authors, among them Dankwart Rustow, Arthur Banks, and Peter Flora, have advocated this strategy. The translation of frozen data into curves allows a direct and visual appreciation of the possibly multiple profiles and evolutions, as well as their points of inflection. The study by Peter Flora, Jens Alber, and Jürgen Kohl[13] on the development of the welfare state in twelve European countries between 1900 and 1970 exemplifies the possibilities of this strategy. In a book edited by Flora and Arnold Heidenheimer,[14] the perspective has been extended to contrast the American and European experiences. With contributions by economists, political scientists, sociologists, and historians, the study promotes the view that the development of the welfare state is part of a secular modernization trend; but it also shows that its determinants have been different on the two sides of the Atlantic.

Longitudinal analyses make it easier to ascertain the sequences of events and to test the key role played by this or that variable. The analysis by Arthur Banks, first of 36 South American states between 1835 and 1966,[15] and later for 106 nations,[16] calls into question the notion that socioeconomic development conditions political development. Historically, at least, such a causal relation is not obvious. On the contrary, the correlation between a premature political development and a subsequent development of communication, urbanization, and education is stronger than the correlation between an early socioeconomic development and a subsequent democratic development. Banks writes that "given the results of the time-lag analysis, it is not evident that the ecological environment really 'explains' anything at all in a deterministic sense. Indeed, it is more plausible to hypothesize that variation in democratic performance is (or has been, historically) a major determinant of socioeconomic change."[17]

The longitudinal study can result in true asynchronic comparisons. The idea in such cases is, for instance, to compare the evolution of Europe in the nineteenth century with the recent development of some Third World countries. There is little doubt that an implicit comparative perspective has stimulated the interest retrospectively devoted to the processes of economic or political modernization in Western Europe; books by Charles Tilly[18] and Raymond Grew[19] well illustrate this growing interest. More limited in scope, the study by Ronald Dore[20] explores the reasons why Great Britain and Japan experienced greatly contrasted industrial developments. According to the author, the main reason was not so much that the two countries were marked by different cultural models, but that, over time, "laissez faire" lost its efficiency. When Japan began to industrialize, the intervention of the state, a bureaucratic organization, and large-scale industrial units promised to be more successful devices. Alexander Gershenkron argues in the same way that the technologies and the patterns of organization that today preside over industrialization are not identical to those that prevailed in the past.[21] Certainly this type of research arouses an interest beyond its historical meaning. It is through this diachronic comparison that we can emphasize the originality of development in the twentieth century.

The typology aims at exhaustivity, the model tends to be selective. The typology tries to cover and rank a multiplicity of cases. The model, to the extent that it clarifies processes, excludes from its field certain cases in order to illuminate others. It is not concerned with the spectrum of political attitudes, but with the agents of socialization. It is not concerned with the range of political forces, but with their genesis. The most incisive models are those that succeed in integrating the idea that causes and factors of change are themselves not permanent. Two discourses are possible. A political scientist of philosophical orientation will talk about dialectical movement. Another, using statistical data, will talk about the intervening of new factors. The models of the Club of Rome show that technological innovations intervene to affect the modalities of a growth that is not necessarily exponential.[22]

In the same way, the comparativist will perceive that solutions for one country are not necessarily appropriate for other countries, that solutions adopted yesterday in Europe (at a certain stage of industrialization) are not appropriate for the Third World countries today. It has finally been admitted that the modalities of economic development in the so-called underdeveloped universe are conditioned by the existence of the advanced countries. This contemporaneity affects the prospects of Third World countries, bringing them technical progress, but also the inconvenience of an ill-suited technology; opening foreign markets, but at the cost of an often dramatic agricultural or industrial specialization. Among the authors who have stressed these problems is René Dumont. The progress of medicine and sanitary conditions raises demographic problems never experienced by the Western countries. The new nations are also inheriting ideologies that encourage them, for instance, to bypass the laissez-faire stage. The new countries have suddenly adopted a number of technologies that impinge directly on their political systems, such as radio and television in countries where the majority of the population is illiterate. The medium, says Marshall McLuhan, is the message. The transistor radio, for instance, does not create the same type of citizens as do the newspapers.[23] The intrusion of a new medium like television could well create a new type of society.

To go further: What significance does a parliament retain in countries catapulted from illiteracy to the era of audiovisual media? What can the place of nationalism be in an epoch where the economic vital space increases every day? These are questions that comparison could clarify, the pertinent question being whether the developed societies are the result of a particular historical gestation or a maturation along compulsory stages.

Some authors have stressed the original aspects of what we are calling developed countries. Other authors denounce, not without some validity, the "linearity" that is implied by the concept of development. It is certainly easier to build a linear model than a retroactive one. But no sociologist would contest the fact that political events influence, and are influenced by, what happens in the economic or the cultural fields. For the analyst, however, the task is to ask not only how socioeconomic conditions might favor the intervention of the military into politics but also how political forces might, in their turn, influence the social and economic factors that initially determined their political role.[24]

An evaluation of various influences becomes more difficult when the segments, artificially isolated, are not considered stable but in motion. How does politics intervene in the developmental process, and how does the achieved development influence the emergence of new political forms? This problem has not discouraged David Apter. His basic hypothesis is that as societies progressively become more differentiated, some social strata appear that favor certain types of participation. The predominance of peasants and landlords will not have the same consequences as the dominance of bureaucrats and the military or intellectuals and union leaders. Modernization creates aspirations that become explosive without a corresponding degree of industrialization. The question is to know what types of regimes may be created by increasing social differentiation. Apter's model brings a kind of dialectical scheme to light and outdates systems that have nonetheless proved their efficiency at a previous stage. When a society reaches a certain level of development, it is communication and not coercion that is the efficient means. "The modernization process creates such problems of coordination and control that *democratic* political systems, in the usual sense of that term, are not very relevant. Moreover, their relevance appears to decrease as a society moves closer to the transition to industrialization."[25]

Apter's model is interesting in that he integrates economic, social, and psychological mutations into the concept of modernization. On the other hand, the immensity of the phenomenon studied sometimes results in excessively abstract analysis. A frequent risk for those who build models is to rise to such a level that empirical verification is no longer possible. It sometimes happens that the logical exigencies of the scholar's human spirit excessively deform processes that are not necessarily marked by logic.

We have tried to point out the limits and advantages of dichotomies, typologies, and models. These formal constructions are nevertheless complementary. Not only do they enhance the perceptive capabilities of comparativists but they cohabit and even communicate in the work of all the more prominent social scientists. The typology summarizes the state of advancement of knowledge in a given field. The model works within this clarifying pattern, helping to solve puzzles identified by the typological ordering and possibly fostering the discovery of new, more accurate, classificatory axes.

NOTES

1. J. Baechler, *Les phénomènes révolutionnaires* (Paris: PUF, 1976), p. 57. See, in English, *Revolution* (New York: Barnes and Noble, 1972).

2. Jean Blondel, *Comparing Political Systems* (New York: Praeger, 1972).

3. Fred Riggs, "The Comparison of Whole Political Systems," in *The Methodology of Comparative Research,* ed. Robert Holt and John Turner (New York: Free Press, 1970), pp. 90ff.

4. On model building, see the important contribution by Raymond Boudon, *L'analyse mathématique des faits sociaux* (Paris: Plon, 1967).

5. Dankwart Rustow, *A World of Nations* (Washington, D.C.: Brookings Institution, 1967).

6. Samuel P. Huntington, *Political Order in Changing Societies* (New Haven: Yale University Press, 1968); see also, with special insight on the role of elites, *Revolution and the Transformation of Society: A Comparative Study of Civilizations* (New York: Free Press, 1978).

7. Reinhard Bendix, *Nation-Building and Citizenship* (New York: Wiley, 1964).

8. Stein Rokkan, "Nation-Building, Cleavage Formation, and the Structuring of Mass Politics," in *Citizens Elections Parties* (Oslo: Universitetsforlaget, 1970).

9. Cyril E. Black, *The Dynamics of Modernization: A Study in Comparative History* (New York: Harper, 1967).

10. Ted Gurr, "A Causal Model of Civil Strife: A Comparative Analysis Using New Indices," *American Political Science Review* 62, no. 4 (December 1968): 1104-24.

11. Donald J. McCrone and Charles F. Cnudde, "Toward a Communication Theory of Democratic Political Development: A Causal Model," *American Political Science Review* 61, no. 1 (March 1967): 72-79.

12. David Apter, "Comparative Studies: A Review with Some Projections," in *Comparative Methods in Sociology,* ed. Ivan Vallier (Berkeley: University of California Press, 1971), pp. 3-15.

13. Peter Flora, Jens Alber, and Jürgen Kohl, "Zur Entwicklung der Westeuropaïschen Wohlfahrtsstaaten," in *Politische Vierteljahresschrift* 4 (1977): 707-22.

14. Peter Flora and Arnold J. Heidenheimer, eds., *The Development of Welfare States in Europe and America* (New Brunswick, N.J.: Transaction Books, 1981).

15. Arthur Banks, "Modernization and Political Change: The Latin American and Amer-European Nations," *Comparative Political Studies* 2, no. 4 (January 1970): 405-18.

16. Arthur Banks, Correlates of Democratic Performance," *Comparative Politics* 4, no. 2 (January 1972): 217-30.

17. Ibid.

18. Charles Tilly, *The Formation of National States in Western Europe* (Princeton: Princeton University Press, 1975).

19. Raymond Grew, *Crises of Political Development* (Princeton: Princeton University Press, 1978).

20. Ronald Dore, *British Factory, Japanese Factory* (Berkeley: University of California Press, 1973).

21. Alexander Gerschenkron, *Economic Backwardness in Historic Perspective* (Cambridge, Mass.: Harvard University Press, 1962).

22. Cf. W.L. Oltmans, ed., *On Growth, the Crisis of Exploding Population and Resource Depletion,* 2 vols. (New York: Capricorn, 1974, 1975).

23. Cf. *Understanding the Media* (London: Routledge and Kegan Paul, 1964).

24. Claude E. Welch, "The Military: Product, Facilitator or Antagonist of Socioeconomic Development" (paper presented at the IPSA World Congress, Moscow, August 1979).

25. David Apter, "Political Systems and Development Change," in *Methodology of Comparative Research,* ed. Holt and Turner, pp. 153ff. See also his book, *The Politics of Modernization* (Chicago: University of Chicago Press, 1965).

CHAPTER 23

FROM COMPARISON TO SYNTHESIS

There comes a time in the construction of a building when the frame disappears; it is entirely covered by the façade and the ornaments. The role of the engineer stops there, while the architect and the decorator continue working until the completion of the building. This image could be transposed to the domain of comparative sociology. To construct a comparison is not exactly the same as to draw a synthetic conclusion. This is so true that sometimes the two operations, analysis and synthesis, are not assumed by the same author.

The explicit synthesis, in the sense we understand it here, is not a plain summary. It is an intellectual construction built on empirical findings and aiming at explanation. But we know examples of theoretical constructions built by one scholar on empirical foundations accumulated by other analysts. Lucien Lévy-Bruhl has thus added to his thinking about the "primitive mentality" by using numerous field studies done by others. In the same manner, Helmut Schelsky, describing what he called the "*skeptische* Generation," has utilized empirical works carried out by other sociologists. Many great comparativists do the same.

What is striking is the fact that almost all political or sociological theories are nourished by comparisons, be they explicit or not. "Pure" theory certainly does not exist, even though systematic efforts at abstraction may result in studies of a high quality.[1]

The balance between comparative analysis and theoretical interpretation can obviously vary from one author to the other. There is a considerable distance between, say, the analytical study edited by Harry Eckstein on the essence and significance of civil struggles[2] and the more philosophical synthesis in which Jacques Ellul contrasted the revolutions of the past to today's revolts.[3] The empiricism is clearly greater in the works of Émile Durkheim than in those of Karl A. Wittfogel.

In all cases, nevertheless, comparison is latent. One would easily admit that books like that of John Kenneth Galbraith on "the affluent society," or Andrew Shonfield on "modern capitalism," or Jean Fourastié on the "*grande métamorphose du XXᵉ siècle*" imply a considerable use of comparative data. All important sociological studies dealing with the great social changes must rest on such empirical and comparative foundations.

The synthesis sheds light on the general traits revealed by comparison. To characterize the "postindustrial" society, Daniel Bell[4] and Alain Touraine[5] have included, each in his own manner, technological, sociological, and cultural elements. They mention the decline of the working class, the development of the tertiary sector, the exponential growth of science, and the privileged place reserved for scientists and experts.

In order to define totalitarian dictatorship, Carl J. Friedrich and Zbigniew Brzezinski[6] have emphasized six characteristics common to all regimes that have historically illustrated this type of rule: a rigorously imposed ideology covering all essential aspects of collective life, a single mass party, a system of physical and psychological terror, a complete control over the mass media and socializing agencies, a monopoly of weapons, and a centralized direction of the entire economy.

The theoretical synthesis proposes a diagnosis that can suggest a prognosis. Considering the functioning of the modern welfare states, Morris Janowitz pointed to contradictions expected to generate serious losses in efficiency.[7] Analyzing the functioning of democratic systems, Michel Crozier, Samuel Huntington, and Joji Watanuki[8] identified an entire series of major dysfunctions. Thus, Crozier noted that European countries, overloaded with demands and participants, no longer succeed in mastering the increasingly complex problems of social and economic development; the bureaucratic organizations in charge of controlling these demands have not increased their capacity for decision making. On the contrary, they have helped foster irresponsibility, and thus to undermine the social consensus. One would find a symptom of this disaggregation in the critical marginalization of intellectual elites.

In the same book, Huntington and Watanuki stressed the growth of similar phenomena in the United States and Japan. Summarizing their findings, the three authors emphasized how most of the perceived dysfunctions—loss of legitimacy, chronic inflation, decline of parties, and so on—are inscribed in filigree in the logic of the system itself. Individualistic values and egalitarian creeds naturally work against governmental authority or legitimacy. The promise of participation arouses foolish demands, the competitive principle leads to an exaggerated fragmentation of interest representation, the responsibility to the electorate brings about a fair amount of aggressive demagoguery, and so forth. At the very moment when they observe what today's situation is generating, the three authors propose an analysis that is already prospective. But they do this more clearly to the extent that an international exchange confirms each national diagnosis.

It would be presumptuous to pretend to review here the great theoretical debates that have been fertilized by comparison. Let us only mention, as illustration, issues such as the future of parliaments, the personalization of power, the spectacular growth of the state, the role of experts, the power of unions, and the rise of neocorporatism.

It is necessary to distinguish, in theoretical explanations, between real tendencies and the ideological discourse that cling to them. Pierre Birnbaum has had no trouble detecting the secret hope that slips into the writings of Talcott Parsons, Karl Deutsch, Edward Shils, Robert Dahl, or Daniel Bell when they evoke the decline of ideologies and the rise of a more consensual society.[9] But Birnbaum's critical appraisal is not immune from personal beliefs and hopes. At the moment the analysis crystallizes into a synthesis, the personality of the author normally reappears. Juan Linz cannot study the manner in which democracies have fallen without remembering the Spain of 1936. That his scientific discourse is colored by considerations about the most appropriate way to prevent antidemocratic subversions would not shock anyone. Political scientists are also citizens. Fortunately!

Almost naturally, the explicit synthesis opens itself to a kind of prospective vision. The manner in which the Marxist analysis has generated the idea of "historical determinism" is symptomatic from this point of view. The identification of sociological rules invites us to predict the future because such laws are essentially designed to transcend immediate observations.

NOTES

1. See, for example, Bertrand de Jouvenel, *De la politique pure* (Paris: Calmann-Lévy, 1977).
2. *Internal War: Problems and Approaches* (New York: Free Press, 1964).
3. *De la révolution aux révoltes* (Paris: Calmann-Lévy, 1972).
4. *The Coming of Post-Industrial Society* (New York: Basic Books, 1973).
5. *La société post-industrielle* (Paris: Denoël, 1969).
6. *Totalitarian Dictatorship and Autocracy* (Cambridge, Mass.: Harvard University Press, 1965.
7. In *Social Control of the Welfare States* (New York: Elsevier, 1976).
8. *The Crisis of Democracy: Report on the Governability of Democracies to the Trilateral Commission* (New York: New York University Press, 1973).
9. Cf. *La fin du politique* (Paris: Seuil, 1975).

CHAPTER 24

FROM COMPARISON TO PREDICTION

In the natural sciences it is easy to predict the results of an experiment carried out in a laboratory. History, by contrast, never repeats itself. The same causes will never produce the same results because they will never be recombined in the same way. Even if the scientific spirit is capable of identifying a large number of factors, "historical events result from a combination of factors which *is* unique."[1]

This does not impede social scientists from leaning toward prediction. This propensity is more visible in economics and demography, which are rich in curves of evolution that seem naturally to call for extrapolation. A birthrate or a production of steel or electric energy seems more predictable than the coming features of political institutions or behaviors. But the desire to forecast the future does not spare any discipline in the social sciences. Oswald Spengler foresaw the decline of the West at about the same time Arnold Toynbee conceived of a more optimistic destiny. The first theorists of "convergence" between liberal and collectivist societies presented their ideas at a time when other scholars expected a far darker conclusion to the cold war.

The contemporary spreading of prospective studies manifests not only an intellectual curiosity but also a real need felt by politicians and planners. The acceleration of technical progress is such that it is necessary at each stage to evaluate its possible repercussions. "We have entered the era of planned economies," states a French economist.[2] Planning is now recognized as a duty for the politician, whom scientists can greatly help. One would not introduce computerized information into a society without inquiring as to its possible economic, political, and human consequences.

"Savoir pour prévoir, prévoir pour pourvoir," said Auguste Comte in a famous maxim: to know in order to predict, to predict in order to supply. "Scientism" is outmoded today. But action and knowledge cannot develop separately. The temptation may even be great for scholars to participate directly in the exercise of power, to make a mark on history. We know examples of such involvement in every Western democracy.

There are several ways to forecast the future. The vulgar manner consists in seeking the model expected for the near future elsewhere. "America is the Europe of tomorrow," some people have said on one side of the Atlantic; "California is the America of tomorrow," some have said on the other side. And it is quite possible that in the domain of refrigerators or cars, Europe has followed the American example. Nobody, however, would argue that this has been the case regarding styles of life, social relations, city living, or even political parties.

Another strategy consists in exploring the future by extrapolating curves on the basis of a battery of hypotheses. This technique of extrapolation does not necessarily imply a comparative approach. It is indeed often applied to a single country. But it is clear that one will better appreciate the evolution on which the prediction relies by multiplying the nations included in the study. One will more accurately imagine the coming trends in birth or divorce rates by considering a cluster of rather similar countries. In a convincing way, Richard Rose and B. Guy Peters have demonstrated that the Western European governments risk being overloaded with debt.[3] Obviously, their prognosis becomes more persuasive in view of the fact that it is not based on observations made in one country only but takes into consideration the evolution of several countries.

To base the forecast on comparative quantified data apparently makes the prediction more reliable, particularly when it is for the short term. But the further the predicted future, the more difficult the prediction becomes. Nobody would say today that Malthus was prophetic, at least as far as Western Europe is concerned. In the best of cases, the analyst can integrate the predictable change of some behaviors into his thinking. That is what Pierre Moussa did twenty years ago as he imagined the "proletarian nations" demanding a better price for their exports of raw materials.[4] These nascent changes, of course, are not always detectable. But the multiplication of examples made possible by international comparison certainly allows one to better conceive of what is coming. The future of the developing nations has been the object of a particularly active and rich research. Political scientists, of course, are in the front line of those who try to predict this future. But in Europe an important contribution also comes from higher civil servants, who have spent many years in these developing countries. This is true especially in the ex-colonial powers, such as France, Great Britain, or the Netherlands.

Predictability is not particularly high in the realm of politics. The only people who would argue the contrary, stressed Bertrand de Jouvenel, are those who see "political change as necessarily flowing from social change, which, being a heavy and slow process, can more easily be predicted."[5] But are we to believe that politics is only an epiphenomenon resulting from social, economic, and technological evolutions? "Politics has reasons that economics does not know." Not to acknowledge this would be to run the risk of misinterpretation and consequently of serious errors in prediction. "Political history is not at all contained in the material transformations of society. To provide evidence for this point, we need only evoke the development of Caesarist regimes in scores of highly different social settings."[6]

Paul Valéry used to say that man advances into the future looking backward. As a matter of fact, man has always nourished his imagination with the experiences of the past, even when he is trying to predict the future.

Now, forecasting is particularly difficult in politics because "accidents" are unpredictable, and politics is full of "accidents." There is no generation that has not experienced such accidents. One example among many: The problem of the "widening gap" between rich and poor countries, as formulated in the 1960s,[7] had to be redefined for several reasons. First, the sudden enrichment of the oil-producing countries gave birth to a new type of country, one financially rich but still traditional in many respects; the increasing price of energy made poorer the poorest nations and reduced the rate of growth predicted twenty years ago for the most developed ones. But these very important changes were not predicted by "widening-gap" theorists. In the same way, French social scientists and politicians in no way foresaw the coming of May '68, although since then they have written 900 books and articles to "explain" the crisis.

All sociologists know that human laws are affected by contingencies. Under these conditions, the best the comparativist can do is to establish a certain number of correlations, which imply that "until now" or "in the past" this or that phenomenon has produced this or that consequence. The establishment of these relationships, considered as constant, permits the evaluation of the probability of certain changes, certain crises, and certain consolidations.

If we are to accept the analysis proposed by Seymour Martin Lipset, it seems possible to predict the life expectancy of a regime according to the two parameters of legitimacy and efficiency.[8] A political system that is perceived as legitimate and that at the same time is efficient will have a great chance of remaining unchallenged; a regime with high legitimacy will probably resist a decline in efficiency (the British case); a regime will certainly collapse under the blows of inefficiency if it is not widely accepted and rooted in the masses (the Weimar Republic or Italy in 1922). Nevertheless, these propositions are not altogether satisfactory for Austria at the time of the Anschluss or for Sihanouk's Cambodia, for example. Coercive power is evidently another central dimension for explaining the longevity of some regimes.

Considering the analysis by Phillips Cutright[9] on the relationship between socioeconomic development on the one side and the development of representative institutions on the other, it might be possible to recognize certain fragile or explosive situations corresponding to a political "over" or "under" development. The Cutright model has also permitted the detection of many abnormal cases, which have not failed to re-equilibrate themselves in one way or another. Democracy collapsed in Chile and the Philippines, yet it was possible to build it rapidly where the ground was solid, for example in Spain or Portugal. This scheme has been so suggestive that it has inspired other analyses, which aimed at predicting probable coups d'état in Africa or Latin America. Not all predictions have kept their promise.

To systematize, writes Alfred Grosser,[10] is "to make an induction with the hope of conquering the possibility to make a deduction." This passage from induction to deduction may be actualized also with regard to the course of time. Comparison leads to prediction precisely because it leads to systematization. But it is also because this prediction can be only general and "systematic" that it remains fragile in face of a future potentially full of pure "events."

It is difficult, as soon as one wants to imagine scenarios for the long term, to master one's obsessions, ideological choices, hopes, and fears. The crisis of today has ended the economic miracle of yesterday; but everywhere in the West optimistic and pessimistic evaluations continue to develop simultaneously. The warnings of the Club of Rome[11] have inspired more emotion among the general public than among experts and politicians. Scholars remain skeptical, probably because they are cautious people. Politicians guard themselves against distant projections, perhaps simply because their preoccupations are with the present or the immediate future. To be a statesman normally requires an ability to consider and foresee the future. But politicians are overloaded with daily activities, and so, paradoxically, they are not in a position to devote enough time to forecasting.

In an interesting article, Sam Cole, Jay Gershuny, and Ian Miles[12] showed the obvious disparity of forecasting studies. The technological optimism of Herman Kahn does not correspond to the pessimism of Paul Ehrlich; the Malthusian views of Jay W. Forrester are different from the more revolutionary perspective of René Dumont. Confronted with the same data, the more eminent futurologists imagine the future in original ways; their representations do not converge, on the contrary they depart from one another. We could probably see in this mixture of divergent hypotheses evidence of the distance existing between a science able to successfully explain the past and an art of prediction that is more difficult to master.

The comparative method is a powerful tool for the progress of knowledge. That is what makes comparison capable, to some degree, of guiding one's comprehension of the future. The prudent person will hesitate to envision the long term; others will take such a risk, conscious that their work, even if full of uncertainties, could help rulers to reach the right decisions in time—to influence the course of events. In any case, the prediction founded on comparisons remains one of the most promising approaches in the "sociology of the future."[13]

NOTES

1. Léo Hamon, *Acteurs et données de l'histoire* (Paris: PUF, 1970), 1:41.
2. Alfred Sauvy, *Conjoncture et prévision économiques* (Paris: PUF, 1977).
3. Cf. *Can Government Go Bankrupt?* (New York: Basic Books, 1978).
4. *Les nations prolétaires* (Paris: PUF, 1963).
5. *L'art de la conjecture* (Monaco: Eds. du Rocher, 1964), p. 297.
6. Ibid., p. 301.
7. See especially L.S. Brown, *World Without Borders* (New York: Vintage Books, 1972).
8. *Political Man: The Social Basis of Politics,* expanded ed. (Baltimore: Johns Hopkins University Press, 1981).
9. "National Political Development: Measurement and Analysis," *American Sociological Review* 28 (April 1963).
10. Alfred Grosser, *L'explication politique* (Paris: A. Colin, 1972), p. 17.
11. D.H. Meadows, J. Randers, and W.W. Behrens, *The Limits to Growth* (New York: Universe Books, 1972).
12. "Scénarios du développement du monde," *Futuribles,* May-June 1978.
13. See Wendell Bell and James A. Mau, eds., *The Sociology of the Future* (New York: Russell Sage Foundation, 1971). This book includes a critical appraisal of 257 studies on the future, nearly all of them based on implicit or explicit comparative analyses.

NAME INDEX

Aberbach, Joel, 126
Abramowitz, Alan, 65
Abramson, Paul R., 115
Adams, R., 81
Alber, Jens, 165, 169
Alker, Hayward R., 111
Allardt, Erik, 15, 106, 126, 162
Almasy, Elina, 101, 105
Almond, Gabriel, 27, 29, 37, 58, 60-65, 82, 101, 144, 147, 155, 156, 159, 162, 163
Althusser, Louis, 62
Amin, Samir, 43
Ancisi, Alvaro, 80
Andreski, Stanislav, 22, 25, 143, 154, 156
Anton, Thomas J., 124, 126
Apter, David, 82, 109, 165, 168, 169, 170
Arendt, Hannah, 128
Aristotle, 161
Armer, J. Michael, 106
Aron, Raymond, 24, 25, 133, 146

Badie, Bertrand, 40
Baechler, Jean, 163, 169
Bailyn, Bernard, 125
Balandier, Georges, 11, 104
Banfield, Edward, 5, 64
Banks, Arthur, 165, 166, 169
Barbu, Zevedei, 128
Barnes, Samuel H., 63, 65, 108, 111, 155, 156
Behrens, William W., 178
Bell, Daniel, 101, 172, 173
Bell, Wendell, 10, 97, 115, 178
Bendix, Reinhard, 22, 49, 107, 113, 128, 145, 164, 169
Bentley, Arthur, 83
Berque, Jacques, 9, 112
Beteille, André, 49
Beyme, Klaus von, 119, 123, 124
Bhatt, Ahmad, 105, 106
Bill, James A., 122
Binder, Leonard, 93, 97
Birnbaum, Pierre, 173
Black, Cyril E., 164, 169
Blanksten, George I., 154, 156
Blau, Peter, 25
Blondel, Jean, 103, 169
Boudon, Raymond, 124, 169
Bourdieu, Pierre, 67

Bracher, Karl Dietrich, 109, 111, 123, 130, 132
Braudel, Fernand, 121
Brinton, Crane, 93, 97
Brown, L.S., 178
Bruyne, P. de, 150
Bryce, James, 5
Brzezinski, Zbigniew, 128, 136, 172
Burnham, James, 42

Caciagli, Mario, 79
Caillois, Roger, 23, 25
Campbell, Peter, 116
Cardoso, Fernando H., 43
Carrère-D'Encausse, Hélène, 54
Clapham, J.H., 116
Clark, Burton, 152
Clastres, Pierre, 130
Cnudde, Charles F., 164, 169
Cole, Sam, 177
Coleman, James, 54, 71, 109, 119, 120, 156, 158, 162
Comte, Auguste, 13, 28, 174
Conradt, David, 65
Cot, Jean-Pierre, 60, 65, 73
Crozier, Michel, 63, 65, 109, 136, 172
Cutright, Phillips, 176

Dahl, Robert A., 23, 25, 85, 102, 122, 125, 131, 133, 159, 173
Dahrendorf, Ralf, 55, 56, 112
Damgaard, E., 126
Darwin, Charles, 154
Davies, James C., 92, 97
Delatte, J., 105
Dennis, Jack, 73
Descartes, René, 1
Despres, Leo, 56
Deutsch, Karl W., 27, 28, 30, 40, 101, 111, 173
Dodd, Lawrence C., 122
Dogan, Mattei, 37, 74, 106, 116, 124, 125, 139, 156
Dore, Ronald, 166, 170
Dumont, Louis, 112, 177
Dumont, René, 167
Durkheim, Émile, 13, 14, 24, 144, 171
Duverger, Maurice, 16, 26, 104, 155, 156, 159

Easton, David, 27, 29 32, 67, 73
Eckstein, Harry, 16, 99, 109, 112, 137, 171
Edinger, Lewis, 112
Ehrlich, Paul, 177
Ehrmann, Henry, 104
Eisenstadt, Shmuel N., 49, 81, 134, 135
Eldersveld, Samuel, 123, 126
Eliassen, Kjell, 125, 126
Ellul, Jacques, 95, 97, 171
Epstein, Leon, 106, 122
Eulau, Heinz, 153, 156
Eysenck, Hans J., 153

Fendrich, J.M., 70
Figgis, John N., 50
Finer, S.E., 161, 162
Finkle, Jason L., 80, 147
Fleming, Donald, 125
Flora, Peter, 165, 169
Forrester, Jay, 177
Foucault, Michel, 28, 96, 97
Fourastié, Jean, 171
Freund, Julien, 30
Friedrich, Carl, 128, 172
Furnivall, John S., 50, 56

Gable, Richard W., 80, 147
Galbraith, John Kenneth, 42, 171
Galtung, Johan, 43
Geertz, Clifford, 52
Germani, Gino, 21, 24, 119, 124, 144
Gershenkron, Alexander, 166, 170
Gershuny, Jay, 177
Glazer, Nathan, 48
Gonidec, P.F., 132
Goode, William. 23
Gottmann, Jean, 52
Gramsci, Antonio, 62, 67
Graubard, Stephen R., 122
Graziano, Luigi, 79, 80
Greenberg, Edward, 73
Greenstein, Fred I., 111, 132, 162
Grew Raymond, 166, 170
Grosser, Alfred, 28, 30, 107, 177, 178
Guasti, Laura, 80
Gurr, Ted, 106, 164, 169
Gusfield, Joseph R., 145

Halévy, Elie, 9, 112
Hallgarten, George W., 145
Hamon, Léo, 25, 178
Harcourt, Robert d', 69
Heath, D., 81
Heberle, Rudolf, 25
Hegel, Georg W.F., 5, 8, 27, 28
Heidenheimer, Arnold J., 40, 165, 169

Heisler, Martin O., 125
Herman, J., 150
Hermet, Guy, 35, 135, 138, 147
Hodge, Robert W., 44
Hoffmann, Stanley, 112
Holt, Robert T., 20, 24, 111, 169, 170
Horowitz, Irving Louis, 120
Hoselitz, Bert F., 137
Hudson, Michael, 91, 109, 122, 137
Huntington, Samuel, 93, 128, 134, 136, 145,
    155, 156, 159, 162, 164, 169, 172
Hyman, Herbert, 71

Inglehart, Ronald, 126, 155, 156
Inkeles, Alex, 63, 73, 153, 156
Ionescu, Ghita, 35
Isaac, Larry, 45

Jackman, R.W., 106
Jackson, R., 51
Jacob, François, 27, 30
Jain, Shail, 49
Janowitz, Morris, 124, 172
Jennings, M. Kent, 70
Jouvenel, Bertrand de, 18, 173, 175

Kaase, Max, 63, 65, 108, 111, 151, 155, 156
Kahin, George McT., 125
Kahn, Herman, 177
Kant, Immanuel, 6, 20
Kindleberger, Charles, 113
Kirchheimer, Otto, 122
Koff, David, 73
Kohl, Jürgen, 165, 169
Kohn, Hans, 128
Kooiman, Jan, 123
Kornhauser, William, 56
Krauss, S., 70
Kravchenko, Viktor, 73
Kriesberg, Louis, 25
Kuhn, Thomas, 26
Kuhnle, S., 126
Kuper, Leo, 55, 56

Lafferty, William, 126
Lambert, Jacques, 59, 119, 124
Lande, Carl H., 77, 80
Lane, Robert, 69, 151, 155
LaPalombara, Joseph, 16, 26, 30, 32, 76,
    112, 125, 155, 160, 162
Laponce, Jean, 108, 111
Laski, Harold, 50
Laslett, John, 110
Lasswell, Harold D., 111
Lavau, Georges, 104
Lawson, Kay, 103

Lazarsfeld, Paul, 124, 148, 154
Leiden, Carl, 122
Lehmbruch, Gerhard, 82, 90
Lemarchand, René, 48, 49, 77, 79
Lemieux, Vincent, 75, 76, 81
Lenski, Gerhard, 44, 49
Lerner, Daniel, 9, 32, 37, 63, 164
Lévi-Strauss, Claude, 11, 28, 143
Lévy-Bruhl, Lucien, 171
Lewis, Arthur, 88
Lijphart, Arend, 15, 83-88, 90, 91, 122, 125, 135, 138, 160, 162
Linné, Carl von, 154
Linz, Juan, 15, 95, 97, 106, 109, 111, 132, 134, 159, 162, 173
Lipset, Seymour Martin, 23, 49, 83, 93, 94, 96, 97, 101, 109, 110, 115, 116, 152, 156, 162, 176
Lorwin, Val R., 82, 86, 90, 91
Louis, Paul, 7
Lukacs, Georg, 42

McClosky, Herbert, 153
Macridis, Roy, 19, 104, 133, 138
McCrone, Donald J., 164, 169
McKenzie, Robert, 152, 155
McKinney, John, 30
McLuhan, Marshall, 167
McRae, Kenneth, 87, 90, 91
McWilliams, Wilson Carey, Jr., 124
Malinowski, Bronislaw, 144
Markovitz, Irving, 43
Marsh, Alan, 151, 155
Marsh, Robert M., 21, 22, 60, 65, 101, 106
Martinet, Gilles, 124
Marvick, Dwaine, 73
Marx, Karl, 27, 28, 44, 92, 143
Mau, James, 178
Meadows, Dennis, 178
Meadows, Donnella, 178
Médard, Jean-François, 75, 76
Mendeleev, Dmitri, 154
Merkl, Peter, 122
Merriam, Charles, 25
Merton, Robert K., 17, 26, 29
Meynaud, Jean, 63, 65
Michels, Roberto, 17
Miles, Ian, 177
Miliband, Ralph, 49
Mill, John Stuart, 13, 14, 118
Montaigne, Michel E.S. de, 6
Montesquieu, 6, 101
Moore, Barrington, 107
Moore, Clement H., 135, 145, 162
Morganthau, Ruth Schachter, 119
Morrison, D.G., 56

Moskos, Charles, 10, 97
Mounier, Jean-Pierre, 60, 65, 73
Moussa, Pierre, 175
Moynihan, Daniel Patrick, 48
Muhll, George von der, 73
Mühlmann, Wilhelm, 11

Nagata, J.A., 53, 91
Needler, Martin, 121, 125
Neustadt, Richard E., 33
Nicholls, David, 51, 55, 56
Niemi, Richard, 70
Nordlinger, Eric A., 82, 90, 152, 155

Olsen, Marvin E., 40
Oltmans, W.L., 170
Ossowski, Stanislaw, 42, 44, 49, 146
Ostrowski, Krzysztof, 115
Ozbudun, Ergun, 78, 81

Paige, Glenn D., 40
Pareto, Vilfredo, 69
Parkin, Frank, 106
Parsons, Talcott, 20, 21, 27, 29, 67, 173
Pascal, Blaise, 6
Passeron, Jean-Claude, 67
Pedersen, M.W., 126
Pelassy, Dominique, 125
Pesonen, P., 126
Peters, B. Guy, 175
Peterson, Richard, 152
Pitts, Jesse, 70
Pizzorno, Alessandro, 66
Polsby, Nelson W., 111, 132, 162
Poulantzas, Nicos, 42, 49
Powell, G. Bingham, 37, 82, 90, 144, 147, 159
Powell, John Duncan, 75, 78, 81
Prewitt, Kenneth, 73
Pride, Richard, 104
Przeworski, Adam, 61, 65, 99
Putnam, Robert D., 121, 125, 126
Pye, Lucian, 39, 65, 93, 94, 97, 109, 125, 129, 136

Rae, Douglas W., 15, 122
Randers, Jorgen, 178
Redfield, Robert, 144
Reischauer, Edwin O., 112
Richardson, Bradley, 112
Richardson, J.M., 20, 110, 112
Riggs, Fred W., 22, 109, 136, 163, 169
Riker, William H., 86
Robinson, Robert V., 115
Rockman, Bert, 126
Rogger, Hans, 108

Rokeach, Milton, 62
Rokkan, Stein, 15, 25, 101, 105, 106, 116
  126, 156, 162, 164, 169
Roniger, Louis, 81
Rosberg, Carl G., 119, 120
Rose, Richard, 40, 74, 111, 112, 175
Rossi, Peter, 44
Roth, Guenther, 56
Rouquié, Alain, 135, 138, 147
Russett, Bruce M., 91, 111, 131, 137
Rustow, Dankwart A., 40, 54, 99, 114, 131,
  133, 164, 165, 169

Said, Edward, 9
Sani, Giacomo, 108, 111
Sartori, Giovanni, 10, 11, 12, 14, 22, 25, 36,
  108, 111, 139, 159, 160, 162
Saussure, Ferdinand de, 133
Sauvy, Alfred, 178
Schelsky, Helmut, 171
Scheuch, Erwin, 11, 12, 59, 65, 106
Schmidt, Steffen, 80
Schoutheete, M. de, 150
Schramm, Wilbur, 125
Schwartzenberg, Roger Gérard, 132
Scott, James, 80
Shils, Edward, 43, 50, 93, 158, 163, 173
Shonfield, Andrew, 171
Siegfried, André, 5
Sigel, Roberta, 74
Silver, Allan, 152, 155
Silverman, S.E., 75
Silvert, Kalman, 119, 124
Simkus, Albert A., 45
Singham, A., 126
Sjöblom, G., 126
Sklar, Richard, 43, 49
Smith, A.K., 138
Smith, David H., 63, 153, 156
Smith, Donald E., 125
Smith, Gordon, 122
Smith, M.G., 50, 56
Smock, Audrey, 51, 55, 56, 80
Smock, David, 51, 55, 56, 80
Sombart, Werner, 110
Spencer, Herbert, 101
Spengler, Oswald, 133, 174
Steiner, Jürg, 90
Steiner, Kurt, 90, 91
Stepan, Alfred, 95, 97, 111
Stephens, John D., 106
Stevenson, H.M., 56
Stirner, Max, 67

Strauss, Leo, 157
Suleiman, Michael W., 91

Tak, Theo van der, 123
Tarrow, Sidney, 6, 114
Teune, Henry, 22, 61, 65, 99, 115
Tilly, Charles, 166, 170
Tocqueville, Alexis de, 6, 17, 92, 112, 137
Tönnies, Ferdinand, 144, 146
Torgersen, U., 126
Touraine, Alain, 172
Toynbee, Arnold, 174
Treadgold, Donald, 116
Treiman, Donald J., 44
Trow, Martin, 152
Truman, David, 27, 50, 83, 102, 106
Tucker, Robert, 128
Tufte, Edward R., 133
Turner, John, 24, 111, 169, 170

Urban, George, 74
Urwin, D.W., 125

Valen, Henry, 126
Valéry, Paul, 176
Vallier, Ivan, 106, 169
Vanhanen, Tatu, 137
Verba, Sidney, 39, 58, 60-65, 101, 105, 106,
  107, 110, 155
Veyne, Paul, 10, 11, 109, 135, 138
Viet, Jean, 101

Wallerstein, Immanuel, 43
Ward, Robert E., 114
Warner, W. Lloyd, 44, 49
Watanuki, Joji, 172
Waterbury, John, 126
Weber, Eugen, 108
Weber, Max, 17, 20, 21, 28, 101, 108, 154,
  161
Weiner, Myron, 94, 97, 125, 160, 162
Welch, Claude E., 138, 170
Welsh, William A., 124
Wiatr, Jerzy, 10, 159, 162
Wittfogel, Karl A., 171
Wolf, Eric, 81
Wuthnow, Robert, 111

Xenophon, 17

Young, M. Crawford, 48, 51, 52, 56

Ziegler, Jean, 10

SUBJECT INDEX

Abstraction, level of, 20, 26, 27, 42, 52, 100, 128
Acculturation, 67, 68
Activists, 152, 155
Administration, high-level, 31
Africa, 22, 43, 47, 88, 119, 120, 121, 130
Aggregation of interests, 24, 33, 34, 36, 85, 130, 172
Alienation, 100
Anglo-Saxon countries, 123
Anthropology, 10, 11, 58
Arab world, 9, 121, 122, 123
Area study, 15, 118, 119, 122, 123, 133
Aristocracy, 113
Articulation of interests, 24, 33, 34, 35, 36, 76, 78, 85, 130
Asynchronic comparisons, 15, 18, 166, 167
Austria, 31, 63, 82, 84-86, 88, 155, 160, 161
Autonomy of politics, 68, 134, 158
Authoritarian regimes, 35, 109, 131, 137, 145, 157, 159, 161

Bangladesh, 53
Belgium, 15, 31, 82, 85, 86, 87, 89
Bureaucracy, 22, 32, 36, 42, 53, 109, 120, 136, 172
Burma, 109

Canada, 72, 83, 87, 153
Case
  abnormal, 129, 176, 177
  clinical, 71, 109
  deviant, 51, 109, 110
  extreme, 143, 144
Center-periphery, 43, 52
Centralism, 123
Centrifugal system, 83, 160
Centripetal system, 83, 160
Chad, 53
Charisma, 11, 21, 23, 54, 120, 158
Chile, 177
China, 76, 114
Churches, 35, 69, 72
Class consciousness, 41, 42, 47
Cleavages
  crosscutting, 17, 83

  overlapping, 17, 48, 53
  vertical, 39, 47, 48, 51, 54, 56, 70, 75, 78, 79, 84
Clientelism, 75-80
Club of Rome, 177
Coalition, 86
Coercion, 161, 168
Columbia, 76, 82, 88
Communalism, 52, 53
Communist countries, 114, 124, 163
Comparison
  asynchronic, 15, 18, 166, 167
  implicit, 112
  longitudinal, 165, 166, 167
Compromise, 50
Conceptual imperialism, 24
Concomitant variations, 14
Contagion, international, 7, 8, 95, 96
Contextual variables, 14, 15, 16
Contiguity, 118, 121
Continuum (progression), 55, 146
Convergence, theory of, 136
Corruption, 40
Crises, accumulation of, 96
Cultural patrimony, 52
Cybernetic models, 26, 27, 29
Cyprus, 82

Deciles of income, 45, 46
Democracy
  façade, 161
  pluralist, 10, 122, 128, 145
  small, 133
  stable, 61
Dependence theory, 43
Development, level of, 10, 21, 40, 47, 167, 168
Domination, hegemonic, 50

Eastern Europe, 10, 35, 43, 68, 96, 124
Egypt, 103
Electoral system, 122
Elites, 31, 4
Equality, quest for, 92
Exclusionary regimes, 159
Experimentation, 13, 14

Factionalism, 53, 136
False equivalence, 60, 61
Familism, 64. 66
Feudalism, 77, 113
Finland, 15
France, 6, 8, 31, 36, 61, 70, 93, 95, 113, 114, 116, 152
Functionalism, 10, 18, 21, 29, 36, 130, 138
Futurology, 177, 178

Generalization, median level of, 20, 28, 120
Generations, indoctrinated, 73
Germany, 63, 155, 160
Gini index, 45
Great Britain, 5, 31, 33, 55, 63, 64, 113, 115, 116, 152, 155, 160, 166

High schools, Europe and America, 70
Holistic theories, 27, 28

Ideal type, 21, 144
Ideology, 11, 62, 72, 123
    decline of, 173
Imitation. See contagion, international
Imperialism, 10, 24
Implicit comparison, 112
Income distribution, 45
India, 76, 105
Italy, 5, 6, 7, 15, 31, 64, 75, 152

Japan, 6, 41, 76, 166, 172

Labels, misleading, 33
Latin America, 47, 59, 75, 106, 117, 154
Legitimacy, 17, 72, 73
Lebanon, 55, 82, 87, 137
Longitudinal comparison, 165, 166, 167

Malaysia, 53, 55, 76
Marginality, cost of, 70
Marxism, 18, 42, 43, 62, 173
Mass media, 15, 32, 52, 73, 89, 120, 68
Mediterranean countries, 121
Membership in parties, 63, 64
Mexico, 60, 64, 76
Military, 103, 120, 151, 161
Ministates, 123
Mobilization, 10, 35, 130, 157
Models
    bipolar, 131
    linear, 21, 167, 168
Modernity, 63, 145, 153
Movements, social, 23, 25

Nation building, 40, 164
Nation-state, 53
Nazism, 130, 131, 146
Netherlands, 31, 85, 123, 155
Nigeria, 53, 55, 82, 87
Norway, 15, 16, 31

Oligarchy, iron law of, 17
Opposition, 120, 122
Overdevelopment, 129, 155, 177
Over-power, 129

Pakistan, 53
Paradigm, 26
Parliament, role of, 104, 153, 167
Participation, 6, 10, 36, 39, 130, 172
Party
    dominant, 34, 159
    hegemonic, 131, 159
    members, 62, 63
    single, 120, 145
Patronage. See clientelism
Persuasion, 161
Philippines, 76, 177
Pluralism
    political, 50, 55, 123, 172
    social, 51
Polyarchy, 23, 131
Portugal, 103
Prejudices, 24
Professional hierarchies, 44
Proportional representation, 16
Protesters, 155
Prototype, 115, 127, 128
Proximity, 9, 118, 123

Quantification, 18, 100, 164, 165

Recruitment, 31
Regimes
    authoritarian, 35, 109, 131, 137, 145, 157, 159, 161
    exclusionary, 159
    semi-competitive, 135
    totalitarian, 69, 71, 72, 73, 128, 130-31, 145
Regional approach. See area study
Rising expectations, 93, 130

Scales of attitudes, 110
Scandinavia, 31, 122, 124, 126
Secularization, 21, 94, 145
Segregation, geographical, 55
Semi-competitive regimes, 135

Site of decision, 34, 85
Socialization, vectors of, 69
Social movements, 23, 25
Society
  heterogeneous, 56, 93, 94, 96
  homogeneous, 56
  postindustrial, 122, 172
  traditional, 144, 145, 164
Southeast Asia, 90, 121
Spain, 15, 75, 177
State, multinational, 53
Stereotype, 24, 59
Structural differentiation, 21, 22, 34
Structuralism, 28
Students
  Islamic, 103
  typology of, 152
Stylization, 128, 129
Sudan, 53
Switzerland, 82, 86, 89

Technostructure, 52, 172
Theory, middle-range, 17, 26

Third World, 43, 46, 94, 128, 129, 151
Tory worker, 152
Totalitarian regimes, 69, 71, 72, 73, 128,
  130-31, 145
Trade Unions, 31, 34, 35
Tradition, 21
"Tree" analysis, 110
Turkey, 76
Type, ideal, 21, 144

Underdevelopment, 24, 129
Under-power, 129, 130
United States, 5, 36, 41, 70, 93, 115-16,
  155

Value explanation, 60
Values, individualistic, 172

Welfare state, 165
Western Europe, 15, 121-23, 129, 137, 172
Western world, 133
Women's rights, 7
World Bank, 45

ABOUT THE AUTHORS

MATTEI DOGAN studied philosophy, history, and political science at the University of Paris from which he received his Ph.D. in sociology. He is director of research at the National Center of Scientific Research in Paris, an institution with which he has been affiliated since 1954. Since 1973 he has been a recurring professor of political science at the University of California at Los Angeles.

A former member of the French National Committee of Scientific Research, he is currently chairman of the committee on political elites of the International Political Science Association and president of the research committee on social ecology of the International Sociological Association. Professor Dogan has published eight books and contributed chapters to thirty others; has served on the editorial boards of several journals; and has published articles in French, English, Italian, German, and Spanish journals. He has been a visiting professor at several universities in the United States, Italy, and Japan.

DOMINIQUE PELASSY received her Ph.D. in political science from the University of Paris. She is a research associate at the National Center of Scientific Research in Paris and has recently published two books: *Helmut Schmidt ou le realisme* and *Le signe nazi: l'univers symbolique d'une dictature*.

Mattei Dogan and Dominique Pelassy are the editors of *La comparaison internationale en sociologie politique* (Paris: Litec, 1980). They are currently writing a book comparing pluralist democracies in Western Europe.